ON NEW TERRAIN

ON NEW TERRAIN

How Capital Is Reshaping the Battleground of Class War

KIM MOODY

Haymarket Books
Chicago, Illinois

Published in 2017 by
Haymarket Books
P.O. Box 180165
Chicago, IL 60618
773-583-7884
www.haymarketbooks.org
info@haymarketbooks.org

ISBN: 978-1-60846-846-1

Trade distribution:
In the US, Consortium Book Sales and Distribution, www.cbsd.com
In Canada, Publishers Group Canada, www.pgcbooks.ca
In the UK, Turnaround Publisher Services, www.turnaround-uk.com
All other countries, Ingram Publisher Services International,
IPS_Intlsales@ingramcontent.com

This book was published with the generous support of Lannan Foundation
and Wallace Action Fund.

Cover design by Eric Kerl.

Printed in Canada by union labor.

Library of Congress Cataloging-in-Publication data is available.

10 9 8 7 6 5 4 3 2 1

CONTENTS

INTRODUCTION

From 1980 through 1982, the world experienced the longest recession since the 1930s. Yet, far from ushering in a prolongation of systemic crisis, this slump laid the basis for a renewed period of capitalist growth and expansion that would last, with ups and downs, until the "Great Recession" that began in 2008. This new "boom" could hardly have been more different from the post–World War II expansion. For this period of growth, "spurred by a sharp drop in interest rates," was sustained by the stagnation of wages across the developed economies and a simultaneous and rapid increase in productivity that sent profit rates upward into the new century.[1]

This new era occurred in the context of accelerating globalization, which, measured by both trade and foreign direct investment (FDI), took off in the mid-1980s. The global wage-earning non-agricultural workforce grew from 1.5 billion in 1999 to 2.1 billion in 2013, composing half of the world's workforce, while despite the Great Recession the number of industrial workers rose from 533.2 million in 1999 to 724.2 million in 2013. Labor's share of world income fell in relation to capital's share almost everywhere, largely the result of increased productivity, on the one hand, and stagnant wages, on the other.[2] At the same time, manufacturing output and employment shifted from the developed economies of the economic North to the developing nations of the East, above all China. The number of industrial workers in the developed economies fell from 122 million in 1999 to 107 million in 2013, while those in East Asia increased from 176 million to 250 million in those years.[3] Alongside this shift came one of the largest human migrations in history, largely the result of dispossession due to rural displacement and war. "Globally, there were 232 million international migrants in 2013," over half of them in Europe and North America, reported the UN Secretary-General.[4]

1

All these trends led to a number of developments that are fundamental to the analysis that follows: 1) the increased productivity that led to labor's falling share of world income also produced much of the decline in manufacturing employment in the developed economies; 2) global migration brought enormous changes in the ethno/racial composition of the working class in many developed economies; and 3) as a consequence of rising trade and FDI, competition became more intense not only globally but within the major developed economies, leading to an unprecedented business consolidation and the rise of the "logistics revolution." These trends would have an enormous impact on the shape of US capitalism in terms of lost manufacturing jobs, rising "service" employment, the changing ethno/racial composition of the workforce, and the consolidation of business on a massive scale that would alter the terrain of class conflict and the composition and power of the working class itself.

In terms of the changing occupational, industrial, and ethno/racial composition of the US working class, we should remember such changes are an almost continuous process as capital itself expands, contracts, moves, and draws in new human material. For example, as Dan La Botz points out, the Great Lakes industrial region that stretched from Pittsburgh to Chicago and Duluth "linked together by a dense network of waterways, railroads, and highways" had been the center of industry and industrial unionism and a "social texture" that supported it until industry began to break up and move after World War II.[5] This is, of course, an important observation about the restructuring of the US working class and the decline of unionism that started even before the neoliberal era that began in the late 1970s as the nation's major industrial region became the "Rust Belt." At the same time, it has to be kept in mind as well that even during the height of the development of the Great Lakes industrial region and the industrial unions it supported in the 1940s and 1950s, the racial, ethnic, and cultural composition of that class was changing.

The autoworkers who rebelled in the plants of Detroit, Flint, or Lordstown in the 1960s and 1970s, for example, were not for the most part the descendants of those who founded the United Auto Workers in the 1930s. Many of those in Detroit and Flint of the 1970s were migrants or their offspring from the South, Black and white, who came to these plants in huge numbers during and after World War II. Those young white workers who made the "blue-collar blues" famous at GM's Lordstown assembly plant came mostly from the rural Midwest to a plant that didn't exist before 1966. Nor by the 1960s were the steel towns of Gary, South Chicago, or Cleveland with their growing black populations the same as they had been in the 1930s. As we will see below, today's working class differs not only in industrial composition and regional concentration from that of the 1960s and 1970s, but in ethnic and racial content as well. The terrain on which the working class and the oppressed fight necessarily changes as the structure and contours of global and domestic capitalism change. It will be argued here that the process of disintegration of the old industrial corridors and regions has been replaced by new and mostly different geographic patterns and structures of concentration with the potential for advances in working-class organization and rebellion.

The late 1970s would see the beginning of the neoliberal era after a decade or more of labor rebellion, low growth, and declining productivity combined with rising inflation—known as "stagflation." Characterized by deregulation of industry, privatization of public services, cuts in the welfare state, tax cuts for corporations and the wealthy, undermining of labor rights, and a general emphasis on "the market" as the salvation of the economy, neoliberalism emerged in the United States as the Democratic Carter administration and Congress defeated labor law reform and passed measures to deregulate truck and air transportation. It would accelerate under Reagan and again under Clinton to become the new norm of economic policy and business preference. Neoliberalism was, as David Harvey has argued, a project to restore class power to the economic elite.[6]

In the period beginning in the 1980s, globalization accelerated, and outsourcing and various forms of workforce "flexibility" increased, along with internationalized production through global value chains (GVC). These developments appeared to fragment and dissolve the power of the traditional working class across much of the industrial North. Yet, under the very same pressures of global competition, just-in-time-driven logistics systems restructured and integrated the movement of materials within the United States (and around the world), and, beginning in the mid-1990s, the biggest wave of mergers and acquisitions in American history reshaped and consolidated capital as businesses sought to reassert their power in global markets and increase control over the workforce. As a consequence, it will be argued here, capitalism has entered a new phase in which the working class is both restructured and, along with capital itself, consolidated, that is, forced together in new ways.

The argument in this work is divided into three parts. The first part examines the industrial and occupational restructuring of the US working class since the beginning of the neoliberal era in the early 1980s as a result of lean production, new technology, and the system's rising requirements of social reproduction of the working class and capital maintenance. Part 2 then analyzes the enormous changes in the terrain on which class conflict takes place. In particular, this involves the major changes in the organization of capitalism in the United States due to the unprecedented wave of mergers and acquisitions that accelerated in the 1990s and the "logistics revolution" that reconfigured transportation and production itself in the twenty-first century. Part 2 will also look at the possibility of a renewed upsurge of labor and social rebellion and what might be done prior to this in order to avoid the weaknesses of the rank-and-file rebellions of the 1960s and 1970s. Finally, part 3 will look at the changes in US politics, the increased importance of the states, the reshaping of the Democratic Party, and the potential for a new radical, class politics in the United States. First, however, the causes of decline in goods-producing employment and the rise of "service" jobs need to be examined.

PART I

The Remaking of the US Working Class

CHAPTER ONE

The Roots of Change

For decades, employment in manufacturing has declined in most of the industrialized economies, while that in "services" has risen in both absolute and relative terms. With the onset of the neoliberal era, increased competition, deregulation, privatization, outsourcing, and lean production methods reorganized the production of goods and services. Production systems were disaggregated, manufacturing workplaces downsized, and existing working-class communities uprooted to such an extent that many have concluded that the working class has either dissolved entirely or at the very least been so fragmented that whatever power for social change once attributed to it has more or less evaporated.

Not surprisingly, theories have been formulated to put social fragmentation at the center of class analysis. One of the most popular recent efforts is Guy Standing's recomposition of capitalist class structure in his *Precariat: The New Dangerous Class.* Terms such as "working class" or "proletariat," he writes, "are little more than evocative labels." Instead Standing proposes a seven-layer "fragmented class structure" for contemporary, presumably Western society. At the top is an "elite," and at the bottom the "precariat" is "flanked by an army of unemployed" and "socially ill misfits." In between these are the other layers, some with a suitable neologism ("salariat," "proficians"), along with the remnants of the "proletariat" somewhere in the middle.[1] At best this and other efforts like it are descriptive—a relayering of the traditional stratification models of society—in which there is no underlying basis for class conflict and no central class large or strong enough to affect social change.[2] A notable exception to the recent popular literature is Tamara Draut's *Sleeping Giant,* which, though its definition of class differs from that in this work, insists that what she calls the "New Working Class" is, indeed, a social class and offers important insights into the reality and potential of today's multiracial working class and its struggles.[3]

If, as is argued here, classes in capitalism are relational in nature, rather than simply stacked uncomfortably one on top of the other, if "the capitalist process of production . . . produces not only commodities, not only surplus value, but it also produces and reproduces the capital relation itself; on the one hand the capitalist, on the other the wage-labourer," then the conflictual nature of that relationship and the way it alters class structure can be analyzed and a different picture of class conflict and contours drawn out.[4] The picture that will emerge here involves the dynamic, often disruptive transition from forms of fragmentation, relocation, and capitalist restructuring to a reconcentration of capital and the working class, albeit with a different internal structure. Although the focus is on the United States, much of what is written here applies to other developed industrial economies as well.

Are Imports and Offshoring the Culprits?

Globalization has meant huge shifts in the world's production from the economic North to the South, or more precisely the East. From 1992 to 2012 the proportion of real value added in manufacturing produced by the developed industrial economies fell from 82 percent to 65 percent, with the fastest growth occurring in East Asia. This dramatic shift, however, is a relative one in which growth in the industrialized nations was 43 percent, compared to 79 percent for the world and 244 percent for East Asia and the Pacific.[5] This relative decline has made trade and imports the most commonly repeated explanations for the decline of manufacturing jobs in the United States and, hence, the shrinking of the traditional industrial "core" of the working class. Without denying the significance of imports and offshoring of production, I will offer a different explanation for the loss of manufacturing jobs rooted in the outcomes of class conflict expressed in rising productivity.

The overall net loss of manufacturing production and nonsupervisory jobs from 1979 to 2010 in the United States was a staggering 5.7 million. To be sure, some industries such as primary metals, textiles, apparel, and electronics have been hit hard by imports and seen huge job losses. From 1980 to 2010 these industries lost approximately 1.5 million production jobs, or about 26 percent of the total decline.[6] Yet it cannot be said for certain that these losses are due entirely to imports or offshoring of production, or, as I will argue below, to repeated crises and productivity gains. Simply looking at the trade deficit for an industry doesn't tell us if the jobs *actually* lost were taken by imports unless the imports outstripped domestic output. Only if domestic output declined or stagnated and imports grew could it be said for sure that imports were the culprit. Otherwise it can only be said that imports destroyed *potential* employment possibilities.

Imports, of course, have risen as a share of GDP and manufacturing products consumed in the United States. So some job losses in those industries listed above are certain. At the same time, as we will see below, manufacturing output in the United States has risen far more than most people realize. If total production job losses in these hard-hit industries explain only a little more than a quarter of the loss of manufacturing jobs plus smaller numbers spread across other industries, then the total impact of imports is certain to be even less. To get a better idea of the impact of trade and trade deals, we will examine the impact of the offshoring of intermediate inputs on manufacturing employment.

The rise of global value chains (GVC) has been well documented, leading to the belief that offshoring has been a major source of job loss in the United States and other developed economies. As the UN observed, however, "Large economies, such as the United States or Japan, tend to have significant internal value chains and rely less on foreign imports."[7] Most of the outsourcing in the auto industry, for example, remained in the US Midwest and South, as Aschoff has shown in great detail for the years 1988–2007.[8] Looking at the proportion of imported material intermediate inputs in total manufacturing output, as opposed to services or energy inputs, since we are trying to determine the impact of imports on manufacturing jobs, we can get an idea of their impact.

Using figures from the Bureau of Economic Analysis (BEA) it is possible to get a reasonably accurate picture of the extent of offshoring in value terms. The value of imports of material inputs as a proportion of all intermediate inputs used by all US manufacturers rose from 16.9 percent in 1997 to 25.1 percent in 2006, a significant increase. This, however, is a percentage of intermediate inputs, not of total production. In value terms, total material intermediate inputs have averaged about 50 percent of total output for those years. Thus, offshore content as a percent of total manufacturing output was 8.4 percent for 1997 and 12.7 percent for 2006, compared to the international average of 28 percent.[9] For much of the period from 1982 to 1997, the percentage was even lower. In other words, while imported parts and components in the supply chains of US-based manufacturing firms have grown since the early 1980s, such as those from the maquiladora plants in northern Mexico, domestic content was still in the 85–90 percent range or more, well above the global average of 72 percent. Manufacturing job losses on a large scale due to offshoring over this period could only be explained if the annual growth of imported intermediate inputs exceeded the growth of total output significantly, but as a percentage of all manufacturing intermediate inputs they grew by less than half a percentage point a year from 1997 to 2006 and probably less from 1982 to 1997.[10]

Recently a trend toward "reshoring" of manufacturing has taken hold, while offshoring has fallen so that in 2014, reshored jobs plus those resulting from inward foreign direct investment grew by sixty thousand, surpassing offshored jobs by ten thousand by one estimate. The reasons for this trend are to be found in the rapidly rising wages and high levels of strike activity in China, as well as slow and uncertain oceanic freight traffic that often disrupts just-in-time production and delivery systems. Among those recently reshoring production were large firms such as Ford, GE, Caterpillar, NCR, and Boeing. While this is a tiny net gain, several research firms believe this trend will grow.[11]

The problem with trade explanations or those rooted in the global shift of manufacturing generally is that manufacturing output in the United States has not declined overall or even slowed down much since the early 1980s but increased at rates close to those of the post–World War II Keynesian epoch of growth, when government spending and even debt were used to induce economic expansion and fund the welfare state. In real terms, measured by the Federal Reserve Board's industrial production index, manufacturing output increased by 131 percent from 1982 to 2007 just before the impact of the Great Recession, three times the average increase for the developed nations, or on average about 5 percent a year, compared to 6 percent annually during the boom years of the 1960s. The real GDP measure of manufacturing growth from the BEA produces almost exactly the same result.[12] This growth did slow down somewhat in the 2000s as two recessions affected output.

It should also be remembered that even industries that lose jobs to imports can see employment eroded by increased productivity as well. The steel industry offers a clear example. Net steel imports measured in tons rose from about 14 percent of total shipments in the United States in 1990 to about 18 percent in 2005 before the recession. Shipments of domestic steel alone, however, rose by 24 percent over this period. Productivity in steel production rose by an annual average of around 5 percent, for a total rise of 75 percent over this period, largely due to the growth of more efficient "mini-mills," while employment fell by nearly half, from 187,000 employees in 1990 to 96,000 in 2005. The major culprit here appears to have been the growth of domestic mini-mills using electric arc furnaces, which are far more efficient, use less labor, and whose proportion of domestic output rose from 37 percent in 1990 to 55 percent in 2005.[13]

As the *Economist* impatiently complained concerning the shift of manufacturing toward China, "For all the bellyaching about the 'decline of American manufacturing' and 'the shifting of production *en masse* to China, real output has been growing at an annual pace of almost 4% since 1991, faster than GDP growth.'" The job loss, which this conservative publication sees "as a good thing," "largely reflects rapid productivity growth."[14] During this period, industrial capacity very nearly doubled, although capacity utilization rates remained below those of the 1960s.[15] While imports did eliminate significant numbers of manufacturing jobs due to their impact on the industries mentioned above, they can at best be said to have slowed the rate of increase of total output, while capital and production shifted to other industries and locations within the United States.

The increased extent of outsourcing associated with lean production and industrial restructuring, which has been part of the experience of fragmentation since the late 1970s, is also sometimes mentioned as a source of job loss. Outsourcing was and remains a common business strategy in the increasingly competitive context of deregulation, shareholder pressure, and international competition—a way to escape expensive union labor and seek lower-paid alternatives. A 2002 survey of global executives reported that 75 percent of firms outsourced food and maintenance, 66 percent legal services, 53 percent Internet services, 45 percent data processing, and 41 percent telemarketing. For manufacturing, 62 percent of executives reported outsourcing some parts and components production. General Motors famously reduced its in-house production from 70 percent to 49 percent during the 1990s.[16]

Despite its growth, however, domestic outsourcing of intermediate inputs to goods production such as parts and components, formerly done in-house, accounted for only 15 percent of such inputs in 2006 and considerably less in the preceding three decades. Indeed, the bulk of outsourcing has been in services such as those mentioned in the survey cited above.[17] This level is relatively low because a large proportion of material intermediate inputs have always come from external domestic suppliers. Outsourcing, understood as work formerly done in-house, simply added some production to this stream. Finally, of course, jobs outsourced within the United States, while highly disruptive to those affected, do not necessarily disappear because they have changed location or ownership title. A more likely explanation for manufacturing job losses on the scale of the last thirty years or so, one that is internal to the workings of US capitalism and, indeed, capitalism generally, is to be found in the rise of productivity extracted after 1980 by the introduction of lean production methods, new technology, and capital's accelerated counteroffensive against labor—an explanation based in class conflict itself.

Before discussing the impact of productivity on job loss, it is important to understand the rhythm of job destruction over the period from 1980 to the present. The loss of manufacturing jobs did not follow the rhythm of the more or less straightforward trajectory of rising imports or offshoring. Rather the big losses occurred, as might be expected, during the recessions of the period, when large amounts of capital were destroyed and firms sought to downsize or reorganize—and when imports also tended to drop. Over two and a half million manufacturing production jobs were lost during the 1980–82 recession, before the acceleration of trade and FDI in the mid-1980s; a smaller number, 869,000 during the shallower recession of 1990–92; a little over two million in the 2000–2002 slump; and about two million during the Great Recession from 2007 to 2010. Between slumps employment levels remained more or less steady (at the lower level) until 2000, while manufacturing output rose by 6 percent a year between 1982 and 1990 and again between 1992 and 2000. From 2002 to 2007 output rose by a more modest 2.4 percent a year until the Great Recession took hold.[18]

The argument here is that while economic slumps destroyed jobs (and capital), productivity increases, extracted mainly through work intensification even where new technology was involved and even during the recessions, prevented the growth of manufacturing jobs when recovery came and output expanded in each decade. Furthermore, as a close look at indexes for real merchandise imports and manufacturing jobs in appendix B shows, when imports fell in recessions, so did the number of jobs, whereas when imports soared between recessions, the number of jobs remained basically flat due to increased output. If it had been primarily imports of either final products or intermediate inputs that had taken these manufacturing jobs, overall output could hardly have been so robust in the years between recessions.

Globalization, of course, does have an impact on US employment and income levels as well as on the developments discussed below. The two major impacts that matter most for this analysis are increased competition faced by US capital at home and abroad, on the one hand, and immigration caused mainly by the dispossession of people around the world by capitalism's expansion and the neoliberal policies that enable it as well as the wars it has spawned. Competition drives the productivity that eliminates manufacturing jobs, while immigrants fill the growing number of lower-paid occupations associated with the rise of service-producing employment as well as some manufacturing and logistics industries. The next two sections will analyze the decline of manufacturing work and the rise of the (sometimes mislabeled) service sector.

Some academics have argued that productivity gains in the period 1987–2007, most of the neoliberal era, are explained almost entirely by those in the computer and electronics product industries, while others have attempted to show that manufacturing production figures such as those calculated by the Federal Reserve System overstate output due to the role of imported intermediate inputs. Such adjustments would, of course, reduce the productivity statistics published by the Bureau of Labor Statistics (BLS) and other agencies. I believe these adjustments are mostly off the mark and highly speculative; therefore, I have used widely published estimates from various sources. I have dealt with both arguments in appendix A in order not to disrupt the analysis here.

Class Struggle, Lean Production, and Productivity

The process of accumulation, as Marx argued, itself leads to "the diminution of the mass of labour in proportion to the mass of means of production moved by it" due to increasing productivity.[19] And, as we will see below, the mass of capital in relation to labor did, indeed, increase over this period. The degree to which increased productivity is extracted and labor thereby relatively diminished, however, is to a large extent determined by class struggle within the labor process as well as by the competition between capitals. While the struggle over wages is always a piece of class conflict, for most of the post–World War II era in the United States it was the fight over relative surplus value, that is, the fight to reduce the time during the working day needed to cover the cost of labor power by increasing productivity that has been capital's major focus.

The late 1960s through the 1970s was a period of intense industrial conflict in the United States, largely in resistance to capital's introduction of hardball management practices in the late 1940s and 1950s, the "management offensive of 1958–63," and the consequent speedup of production in the 1960s.[20] This was the era of rank-and-file rebellion in which blue-collar workers went on the offensive against their bosses, and often their union leaders as well, in a fight against speedup and deteriorating working conditions and real wages, while millions of public-sector workers joined unions for the first time.[21] Partly as a result of high levels of conflict productivity, growth during the 1970s virtually collapsed in US manufacturing, and profit rates fell.[22] The rebellion came to an end with the recession induced by Federal Reserve chairman Paul Volker's sudden increase in interest rates in 1979, which announced the neoliberal era and created the opportunity for capital's new counteroffensive against organized labor.[23]

In the three or so years of this recession 2.5 million manufacturing jobs were lost, the unions that had been the major sites of the 1960–70s rebellion lost more than two million members, while the number of all private-sector union members dropped by 26 percent, and strikes all but disappeared.[24] This became an opportunity for capital to launch its new offensive to undermine collective bargaining arrangements, compress real wages, reduce benefits, and, most importantly, extract continuous increases in productivity that would eliminate millions of manufacturing jobs. The major weapon in capital's struggle to increase the extraction of surplus value through the intensification of work in this period was lean production, often accompanied by new technology.[25]

Lean production was introduced from Japan into the United States in the 1980s, and its stated object was always to eliminate "waste," meaning buffers that slowed production, high inventory levels, imperfect parts, and "idle" labor time in the production process. Appropriately dubbed "management by stress" by Mike Parker and Jane Slaughter of *Labor Notes*, lean methods constantly stressed the production system to locate and eliminate all non-value-producing labor. As Toyota's lean pioneer Taiichi Ohno put it, "Manpower reduction means raising the ratio of value-added work."[26] Here lean production will be used as shorthand for the multitude of programs introduced over time in this long period to impose measurable and standardized work processes (metrics) and further reduce labor input in relation to output, such as total quality management (TQM), statistical process control (SPC), Six Sigma, and so on. Virtually all these methods of control came into practice in the 1980s along with human resource management (HRM) and supply chain management (SCM) as new disciplines and are now global in their application. While the various lean methods were often applied selectively or partially, most, like Six Sigma, have "come to be integrated with lean principles," as one recent study of the auto industry noted.[27] Although the auto industry led in the application of lean production norms, innovations sometimes came from elsewhere. "Data-driven" Six Sigma was developed by Motorola in the mid-1980s and soon adopted by General Electric, but not adopted by Ford, for example, until 2000. By now it is used "all over the world, in organizations as diverse as local government departments, prisons, hospitals, the armed forces, banks, and multinational corporations."[28]

While in its classic form lean production was characterized by a number of features, such as the Andon Board, *kaizen* or continuous improvement teams, job rotations, just-in-time delivery of parts, et cetera, at its heart was the fight over time. The just-in-time (JIT) standard for the auto industry, and by implication most manufacturing, went from a three-day delivery "window," to "a thirty-minute time frame."[29] This obviously put enormous pressure on suppliers and their workers. This emphasis on time was not merely the lengthening of hours for some and their shortening for others involved in the new "flexibility" demanded by capital, but the time worked actually producing value within each day, hour, and minute. It is, in short, about the *intensification* of work.[30] This is one reason why the introduction of programs designed to measure performance, such as SPC and Six Sigma, have become so important. Ostensibly meant to reduce errors and variations in outcomes, they aid in the standardization, measurement, and intensification of the labor process.

Hence the lax American standard of 45 to 52 seconds of actual work per minute in automobile assembly was to be replaced by Toyota's 57-second minute; thereby, "filling up the pores of the working day."[31] An indication of just how employers would implement the 57-second minute is found in the November 1997 issue of the rank-and-file newsletter *The Barking Dog*, distributed at the GM-Toyota NUMMI plant in California, which reported the introduction of a "pilot team in charge of figuring out how to add six seconds of work to our jobs."[32] In other words, 57 seconds was a goal to be achieved piece by piece to reduce resistance. What began in the auto industry rapidly spread to other manufacturers and beyond. Aside from adding seconds to each job, management also reduced break time.

A recent study of work intensification in the United States based on time used diaries of more than 43,000 men and women employed mostly in routine "middling" goods and service-producing jobs found that from the 1980s to the 2000s the number of breaks during the workday fell by 30 percent for men and 34 percent for women, while the time in breaks decreased by 29 percent and 25 percent, respectively. The time at work until a break was taken rose by 20 percent and 27 percent, respectively, for men and women. In other words, the time before any break rose by over an hour, while the breaks were fifteen minutes shorter for men and nine minutes shorter for women. Total break time went from 13 percent of the work day in the 1980s to 8 percent in the 2000s, which is to say that within the average eight-hour day capital gained approximately twenty-four minutes or almost half an hour of extra work at no extra cost in wages, benefits, or employment taxes! Furthermore, the authors concluded that the major driving force behind shrinking break time was "technological change," which drove the increase in time actually worked.[33] For the routine jobs measured with their constant repetition, this amounts to a stressful and fatiguing extension of time actually worked.

If the reduction in break time were combined with the Toyota 57-second minute, the employer would have gained almost two extra hours of work within the eight-hour day. While it is unlikely that most employers reach the full Toyota standard and even allowing for a slowing down of performance during the extra work due to fatigue, this amounts to a significant increase in productivity and the rate of surplus value. And the push to fill up "the pores" continues. The 2015 contract agreement between Ford and the United Auto Workers grants the company one minute less in break time for each hour worked each day by each of Ford's 53,000 unionized workers.[34] That amounts to more than seven thousand extra hours work per day for the entire workforce, the equivalent of almost four years for the company at no extra cost.

There is another feature of lean production introduced first by General Motors in Belgium in 1989 and then spread to the United States in the 1990s: the alternative work schedule. This innovation did away with the traditional two crews working five-day-a-week, eight-hour shifts, and replaced them with three crews working ten hours a day for four days. Two crews worked regular day or night shifts during the week, but the third crew worked Friday and Saturday days and Sunday and Monday nights. This meant that weekday shifts went from a total of sixteen hours a day to twenty, while each weekend day had a regular ten-hour shift not including overtime. When this schedule was implemented at GM's Lordstown, Ohio, plant capacity utilization grew by 43.5 percent in the first two years of operation and the number of cars built per hour rose from seventy-six to eighty. The number of hours worked increased, but weekends were now "regular" shifts of forty hours with no Sunday premium, and the number of workers fell from 9,119 to 8,800. Cost savings were enormous. By spring of 2016, on its fiftieth anniversary, the Lordstown plant employed just 4,500 workers at what *Automotive News* called "one of GM's most productive North American plants."[35] Since the introduction of longer shifts of this sort at GM, they have become more common. While the percentage of all manufacturing workers doing evening or night shifts has remained around 18 percent, the hours of those working longer evening or night shifts have clearly increased. According to a recent survey of four hundred shift work operations by the consultancy Circadian, only 34 percent, just about a third, worked eight hours. Nearly half worked ten- or twelve-hour shifts, while another 15 percent worked between eight and twelve hours and 4 percent "other" hours.[36]

The GM alternative work schedule, however, increases the hours of *all* shifts or crews. The logic of lengthening the workday (or night) lies in the fact that, as Shaikh points out from empirical evidence, "the productivity of labor generally increases with the length of the working day, at least until exhaustion sets in."[37] Just where exhaustion sets in is determined by the intensity and difficulty of the job and is a matter of some controversy. Interestingly, Shaikh's argument on the effects of different shift lengths concludes that two ten-hour shifts provide "the highest total daily output of any shift combination" for a twenty-hour day, which, excluding overtime, is exactly what the GM alternative work schedule involves.[38] Thus, the average level of productivity is almost certain to increase with the length of the shift at ten hours so that each crew will produce more output, as they did at Lordstown, even if the rate of growth diminished toward the end of the day due to exhaustion. Shaikh's detailed and empirically based argument shows that even at the end of the shift unit labor costs will be below the starting point and average of the day. Since productivity will fall significantly at the beginning of each shift, the lengthening of the shift is important to capital in increasing the overall average level of productivity per day.[39] Thus, whatever damage it does to the worker, it is in the interest of capital to extend the workday beyond the previously acceptable eight hours. As we saw in the example of GM's Lordstown plant, this also means the inevitable loss of jobs. By the late 1990s, alternative work schedules had become widespread across many industries.

More recently, supplementing or even supplanting the various innovations in lean production have come electronic forms of surveillance, work measurement, and monitoring such as radio frequency identification (RFID), global positioning systems (GPS), and biometric measurements that drive just-in-time norms within production processes and along supply chains maintaining management by stress all along the line.[40] It is precisely this sort of monitoring that allows employers to seek and measure a reduction of rest time per minute beyond even the shrinking of official break time, and to calculate the impact on productivity of a lengthened workday.

Technology, including that in the actual production process, also plays a role in this beyond surveillance, but, as is almost always the case, not as a substitute for the burdens of labor but as the enabler and enforcer of its intensification. Given the limits on the length of the workday imposed by law, custom, or union agreement, as Marx put it, "machinery becomes in the hands of capital the objective means, systematically employed, for squeezing out more labor in a given time."[41] Since Marx's day, works by Nobel, Braverman, and others have shown that the design and use of technology is socially constructed to intensify management control, reduce worker skills, and increase efficiency and output. As Noble put it writing about post–World War II developments in automation, the concerns of those who designed and deployed the new technology were "reflected in a general devaluation of human skills and a distrust of human workers and in an ongoing effort to eliminate both" in the name of efficiency and, of course, reducing human toil.[42]

All of these changes taken together have led to one of the biggest job-destroying intensifications of labor in the history of capitalism. By the second decade of the twenty-first century, if you survived the process, your job had been stressed, reengineered, measured, monitored, standardized, intensified, and connected just in time to another stressed, reengineered, etc., job while you and your fellow workers had been informed that you were the organization's most valuable asset. After all, who could produce so much surplus value so fast at virtually no extra cost?

There can be little doubt that management by stress, work reorganization, extended workdays, measuring and monitoring, new technology, and, of course, the undermining of unions fostered by lean methods had a major impact on productivity. In the early phase of lean production during the 1980s, manufacturing productivity grew by 5 percent a year on average.[43] In the automobile industry labor productivity rose by an annual average of 3 percent from 1987 through 2009, jumping to 3.6 percent a year from 2001 to 2009.[44] A European Union study of manufacturing as a whole put the average annual increase in the United States at 3.6 percent from 1979 to 2001, while a Conference Board analysis calculates the increases in real value added per worker in manufacturing at 4 percent a year from 1979 to 2012, with that rate jumping to 6 percent from 2000 to 2007. For the periods of 1990–2000 and 2000–2007, the BLS estimates average annual productivity growth in manufacturing at 4.1 percent and 4.7 percent, respectively.[45] It stands to reason, therefore, that a more than doubling of productivity since the early 1980s can well explain much of the 50 percent drop in manufacturing production worker jobs over that long period. The payoff for US capital was enormous as unit labor costs in US manufacturing fell consistently from 1990 through 2010.[46] What then of the rise in service jobs?

Service Jobs: Short Hours, the Social Reproduction of Labor Power, and Dirt

The rise of employment in occupations and industries labeled as "services" is not new. Service employment surpassed that in goods production by mid-century in the United States. One reason why service jobs tend to outstrip those in goods production is the difference in hours worked and productivity. Workers in manufacturing, construction, transportation, and warehousing and utilities work an average of forty hours a week, while those in administration, waste, health and social services, food services, and accommodations average about thirty hours per week—hence the growing number of part-time workers.[47] While some services have achieved high rates of productivity under lean conditions, others, such as food services and accommodations (0.8 percent) and janitorial services (1.9 percent), fall well behind the 3 percent annual rate for manufacturing.[48] It is precisely this low productivity that makes it possible to employ part-time workers because any rise in productivity over the workday, such as we saw in manufacturing above, will be minimal, so that shorter hours are profitable in this case. Low wages, on the other hand, keep unit labor costs down, making workforce expansions economical for the employer. As a consequence of shorter hours and low productivity, an increase in output in services requires proportionately more workers than in manufacturing or transportation. But which services are driving this growth?

Those service jobs that grew over the years were largely the creation of the internal dynamics of capital accumulation and two of its ongoing cost problems resulting from the postwar growth of the US economy: the social reproduction of labor power and the maintenance of its expanding fixed facilities—not primarily or even significantly as a result of the personal spending habits of the rich. Social reproduction is the labor expended in child rearing, family maintenance, elder care, and other forms of labor required to reproduce the species. Historically, this was unpaid labor performed by women mostly in the home, though, as we will see, it has now been partially transformed into commodity production, also often performed by women. Looking at those private-sector services most likely to employ working-class people (excluding finance, insurance, and real estate [known collectively as "FIRE"] and professional services), service jobs grew by 14.2 million from 1990 to 2010. Some eight million of those jobs or 57 percent of total growth were in employment associated with the labor of social reproduction, such as health and social care and food services. In other words, much of the increase in service work centers on society's need to reproduce its workforce—both active and potential.

Ironically, much of the increase in demand for the commodified reproduction of labor power is due to the increased participation of women in wage labor, including women with children, that began in the 1950s. As the economy expanded following World War II, capital drew increasingly on those engaged in social reproduction in the home or family as part of the unpaid reserve army of labor. Not only did more women enter wage labor, but the number of hours they worked also rose dramatically: from a median of 925 hours per year in 1979 to 1,664 in 2012; for women with children the increase was even greater, more than doubling from 600 hours per year to 1,560 over this period.[49] The resulting relative shortage of unpaid female labor of reproduction in the home opened the door to the commodification of the labor of reproduction outside of the family in the market. The fall in real wages that began in the 1970s became an additional push for women with children to turn to wage labor, hence further reducing their ability to perform the labor of social reproduction in the home, which despite some improvements in male participation remain largely the responsibility of women.

In the United States to a greater degree than other developed economies, many of the services involved in the social reproduction of labor power fell to the private sector. Capital, ever ready to extend the hand of exploitation, and as Marx put it, "always seeking out new areas of investment," moved to fill the gap.[50] As a result, a growing proportion of the labor of reproduction—child and elder care, health maintenance, food preparation, and so on—once done in the home or family has been commodified and provided by profit-making businesses as families had to buy more of the services that underlie social reproduction. For example, in 1982 Americans spent 40 percent of their food expenditures eating out, while by 2010 this was up to 49 percent. Health care expenditures grew from 4.7 percent of average consumer income in 1985 to 6.4 percent in 2009.[51] The workforce delivering most of these services outside of the home, however, remained disproportionately female.

At the same time, the growth in jobs needed to maintain capitalism's facilities and buildings (part of its growing fixed nonresidential stock), work its ancillary functions via temporary employees, and clean up its growing mess increased by an additional five million jobs from 1990 to 2010.[52] Many of these jobs were those outsourced or subcontracted from manufacturing and other industries in the last thirty years—when many formerly appeared in the BLS's "manufacturing" column. Thus, aside from managerial and professional jobs, altogether 90 percent of the growth in major private-sector, service-producing job categories from 1990 to 2010 came from the reproduction and maintenance of capitalism's workforce and fixed capital, the result of capitalist accumulation itself and all now done by profit-making (or -taking) firms, even when, as in health care, they are partly publicly funded.

Many of these jobs are low-skilled and low-paid. As they have grown as a proportion of the workforce, fully 43 percent of all private-sector jobs fell below the BLS definition of "low wage" by 2010.[53] On the one hand, few of these jobs are white-collar; most are physical in nature, require little training, and are more likely to be held by women, immigrants, Latinos, or African Americans. On the other hand, they are landlocked and seldom susceptible to offshoring. While not all of these workers produce surplus value, they are nonetheless essential to contemporary capitalism. As they possess no means of production, must sell their labor power on the market, work more hours than covers their wages, and work under the rule of capital, they are working class.[54]

Finally, the arbitrary separation in government statistics of many of these so-called service jobs from material production is misleading in that most of the jobs in industries or occupations such as those in hotels, hospitals, food services, building cleaning, waste management, maintenance and repair of many kinds, entertainment, and so on, both use up physical inputs, as Ursula Huws has pointed out, and produce a material good or effect—a material change.[55] While Marx was clear that a service did not have to be material in this way to be a commodity, it is nonetheless the case that much service work does produce a material commodity. What determines whether or not they produce surplus value is whether, as Shaikh and Tonak argue, they "are capitalistically organized," that is, paid out of capital as variable capital.[56] And what we see here is that more and more social activity is, indeed, capitalistically organized. Because these jobs are not so different from those officially tagged as "goods producing," they have come to face the same lean reorganization as their high-tech enablers. As Joan Greenbaum wrote of reengineered office work at the dawn of the twenty-first century, "The restructured world of work was held in place through computer and communications networks, as well as by other now familiar varieties of office technology, which, like schemes for reorganizing work, were designed to get more work out of remaining workers."[57] By 2010 Sameer Kumar could write approvingly of America's specialist hospitals, "They have adapted Lean Manufacturing, Six Sigma, and supply chain strategies in order to become more efficient as well as improving patient care and satisfaction."[58] This includes the use of GPS to track the movements of nurses and the introduction of electronic clinical decision support systems, which are derived from critical path analysis and standardize treatments and remove judgment from caregivers. Lean methods have also penetrated America's public schools, where teams promote speedup in the name of "continuous improvement" and teachers are evaluated by how their students do on standardized tests.[59] Just as much as those who produce things "you can drop on your toe," as the *Economist* famously put it, these service workers are being stressed to the max.[60]

CHAPTER TWO

Precarious Work: Growth but Less Than You Thought

As any number of commentators have noted, the era of lean production saw an increase in workforce flexibility and nontraditional employment. On examining the growth and extent of contingent and insecure work in the United States, however, it is well to keep in mind what one international study of precarious jobs cautioned: "The assumption that the principal norms regulating work are those of full-time permanency has never reflected the full variety of working relationships present in industrial economies."[1] In other words, there has always been a strong element of contingency in working-class reality.

Indeed, for Marx and Engels, precariousness in the broadest sense was the normal condition of the working class. The process of capital accumulation necessarily spins off a part of the workforce, as we saw above in the extreme case of manufacturing in the United States where productivity destroyed millions of jobs. In Marx's words, "It is capital accumulation itself that constantly produces, and produces indeed, in direct relation to its own energy and extent, a relatively redundant working population, i.e., a population which is superfluous to capital's average requirements for its own valorization, and is therefore a surplus population."[2] This ongoing process forms and reforms a vast industrial reserve army of labor composed not only of the unemployed but of those "marginally attached to the labor force," as the BLS puts it, those between jobs, discouraged workers, those outside the labor force at any moment, those in temporary employment, women in the home, students, and so on. This is not a permanent body of individuals, some precariat separate from the working class as a whole. As Marx argues, the rise of new industries and the system's periodic crises depend on "the constant formation, the greater or less absorption, and the re-formation of the industrial reserve army or surplus population."[3] Thus, this army constantly drafts and discharges from the ranks of the working class as a result of both long-term and cyclical trends.

This being the case, any individual is likely to experience different degrees of short-term and long-term employment as well as bouts of unemployment in a lifetime. Indeed, the average number of jobs held by persons eighteen to forty-four years of age over thirty years between 1978 and 2008 was around eleven regardless of gender, race, or education, with the exception of those with less than a high school diploma, who averaged 13.3 jobs during those years.[4] The younger the worker, the more jobs mostly of shorter than average duration she experienced; the older, the fewer, with longer duration. Some of these jobs will be short-term, particularly for younger workers, others long-term, but both a lifetime job with the same employer and endless multiple short-term jobs were always the exception. There is nothing new about this.

What is under consideration is the degree of change. One of the results of the ongoing accumulation process and the increased flexibility of the workforce demanded by lean production and the growth of extended supply chains in both services and goods production has been the increase in precarious or contingent employment such as temporary agency work, short-term contracts, on-call work, independent contracting (that is, bogus self-employment), involuntary part-time work (part-time for economic reasons by those who usually work full-time), and so on. By the 2005 BLS estimates, the most recent available, adjusted for some undercounts of temporary and involuntary part-time workers and overlap of categories, some 21.6 million employees worked in precarious situations, compared to 18.7 million in 1995, an increase of nearly three million precarious jobs over a decade. Yet, surprisingly, the proportion of precarious workers hardly rose at all, from 15.2 percent in 1995 to 15.5 percent in 2005, the last BLS count.[5]

This seems counterintuitive, and one can almost hear the protests of disbelief from many of those who read this. Nevertheless, contingent workers, those who told the BLS survey they didn't expect their job to last a long time, dropped slightly from 1995 to 2005. All the other measures of precariousness rose somewhat, but not enough to increase the proportion by much. While the 1995 survey was the first, so that there are no comparable figures for earlier years, we can get an idea of how much precarious employment grew prior to

1995 by looking at one available statistic that would indicate a rise in precariousness. In 1980 all personnel supply services, which includes temp agencies but is broader, supplied only 543,000 workers. By 1990 those working for temp agencies alone rose to 1,288,000 and then to 2,189,000 in 1995. Similarly, the number of unincorporated self-employed, most of whom would be "independent contractors," increased by 1.6 million between 1980 and 1995.[6] Thus, it is most likely that the biggest jump in precarious work came with the initial spread of lean production in the 1980s and early 1990s, at which time it was part of the fragmentation experienced by many.

It is, of course, also possible that precarious jobs have increased since 2005. The little data available on this, however, don't point clearly in this direction.

Table I: Precarious Employment, 2005–2015

Type of Work	2005–6	2009–10	2015
Temp Agency	2,539,000	1,823,000	2886,300
Unincorporated Self-Employed	10,464,000	9,831,000	8,551,000

Source: US Census Bureau, *Abstract of the United States 2007* (Washington DC: US Government Printing Office, 2006), 383, 386; US Census Bureau, *Abstract of the United States 2012* (Washington DC: US Government Printing Office, 2011), 388, 391; BLS, "Labor Force Statistics from the Current Population Survey, Household Data, Seasonally Adjusted, Table A-7, 2016," www .bls.gov/web/empsit/cpseea07.htm; BLS, "Household Data, Annual Averages," Table 22, www .bls.gov/cps/cpsaat22.pdf.

As table I shows, temporary agency employment dropped during the recession and then rose to slightly above its previous number, while unincorporated self-employment (mostly independent contractors) fell significantly, more or less back to its 1995 level. So, while there might have been some overall net gain in precarious jobs over this period, it seems unlikely that the proportion of precarious workers in the total workforce could have risen much since 2005. Give or take a couple of percentage points, it is hard to avoid the conclusion that at least since the mid-1990s, precarious work in the United States has not grown as much as many impressionistic accounts imply and that the large majority of workers, about 85 percent, are still in "traditional" employment arrangements. The same is true in Canada and Europe, where estimates put the average percentage of precarious jobs slightly higher, at about 20 percent.[7]

This limited growth in precarious work is further supported by the fact that although people change jobs over time, job tenure has not changed much in the United States since the introduction of lean production norms and neoliberalism in general. Those who stated they had been in the same job for ten years or more fell by 5 percent from 1973 to 2006, and then, surprisingly perhaps, rose again for all age groups from 2006 to 2016. In any case, average job tenure was still measured in years. For those ages 25 to 34 the average length of job tenure fell from 3:8 years in 1979 to 3.5 in 2006, while those in the 35 to 44 age range saw it fall from 7.1 years to 6.6, and those ages 45 to 54 from 11.3 to 10.3.[8] These figures, of course, don't include the crucial 18 to 24 years of age cohort, precisely when new entrants to the workforce will experience the most precarity and shifting of work in hopes of finding something better. The median years of tenure for all wage and salary workers with the same employer actually rose from 3.5 years in 1983 to 3.8 in 1996, 4.0 in 2004, and 4.8 in 2014. The trend was the same for all age and gender groups.[9] None of this is to deny the fact that more and more jobs are dead end in that they don't offer a clear path to higher earnings, as wages remain low over time and benefits become rarer. Nevertheless, on average, workers still hold jobs for a number of years—the longer one is in wage labor, the longer the job lasts on average. The idea that workers change jobs all the time, making organizing impossible, is misleading. Nevertheless, the variety of impressionistic theories or at least neologisms about employment trends continues to proliferate.

The Gigariat

In the last few years, various academics and commentators have offered a series of neologisms in explanation for perceived changes in employment, including the "gig economy," the "sharing economy," the "servant economy," and the "age of self-employment," as well as the "precariat." More people are moving from job to job, more are self-employed, and more jobs are insecure. Or so these stories go. Speaking of the alleged rise in self-employment, economist Robert Solow summed up the problem with many of these propositions when he said, "You can see the age of self-employment everywhere except in the self-employment statistics."[10] In fact, if we look past the neologisms, we will see that many of these characterizations of the recent changes in capitalism do not hold up well.

Take the gig economy. To situate ourselves in the parade of economic neologisms we will call these nomadic workers the "gigariat." The term *gig*, of course, was coined by jazz musicians who had to go from job to job to make a living. The gig economy is usually said to have emerged in the wake of the Great Recession of 2008. In this emerging economy, job seekers cobbled together a living by taking and letting go of two or more jobs, sometimes through Internet outfits like TaskRabbit, Fiverr, or Uber. Although it denies it, Uber is an employer, while most of the others are simply digital "platforms" that provide a link between employers and gigsters. Some accounts throw in outfits like Airbnb, eBay, or Etsy because they can bring in income, but these are digital marketplaces, not labor markets. As a JP Morgan survey found when it looked at what it called "capital platforms," such as Etsy, eBay, and Airbnb, versus "labor platforms" such as Uber and TaskRabbit, was that it was the capital platforms that captured the lion's share of the 1 percent of adults who used any income-generating digital platform. By mid-2015, those who used labor platforms accounted for .04 percent of adults surveyed.[11] To get a broader look at the gigariat, we will seek them out, beyond just the "labor platforms," in the economy as a whole.

Not surprisingly, the BLS does not enumerate the gigariat. But assuming these peripatetic workers do actually work someplace for someone—even if themselves—they must show up somewhere in the BLS's statistical series. An obvious place to start is with the BLS category of multiple jobholders since gigsters famously hold multiple jobs. Already, however, there is a problem. While there are millions of multiple jobholders, their numbers haven't grown since the early 1990s. Since the alleged acceleration of the gigariat is usually placed in wake of the Great Recession, when the number of multiple jobholders fell to 6,878,000 by 2010, the subsequent increase in these workers to 7,262,000 by 2015 appears as a trend. The problem is that in 2007, just before the recession, there were 7,655,000 multiple jobholders, while in 1994 there were 7,260,000. In other words, in more than twenty years the number of these workers has not grown much, and their percentage of the workforce has actually fallen from an average of 6 percent in the 1990s to 4.9 percent from 2010 to 2015. Furthermore, 55 percent to 58 percent of these are full-time workers who hold one or more additional jobs.[12]

Far from emulating the lifestyles of Charlie Parker or Thelonious Monk, these overworked employees are engaged in the age-old and, despite its name, unromantic practice of "moonlighting" to make ends meet. In fact, the percentage of multiple jobholders in the employed workforce, with some ups and downs, has not changed significantly since the 1970s, when they averaged 4.9 percent of those employed just as they do today.[13] This is a sign that a good deal of the working class has never held jobs sufficiently well paid to meet their daily needs, which is not some new phenomenon.

Self-employment is often mentioned as part of the gigariat. For example, the Freelancers Union/Upwork claimed in a 2015 report that some fifty-four million Americans were freelancers—that is, self-employed people "engaged in supplemental, temporary, project-or contract-based work, within the past twelve months." As Lawrence Mishel of the Economic Policy Institute points out, this includes people with regular jobs who earn supplemental income in almost any way. By this definition I would have been a freelancer when I worked full time at *Labor Notes* or Brooklyn College because I received some royalties on a book I wrote. This is clearly absurd. As Mishel points out, as of 2015, "Only 11.3 million self-employed persons, representing 7.7 percent of total employment, work for themselves and have no employees," down by 1.8 million from 2014 to 2015—not fifty-four million.[14] In fact, the number of unincorporated self-employed workers, who form about two-thirds of the self-employed, has fallen for some time. The greatest increase in these workers came in the 1980s, leveled off, and then declined. What is more, they have declined in numbers since 1990 and as a proportion of the workforce since 1967.[15] The incorporated self-employed, on the other hand, have grown since the late 1980s both in numbers and as a percentage of the employed labor force, although they remain only about 4 percent or less of the workforce. These are mostly small business entrepreneurs, some with employees, however, and don't fit into our picture of the working class even if some conform to the image of the gigster.

It seems that the enthusiasts of the gig economy have looked at job trends for a few years since the Great Recession and generalized the future. What they saw, however, was not a trend but a long-standing cyclical feature of multiple jobholding that happened to be accompanied by an as yet marginal rise in those seeking work through the Internet rather than newspaper want ads, old-fashioned employment agencies, or vanishing state employment services. Even if this latter trend grows to be the norm among job seekers, it will not by itself define the nature or stability of future employment, a power that still resides with capital, which is the shaper of the labor market and the jobs in it, and the actual employer of more and more workers.

There are, to be sure, millions of working-class people, such as construction workers, taxi drivers, some truckers, and others, misclassified as self-employed independent contractors. While some of these might fit the gig profile, such as the 150,000 or so Uber "driver-partners," many are simply in industries long characterized by intermittent or seasonal employment and dominated by contractors who are, large or small, capitalist employers.[16] The independent contractors who work for them or others who employ this dodge are not really self-employed at all. This is a legal fiction exploited by employers to evade paying benefits, employment taxes, insurance, the cost of layoffs, unions, and so on. Overall, there isn't much evidence of a burgeoning gigariat. What there is for many, particularly younger workers, is a labor market still characterized by high levels of unemployment and a growing proportion of low-paid jobs, whether they are precarious or not, and a bleak future. The idea that this is the equivalent of jazz musicians seeking club dates only trivializes this reality.

The *experience* of increased precariousness in the last several years is almost certainly not based solely in the nature or multiplicity of the jobs one has held. Whether voluntary or not, each change in employment implies a period of unemployment with a decline or absence of income—a draft into the reserve army, whether brief or prolonged. Since 2007, however, this has been a period of economic crisis and high unemployment. The official rate jumped from 4.6 percent in January 2007 to 9.8 percent in January 2010 as the Great Recession took hold. In three years the number of unemployed increased by 7.6 million people, reaching 14.8 million in 2010—most of them looking for work. Not surprisingly, the duration of unemployment for those who found work rose dramatically, from a median of 5.2 weeks in 2007 to 10.4 in 2010, and it was more than twice that for those who didn't.[17] Looking at the whole neoliberal period since the early 1980s and smoothing the data for incremental trend purposes, Anwar Shaikh shows that not only did the average unemployment rate double over time, but also the duration of each experience of unemployment quadrupled, with over half that increase coming with the recession in 2008.[18] Thus, the *experience* of precariousness or gigging since the beginning of the crisis is as likely to have been formed by the high level and increased duration of unemployment between jobs as by the contingent nature of many of the jobs themselves. In an economic slump all kinds of jobs become more contingent or precarious. Most of the two million manufacturing production workers who lost their jobs from 2007 through 2010 were traditional full-time employees—not temps, independent contractors, or gigsters—and few of them will return to those same full-time jobs. Nevertheless, as we saw, on average most jobs will last a number of years. The only really new as opposed to cyclical aspects of all of this are the appearance of Internet platforms as a way to find employment, the above trend rise in the duration of unemployment, the persistent increase in productivity, and the secular decline in real wages discussed below, all of which apply to traditional as well as to contingent forms of employment.

Of course, twenty-two million or more workers in contingent jobs is no small number. Nor is the influence of so much insecure work on the conditions of those in traditional employment situations likely to be negligible even in times of growth. As a result of lean methods of work, including those that promote precarious and flexible employment, most jobs have been characterized by declining working conditions due to years of labor intensification and job standardization and falling real wages and declining benefits.

The End (of Good Jobs) Is Nigh!

In a sense, the debate over just how much employment is or isn't precarious misses the bigger change in working-class life over the past three decades—the decline in living standards and working conditions experienced by the vast majority of this class. As we saw above, work intensification has become the norm, while the standardization of work has, if anything, increased the deskilling and degradation of work analyzed years ago by Braverman.[19] Looking at the economic side of working-class life, one measure of declining living standards is the fall in both hourly and weekly real wages, which despite some ups and downs remain below their 1972 level.[20] By 2011 28 percent of all workers earned less than the official poverty-level wage of $11.06 an hour. So stagnant has been the income of the working-class majority that 30 percent of the workforce, and clearly a higher percentage of those in working-class employment, now relies on public assistance to get by.[21]

Income inequality has increased dramatically. From 1982 to 2012 the share of total income that went to the top 10 percent increased from 35 percent to 51 percent, while that of the top 1 percent rose from 10 percent to 23 percent. Furthermore, the labor share of income in GDP has declined in relation to capital, whose piece of the pie climbed from 18.8 percent in 1979 to 26.2 percent in 2010.[22]

While precarious and part-time workers have always done worse on employee benefits, these have declined for all groups of workers. In 1979 69 percent of all employees had some form of employer-provided health care benefits. By 2010 this was down to 53 percent, much of which went to managerial and professional employees. By 2010 only about 43 percent of employees had employer-provided pensions, and the percent of defined benefit plans had fallen from 39 percent in 1980 to 18 percent by 2004.[23] Since the early 1980s employers have been turning away from defined benefit pension plans, in which a worker's retirement income is predictable and secured by the employers, to defined contribution plans, which are essentially savings plans such as 401(k)s. These are based on financial investments such as stocks, bonds, and frequently mutual funds. One result is that the rich have done well with such savings, while the majority of working-class people have lost ground. Naturally, the financial crisis of 2007 wiped out a good deal of the savings of those nearing retirement. As New York Stock Exchange and the S&P500 indexes dropped by 37 percent from 2007 through 2009, retirement savings also fell.[24] Fidelity Investments, which manages many 401(k)s reported that the average work-based savings account fell by 27 percent. The well-to-do actually lost more on average because they have more savings in equities, but even those in the modest $5,000-to-$100,000 range lost 15 percent in those years.[25] According to an Economic Policy Institute study, however, those fifty-six to sixty-one years of age who would have retired in 2013 saw the median family savings plunge from a meager $35,929 in 2007 to $17,000 in 2013, a drop of more than 50 percent. These low median figures are in part because nearly half of US families have no retirement account savings at all. African Americans and Latinos are disproportionately among this latter group. The median savings among those families who do have retirement savings was $60,000 in 2013, clearly not enough to live on for long. Except for the shrinking minority with defined benefit plans, most working-class people must rely primarily on Social Security payments.[26] If anything in American society is precarious for the vast majority of working-class people, it is retirement, both for those now retired and perhaps even more so for those who retire in the future.

Furthermore, benefits, like income, are not distributed equally. By March 2015 only 7 percent of those employed in manufacturing had defined-benefit pensions, 10 percent in construction, and 9 percent in trade, transportation, and utilities, compared to 33 percent in finance and insurance. Among families in the 32-to-61 age bracket, the richest 20 percent are ten times more likely to have a retirement savings account such as a 401(k) or IRA than those in the bottom 20 percent and almost three times as likely as those in the second lowest quintile. In terms of health care benefits, the higher the earnings, the better the coverage. Ninety-three percent of the top 25 percent of earners had access to health care benefits, compared to 75 percent for those in the 25–49 percent range and 35 percent for the bottom 25 percent of workers, little more than a third of the access that the top earners had. Part-time workers, of course, did worse than full-timers.[27]

Much conventional analysis based on Current Population Survey occupational data argues that it has been both high-paying managerial jobs and the lowest-paying jobs that have grown rapidly while middle-income jobs have declined. Using the BLS's Occupational Employment Statistics (OES) survey, which excludes self-employed and nonwage or salary workers, Abraham and Spletzer concluded that by far the fastest growth since 2000 occurred not among managers but among the lowest-paid third of the workforce, with middle-income jobs declining as a share of employment.[28] Their study only goes up to 2004, but if the BLS employment projections for 2014–24, which are also based on OES estimates, are any guide, 70 percent of *all* the gains in nonmanagerial and nonprofessional jobs will fall in the official low-income range at or below $32,390 a year, and over a third of those in the very low range below $21,590.[29] These, of course, are the jobs that offer the least and the worst in terms of health care and retirement benefits. If employment tenure is not much less than twenty years ago, *economic* precariousness certainly is much greater for the vast majority of those who must work for a living. Most of this 70 percent of predicted new jobs are also low-skill and require little training or education, meaning, among other things, that they offer no path to improved income or skills. The end of good working-class jobs is nigh!

Work for the vast majority of working-class employees is far more intensive and demanding, likely to pay less and offer fewer benefits, with less state provision to fall back on, so that the rate at which workers are exploited is much greater than during the last period of upsurge in the 1960s and 1970s. Even growing numbers of professionals face the contagion of capitalist exploitation along with job standardization and degradation. On the outer edges of the working class, experiencing many of the same problems are the "proletarianizing" professionals such as teachers, nurses, and various technicians and engineers whose traditional autonomy has been crushed in the vice of measured and monitored standardization and lean just-in-time requirements as capital extends and deepens its authority over an increasing number of professions. The rebellion of such professionals, notably teachers and nurses in recent years, is a sign of how capitalism's expansion inevitably ensnares and encloses more and more of those who must work for a living.

The results for capital have been dramatic. That the growth of extreme economic inequality in the United States is the result of the trends discussed above that began as the neoliberal era opened are confirmed in Thomas Piketty's monumental study where he writes: "Since 1980, however, income inequality has exploded in the United States. The upper decile's (10 percent of the population) share increased from 30–35 percent of national income in the 1970s to 45–50 percent in the 2000s—an increase of 15 points of national income."[30] In fact, as he shows, the bulk went to the now notorious "1 percent," who alone gobbled up half that increase. This makes the United States more unequal economically than any European nation, even though inequality has grown there as well. The starting point for this soaring inequality is found in the capital-labor relationship.

Table II: Real Profit/Wage Ratio Selected Years, 1975–2011 (in $billions)

Year	Real NOS	Real EC	NOS/EC
1975	227.5	1069.7	21.3
1985	341.2	1391.7	24.5
1995	480.1	1648.0	29.1
2005	658.4	2036.0	32.3
2011	711.0	1988.8	35.8
Growth	213%	86%	68%

Real NOS = Net Operating Surplus adjusted by PPI
Real EC = Employee Compensation adjusted by CPI-U

Source: Council of Economic Advisers, *Economic Report of the President 2013* (Washington DC: US Government Printing Office, 2013), 342, 393, 399.

Table II shows that the ratio of profits (net operating surplus or the money equivalent of surplus value measured in conventional terms) to wages (total employee compensation, including benefits) has risen significantly, by more than two-thirds, since the mid-1970s. In fact, this table understates the degree of exploitation since total employee compensation covers managers and professionals as well as working-class wage earners, and net operating surplus significantly understates surplus product as measured in both Marxist and Classical terms.[31] Nevertheless, the profits/wage ratio indicates a rising rate of exploitation, which along with a dramatic fall in interest rates has meant a rising rate of profit since the early 1980s, even into the crisis that began in 2007. Furthermore, as Anwar Shaikh points out, "The overall degree of income inequality ultimately rests on the ratio of profits to wages, that is, *on the basic division of value added.*"[32] Thus, it is in the sphere of wage labor that social inequality finds its deepest roots, though, of course, this inequality affects different sectors of the working class to varying degrees, a crucial matter as the working class itself is changing in ethno-racial composition.

CHAPTER THREE

Growing Diversity in the Midst of Change

The drawing into the workforce of immigrants (the global reserve army of labor), particularly in lower-paid jobs in the last thirty years or so, like the absorption of women with children into wage labor that accelerated in the 1950s, is a consequence of the process of expanded reproduction or accumulation in the United States and abroad, on the one hand, and the consequent dispossession abroad, on the other.[1] Here most immigrant workers join many native-born African American, Latino, and women workers in the lower-paid ranks of the workforce, where often productivity is lower and more labor required. Both foreign and domestically born Blacks, Asians, and Latinos composed over a third of the US population in 2010, compared to 20 percent in 1980, with the Latino and, on a smaller scale, Asian populations growing fast due to immigration.[2]

These racial and ethnic groups now make up a large and growing proportion of working-class occupations. Blacks, Latinos, and Asians, including immigrants, composed about 15–16 percent of the workers in production, transportation, and material moving occupations as well as in service occupations in 1981 and now make up close to 40 percent of each of these broad occupational groups. Furthermore, these groups are spread throughout these occupational categories to a much larger degree than in the past. In construction trades, for example, workers of color composed 37 percent in 2010, compared to 15–16 percent in 1981. Below we will see that Blacks, Asians, and Latinos together composed about 35 percent of the employed working class, compared to 22 percent for the middle class and 11 percent for the capitalist class.[3] It is also the case that these groups of workers are disproportionately concentrated in urban areas. As shown below, they are central to the logistics clusters, with African Americans making up almost half of the warehouse workforce in the Chicago area and Latinos likewise in the Los Angeles and New York–New Jersey clusters, as well as to the commodified labor of social reproduction and capital maintenance.

To a certain extent, these increases in the proportion of workers of color have been reflected in the unions. In terms of union density, the percentage of workers in employment who belong to unions, men, women, and every racial and ethnic group lost ground after the early 1980s. Yet among those who do join unions it is women, Blacks, Latinos, and Asians who are more likely to win an NLRB representation election, thus bringing growth. Women, women of color in particular, are more likely to become union members than any other group.[4] Women now compose 46 percent of all union members. The proportion of Blacks, Asians, and Latinos in union membership also rose from about 23 percent in 1994 to 33 percent in 2014, about 13 percent of total membership being immigrants.[5] While Blacks are more likely to be union members than white workers, the biggest growth, after women in general, has been among Latinos, many of them immigrants. Between 2011 and 2014 alone some two hundred thousand Latino workers joined unions. While the rate of unionization among foreign-born workers who are not citizens is only half the national rate of 12 percent, for those who are citizens it is 13 percent. Furthermore, the longer immigrant workers are in the United States, the higher the rate of unionization, eventually surpassing the rate among whites and pointing toward large-scale future growth among the foreign-born.[6]

To some extent this rapid growth in unionization among immigrants and Latinos probably reflects the growing activism in the Latino community, much of it around immigrants' rights and organization. Asians and Pacific Islanders, however, also saw a leap in union membership by ninety-six thousand in one year from 2013 to 2014.[7] Black workers have remained about 13–15 percent of union membership since the early 1980s and unable to increase as a proportion largely due to the loss of manufacturing jobs that hit African American communities particularly hard. Yet in the last decade or so there has been an increase in community-based Black worker organization and more recently mobilizations around the Black Lives Matter movement. It seems likely that just as activism in the Latino community contributed to increased union membership, this new Black activism may also lead to a growth in union membership and organization among Black workers.[8]

It seems clear that these workers are central to organizing in areas such as warehousing, hotels, hospitals, building services, meatpacking, and others where they form a growing proportion of the workforce—indeed, those sections of the workforce that are actually growing. For such organizing to be successful, however, it must address the enormous inequalities within the working class as well as those in society in general. To argue that today's working class is far more diverse than that of three or so decades ago is not to say that inequalities of gender and race have disappeared. Even for full-time workers median weekly earnings differ by gender and race. As of 2010, male full-time workers earned $824 a week, compared to $669 for women. Whites took home $765 a week in wages, compared to $611 for African Americans and $535 for Latinos.[9] In 2011, 23.4 percent of white workers' earnings were below the poverty line, while 36 percent of Blacks and 43.3 percent of Latinos fell below that line. The difference between men and women was 24.3 percent.[10] Race and gender lines remain major fault lines in the structure of the changing working class.

While many unions have made efforts to incorporate more workers of color, immigrants in particular, the perpetuation of business union norms and institutions continue to make it difficult to confront racism in the ranks and in society. A focus on organizing these low-paid industries and occupations can begin to address this, but internal challenges will also be needed to transform "diversity" into interracial unity.

A Reconsolidated, Restructured, More Diverse Working Class

Today's working class does not look like that of half a century ago. Using Hal Draper's representation of the working class as concentric circles from an industrial "core" to outer rings of workers presumably less concentrated or less likely to be direct producers of surplus value, we can see the differences from the beginning of the era of transition in the 1980s.[11] The employed working-class private industrial core, consisting of production and nonsupervisory workers in mining, manufacturing, construction, utilities, transportation and warehousing, and information numbered 22.9 million in 2007 before the impact of the Great Recession, compared to 20.2 million in 1983. In relative terms, of course, it has shrunk. This industrial core accounted for 24.3 percent of the total production and nonsupervisory workforce in 2007, down from 33.2 percent in 1983.

Furthermore, the composition of the core has also changed with the number of mine, mill, and factory workers shrinking from 64 percent in 1983 to 47 percent of the core in 2007. On the other hand, those in transportation and warehousing, at the center of logistics, whose numbers grew by 68 percent over this period, increased from 12 percent to 17 percent of the core, while those in the information sector increased by over half, rising to 11 percent of the core.[12] As we shall see, logistics workers are part of the overall production process of goods output, including even that of many imports. It is fair to say that these logistics workers have at least as much leverage in the economy of today as autoworkers did in the 1970s. Naturally, the Great Recession had a severe impact on manufacturing in particular, so that the core shrank to 20 percent of the private workforce. The degree to which it grows again remains to be seen.

In the minds of many this core is the domain of the white male worker. Gender segregation in employment, like that of race, is, of course, still a reality, and the majority of women workers, now almost half the workforce, are found in service, sales, and office work. But the proportions have changed. In 2010 in manufacturing, women composed 28 percent of the core workforce. In transportation and warehousing, women are almost a quarter of the workforce, while in utilities they are 22 percent of the workforce. Construction has the smallest percentage at only 9 percent. On the other hand, women compose 41 percent of the information sector. If construction is excluded, women are almost a third of the core. Together with minority workers, even allowing for considerable overlap, nonwhite male workers probably account for about 40 percent of the core and are certainly likely to increase in the coming decade or so.

At the same time, as we will see below, millions of workers beyond the traditional core are employed by companies that are larger than they were a quarter of a century ago, work in more capital-intensive situations, work and live in large urban concentrations, and are even more diverse. Workers in call centers, hospitals, hotels, many large retail stores, and Internet retailers that are basically warehouses plus call centers work in numbers and under conditions that might well qualify them as part of today's core as much as many factory workers. This is not just the case for workers directly involved in logistics and vulnerable supply chains. The growing number of workers employed to maintain and clean capital's fixed assets, including not only factories and warehouses but its office buildings, airports, bus and railroad stations, hotels, hospitals, schools, universities, and so on have power not only by virtue of the embeddedness of these facilities but also as a result of the massive and constant reproduction of waste and filth such agglomerations create when profit is more important than the prevention of waste and pollution. The same is true of much of the labor of reproduction now performed in capitalist institutions, many of them having large concentrations of workers. The relative success in recent years in organizing building cleaners, hotel workers, and hospital employees gives testimony to this power. Indeed, some of the most militant strikes have been conducted and led by women outside the core in the proletarianizing professions, such as the monthlong strike by 1,500 members of the Pennsylvania Association of Staff Nurses and Allied Professionals against Temple University Hospital and the nine-day 2012 strike of the 30,000-member Chicago Teachers Union.

Table III summarizes the shape of US class structure today in very rough terms. Although I have not attempted to track the detailed shifting of some workers from working-class jobs to those in the middle class and vice versa conducted by Michael Zweig, the proportional results are almost the same, at about 63 percent of the workforce, and close enough for our purposes here.[13] Counting up the numbers does not tell us much about class relations in itself, but it can help us conceptualize the proportions, demographics, and occupational distribution between and within the three major classes of modern capitalism. Broad occupational categories are used rather than industry figures, in part because they sort out management from labor and give us a fairly good idea of those who must sell their labor power, work under the control of capital, and work longer hours than it takes to produce their own compensation, whether or not they directly produce surplus value. In relation to the core/concentric circles model mentioned above, the twenty-nine million or so workers involved in the production and movement of material commodities represent the core, larger here because these categories cross various industry lines, while service occupations, most of which involve a mixture of material change as well as direct service, reflect the next circle, many of whose members work in large firms and workplaces and possess significant social power. The third circle is composed of the millions of office and sales workers, some of whom are concentrated in large offices, retail outlets, call centers, and so on.

Table III : Rough Guide to Class Structure in the United States, ca. 2010 (in thousands)

Occupational Sector	Employed	%Women	%Black, Asian, Latino	% of Class	% of Total
Total Employed	139,064	52%	22%	100%	100%
Capitalist Class					
Wealth $2 million +	1,500*	44%	11%	100%	1%
Middle Class					
Managerial	19,438†	40%	20%	39%	14%
Professional	30,805	57%	23%	61%	22%
(Proletarianizing)	(11,471)	(80%)	(24%)	(23%)	(8%)
Subtotal	**50,243**	**50%**	**22%**	**100%**	**36%**
Working Class					
Production, Transport, and Material Moving	16,180	21%	39%	19%	12%
Extraction, Construction, and Maintenance	13,073	5%	34%	15%	9%
Service	24,634	57%	42%	28%	18%
Sales and Office	33,433	63%	28%	38%	24%
Subtotal	**87,320**	**45%**	**35%**	**100%**	**63%**

* Based on CEOs and those with $2 million or more in financial assets
† Minus CEOs who go to capitalist class

Source: US Census Bureau, *Statistical Abstract of the United States: 2012* (Washington DC: US Government Printing Office, 2011), 393–97, 467–68.

In table III, the capitalist class is defined not by income but by the ownership of capital, in this case the admittedly somewhat arbitrary net wealth of over $2 million. "Middle class" refers not to those statistically in the middle-income range or all those between the rich and the poor, but those socially located between capital and the working class in terms of the production of society's wealth. These are mostly managerial and professional people. The working class, of course, comprises those employed directly by and paid from capital. What we see in table III is not only that the working class embraces nearly two-thirds of those employed but is far more racially diverse than the middle class and more than three times that of the capitalist class. In numerical terms, although the working class is still majority white, the vast majority of employed people of color are working class. Workers in traditional goods or extractive producing jobs compose just over a third of the employed working class as it is today. Many of the 28 percent who work in service jobs in fact produce materials goods or results, and many are now concentrated in the large workplaces that reproduce many of the conditions of factories of old and the lean methods of the neoliberal era.

Even many of those among the sales and office workers are now often concentrated in relatively large work settings such as big-box retailers, supermarkets, Internet retailers, call centers, and so on. Given the dynamics of capital's constant push to control and standardize all forms of work, many in the middle class, who belong in proletarianizing professions such as teaching and nursing, who compose almost a quarter of the middle class, are increasingly approximating the conditions of working-class work and existence. We see this in the successful organizing and many strikes of nurses and teachers in particular. If these two groups and the leaps in consciousness they have displayed in recent years are at all typical, the numerical growth of the working class will be accompanied by increased militancy and class consciousness.

The working *class*, as opposed simply to the workforce, of course, is composed not only of its employed members but of nonworking spouses, dependents, relatives, the unemployed, and all those who make up the reserve army of labor. If working-class people in employment make up just under two-thirds of the workforce, those in the *class* amount to at least three-quarters of the population—the overwhelming majority. As teachers, nurses, and other professionals are pushed down into the working class, the majority grows even larger. If the "99 percent" popularized by the Occupy movement is not quite accurate, there being too many middle-class people tied materially and mentally to the capitalist class, the percentage of those whose fundamental interests are opposed to capital nonetheless moves in that direction.

The industrial, occupational, and ethno-racial changes in the demographics of the working class over the past three decades or more tell only half the story of the remaking of the US working class. Equally if not more important are both the new terrain on which class conflict occurs and the new sources of power this brings to many sections of the class formerly thought of as peripheral; closer to the core in their conditions and settings of work and in the leverage they have over capital's restructured and reorganized processes of production. Millions of service, sales, and even office workers now work in larger, more capital-intensive workplaces, embedded in larger concentrations of capital, and owned by fewer capitalists. They are increasingly linked together in vulnerable technology-driven supply chains, themselves organized around enormous logistics clusters that concentrate tens and even hundreds of thousands of workers in finite geographical sites. It is to this side of class formation that we now turn.

PART II

The Changing Terrain of Class Struggle

Competition and the Concentration and Centralization of Capital in the United States

The increase in both international and domestic competition, enabled and driven by deregulation and globalization, the repeat of decennial crises that encourage industry restructuring, and the rise of profit rates after the economic recovery began in 1982 that enabled reorganization have together brought about one of the most extraordinary waves of business consolidation via mergers and acquisitions (M&As) in the history of US capitalism. M&A movements tend to come in waves. They are part of the ongoing reorganization of capital under the pressures of competition, their rhythms determined partly by falling and then rising rates of profit. In the United States there have been six major waves of mergers and acquisitions in which business has been reshaped: 1897–1904, 1916–29, 1965–69, 1984–89, 1992–2000, and 2003 to the present.[1] Each of these merger movements attempted to resolve problems associated with falling rates of profits leading to recessions and to take advantage of the resumption of profitability to increase efficiency and market share through mergers.

In conventional terms merger waves are the product of economic expansion, on the one hand, and capital liquidity, on the other.[2] From a Marxist perspective more particularly, they rise and fall with the rate of profit. Using the rate of profit-of-enterprise calculated by Anwar Shaikh and the empirical information on merger numbers and value provided by Gaughan and Pautler, the four post–World War II merger waves (1965–69, 1980–90, 1992–2000, and 2003–present) correspond to a remarkable degree with the rise and fall of profit-of-enterprise rates over this long period.[3]

The process of the concentration and centralization of capital during the neoliberal period follows the course suggested by Marx in his brief discussion of these tendencies and the contradictory course they follow in *Capital*.[4] As capitals grow, "offshoots split off from the original capitals and start to function as new and independent capitals . . . therefore the number of capitals grows to a greater or lesser extent." This shows up to some extent in those M&A deals that are, in fact, divestitures, as well as in new business formations. These capitals, however, must grow or merge. "It is concentration of capitals already formed, destruction of their individual independence, expropriation of capitalist by capitalist, transformation of many small into few large capitals."[5] This is precisely the course followed during the era of lean production as fragmentation, often via outsourcing or divestures, turned increasingly to concentration and centralization via mergers and acquisitions in the 1990s and beyond.

While mergers and acquisitions are generally pushed by the desire to increase profits through increased efficiencies and by expanding in new or old markets, on the one hand, and enabled by increased profit rates, on the other, each wave tends to have its own characteristics. Most recent waves of the 1960s and 1970s were characterized by "conglomerate" mergers involving companies in different industries, while that of the 1980s was noted for corporate raiders, hostile takeovers, leveraged buyouts (LBOs), and lots of debt. It was during this decade that outsourcing took off, and divestitures composed 35 to 40 percent of all M&As. The fifth merger wave that began in the early to mid-1990s, in contrast, was characterized by strategic mergers and acquisitions within specific industries leading to increased centralization and consolidation within a wide range of industries, with relatively little debt incurred. During this wave, divestitures fell to about a quarter of all deals, even though many of these were sales to acquiring firms seeking increased market share in their core line of production. The sixth wave, beginning in 2003, with ups and downs to the present, has been similar to that of the 1990s, although LBOs made somewhat of a comeback for a brief time in 2006–7, many carried out by private equity firms. For the most part, however, in value terms these remained a relatively small proportion of M&As, with debt far less than in the 1980s. Measured by the number of mergers and acquisitions these last two waves surpassed those of 1897–1904, 1916–29, 1965–69, and 1984–89.[6] Unlike the previous waves, these last two have been international, with Europe following a similar pattern to the United States in acquiring firms at home and abroad. Altogether cross-border M&As rose in value from $151 billion in 1990 to just over $1 trillion in 2007 before the recession brought this activity down for a time. In 2007, 88 percent of sales and 83 percent of purchases were between developed nations. US firms accounted for about 20 percent of both sales and purchases, by developed countries, with the UK slightly behind on sales but ahead on purchases, at 27 percent. Clearly the impact of increased global competition was forcing business consolidation across the developed economies.[7]

While much of the literature on mergers emphasizes the financial side due to its impact on stock prices, debts incurred, and the big fees made by banks and other financial enablers, M&As since the mid-1990s have been primarily a means of increasing profitability by capturing increased market share in specific lines of production. In order to survive the increased competition of the era, firms have had to increase in size, productivity, and market share. As Marx argued, "The battle of competition is fought by the cheapening of commodities. The cheapness of commodities depends . . . on the productivity of labour, and this depends on the scale of production. Therefore the larger capitals beat the smaller."[8] The increase in productivity through labor intensification, application of new technology, and of the size of concentrations of capital through competition and mergers is precisely what has happened over the last quarter century. What began as a process of fragmentation in the 1980s has become one of concentration and relative centralization impelled by global and domestic competition since the mid-1990s.

The first large merger wave of the post–World War II period came in the late 1960s, peaking at about 2,500 transactions a year, many producing "conglomerate" corporations, and then rapidly falling in the early 1970s. The next wave began in the 1980s as competition intensified due in large part to the acceleration of globalization in the mid-1980s, as FDI and trade both took off. This wave saw many LBOs and hostile takeovers financed by debt, but also a move away from conglomerate mergers.[9] In 1980 M&As numbered 1,560, at a value of $32.9 billion, after which they rose to 4,239 worth $205.6 billion in 1990 and then in the fifth wave to 11,169 valued at $3.4 trillion in 2000, the highest level ever. After 2001 M&As leveled off at about seven thousand a year, still well above pre-1990s levels, until the crash of 2008, and then rose again after 2012. By late 2015, it was estimated that the number of M&As would reach ten thousand for that year at a value of about $2 trillion.[10]

To be sure, some of this activity involved outfits like private equity firms, particularly in the 1980s, that preferred to "strip and flip" a company rather than actually run a business, but as the examples below show, most M&As since the mid-1990s are about improving competitiveness and profitability by capturing market share through gobbling up the opposition. Furthermore, the wave of M&As that began in the mid-1990s, unlike that of the late 1960s, has been directed toward strengthening the firms' "core competencies," that is, their basic line of products, bringing about an increase in both the concentration and centralization of capital in many industries. Indeed, leading up to the most recent wave, the years from the early 1980s into the 1990s were, as Doug Henwood wrote, a "period during which many of the conglomerates were broken apart, and combinations between firms in the same or related industries predominated."[11]

As this suggests, the trend toward greater industrial focus necessarily also includes divestitures, and indeed the number of divestitures has run at an average of about three thousand a year since the mid-1990s.[12] In some cases, companies downsize to gain greater focus. Nevertheless, one company's divestiture is another's acquisition, so that on average companies will tend to grow in order to increase market share. Three recent examples of divestitures aimed at increasing industrial focus by divesting financial services units are General Electric (GE), General Motors (GM), and Chrysler. In GE's case the divesting of financial units has been accompanied by acquisitions of manufacturing firms in its power and aerospace lines.[13] GM sold control of its car financing unit, GMAC, to Cerberus Capital Management in 2006. GMAC became a bank holding company, which was renamed Ally in 2010 and operates as an independent firm. As a result of the financial bailout, the US Treasury owns a majority share in Ally. GM retains a small minority share of Ally and still has a small subprime financial unit.[14] Chrysler sold its financial division to Toronto-Dominion Bank in 2010, where it was renamed TD Auto Finance.[15] As troubled companies, both GM and Chrysler simply downsized, while GE continued to aggressively buy up manufacturing units. In any case, the era in which big manufacturing firms like GE, GM, and Chrysler depended on their financial businesses appears to be coming to a close. At the same time, USX, as US Steel became known with its acquisition of Marathon Oil in the 1980s, became US Steel again in 2001 as it spun off its energy interests. In the 2000s it purchased assets from bankrupt National Steel, Lone Star Company in 2007, and other steel-related companies.[16] Conglomeration was on its way out.

Pros and Cons for Labor

The direction of mergers is crucial because different configurations promote different balances of class power. In general, as Marxist political economist Howard Botwinick notes, "a number of writers have argued that the increasing conglomeration of U.S. corporations in the 1960s and 1970s played a major role in tipping the balance against labor in industries such as coal, meat-packing, printing, and steel."[17] Conglomerates are better placed to resist strikes or even unionization in any one line of production because of their resources in other subsidiaries. Here is what labor economist Charles Craypo wrote about the advantages to management of conglomerates just as conglomeration reached its apex:

> The conglomerate employer is, by definition, a multi-industry enterprise. This results in greater employer-operating mobility than that of a union whose bargaining structure and representation rights rarely cross industry lines, greater financial leverage than that of a union whose members depend on a single business operation for their livelihood, and greater administrative range than a union whose decision-making options are limited to a single plant or industry. These administrative, financial, and mobility advantages enable the conglomerate to frustrate the collective bargaining process and impair the bargaining strength of the unions.[18]

The movement of mergers and acquisitions away from conglomeration and toward a focus on a single industry or line of production since the mid-1990s potentially reestablishes the bargaining power of workers, providing, of course, that the unions organize the workforce and take full advantage of this renewed condition. So far, only in a few industries, such as hotels, hospitals, and to a lesser extent meatpacking, has this even begun.

There are downsides to consolidation through M&As. For one, merged companies typically close some plants or facilities, which can lead to workforce reductions. An example is found in the case of flour products, where 131 plants out of 480 acquired were closed, and there were production job losses of about 12 percent by 2000.[19] Downsizing of the workforce is another typical part of restructuring in the wake of a merger. In addition, experience shows that the new owners will try to undermine existing conditions and pay and to squeeze even more work out of the remaining workforce. Industry consolidation is not a free ride for labor. Nevertheless, the outcome is necessarily an industry in which fewer but larger firms compete, the combined workforce of more and more firms is relatively larger, and the new production methods and links more vulnerable. In the long run, this is a situation that makes the industry more susceptible to unionization, as was the case in the 1930s after the 1916–29 merger wave that produced corporate giants such as General Motors, John Deere, and Union Carbide.[20] Consolidation through mergers and acquisitions has affected almost every major industry in the United States. This included the FIRE industries, which saw some of the highest levels of concentration and centralization. Our concern here, however, is with those industries that most affect the structure and potential power of the working class. Below are examples of consolidation in some of these industries that took place in the wave of M&As from the 1980s up to the Great Recession in 2008 and beyond.

Consolidation in Major Industries

In the United States, consolidation accelerated in manufacturing industries beginning in the 1980s and 1990s. Two industries deserve particular attention due to their continuing relative importance in the US economy: the auto parts industry and meatpacking. Auto has been the trend-setting industry in the introduction of lean methods, outsourcing, and industry reorganization throughout this period. The decline of the "Big Three" US assemblers and the growth of internationally owned "transplants," which now produce 45 percent of all automobiles and light trucks and 59 percent of sales in the United States, is well known.[21] During this period, the Big Three ended assembly on the East and West Coasts, reconcentrating in the Midwest, while the new transplants moved into the upper South (Kentucky and Tennessee) and Southeast—both facts that would affect the location of parts suppliers.

For reasons of relocation and competition, a dramatic restructuring of the auto parts industry has accelerated since the recession of 1980–82. This occurred in two overlapping phases. In the 1980s, the number of parts plants proliferated in response to outsourcing and the growth of mainly Japanese-owned transplants. Much of this growth was in the South as the automobile industry as a whole stretched into an industrial corridor reaching from Canada to Mexico. By the census measure of the automobile parts industry, the number of "establishments" (plants) grew by almost 1,300 from 1979, reaching 5,826 in 1989 as outsourcing increased. Given the volatility and limits of the US car and light truck market on which these suppliers depended and the high levels of competition introduced by the internationally owned transplants, however, this was not sustainable. In the second phase of reorganization from the mid- to late 1990s to 2013, according to the same measure, the number of parts plants fell by nearly 800 to 5,146.[22] While the stretching of the industry southward continued, the Midwest, now extended into the contiguous upper South, and connected by the network of interstate highways (I-70 East–West, I-65 North–South from Chicago, I-75 North–South from Detroit) remained the geographic heart of the parts industry.[23]

Beginning in the 1990s, the Big Three automobile assembly companies, Ford, Chrysler, and General Motors, following the Japanese model, reorganized their supply chains into three tiers, establishing just-in-time schedules and reducing the number of suppliers each used, with Tier 1 firms making larger components, such as entire car interiors. As a result, the number of Tier 1 suppliers earning $2 billion or more a year grew from five to thirteen within a few years. By 2012 twenty-nine Tier 1 companies had passed the $2 billion mark.[24] Downward pressure from the assemblers and the Tier 1 suppliers, however, produced a wave of failures and mergers throughout the parts sector. Using the much broader definition of the industry, which includes all firms involved in the automobile supply chain, the Original Equipment Suppliers Association (OESA) estimates that the number of supplier firms (not establishments or plants) declined by 80 percent from 1990 to 2010, particularly in the 1990s as many smaller Tier 3 suppliers either went bust, exited the parts business, or merged with others to defend or gain market share. By 2008–9 the top ten North American auto parts supplier firms controlled a third of the original equipment market that supplied assemblers. Continuing into 2015, mergers in the auto parts sector grew larger and larger, such as German-owned ZF's $12 billion purchase of TRW. In most cases, reported Price Waterhouse Cooper, the most acquisitive companies saw improved profits.[25]

To a large extent, the parts industry is still centered in the Midwest and upper South, though production has often moved out of inner cities to rural or semirural locations. Remarkably, production worker employment levels in the automobile industry as a whole grew, with ups and downs from 575,000 in 1980 to 770,000 in 2000. Although the Great Recession in 2008, which killed car sales, took a heavy toll, by late 2015 production worker employment was up to 733,000.[26] Today the auto industry as a whole is more centralized, structured, and tightly linked, with its parts suppliers fewer and larger, and more geographically concentrated in two regions than was the case in the glory days of the Big Three. By the new century most of these changes seen in the auto assembly and parts industry had become "characteristic of much of U.S. manufacturing, even outside the automotive sector."[27]

The meat processing and packing industry went through a dramatic restructuring in the 1980s, where between 1982 and 1992 some 1,112 plants were acquired, while 228 were closed and another 214 sold off by 1992.[28] As meat processing and packing was a growing industry, the number of production workers actually increased from 298,000 in 1980 to 359,000 in 1990 and 429,000 in 2000.[29] The reorganization of the 1980s was characterized by the entrance and growth of the major nonunion packer IBP and was a disaster for the unions. Reorganization and company exits, however, soon turned to centralization and consolidation through mergers and acquisitions and concentration through the growth of larger plants. By the early 1990s four companies produced 71 percent of beef shipments, 43 percent of hogs, and 41 percent of chickens. The share of total output of large plants employing four hundred or more workers accelerated to 72 percent of beef slaughtering, 86 percent in hog plants, and 88 percent of chickens by 1992. Production became somewhat more geographically concentrated, moving westward, with beef into the Great Plains states and hogs moving west of the Mississippi into the "Western Corn Belt," on the one hand, and south to the Carolinas, on the other.[30] By 2011, as a result of ongoing mergers, the top four companies—Tyson, Cargill, JBS, and National Beef—controlled 75 percent of total meat production. Overseas firms played a growing role, with Brazilian-owned JBS buying up Swift, Smithfield Beef, Pilgrim's Pride, and, subject to regulatory approval, Cargill's entire pork business, while in 2015 Chinese giant Shuanghui International bought Smithfield's entire hog production.[31] Despite the Great Recession, by late 2015 production worker employment in the industry, now concentrated in larger plants and fewer companies, remained near the 2000 level at 416,000.[32]

The steel industry, under enormous global pressure, also saw a consolidation in the early twenty-first century. Under heavy international competition, the old major US steel companies withdrew from the conglomerate strategies of the 1980. USX, as we saw above, became US Steel again in 2001 as it spun off its energy interests. In the 2000s it purchased assets from bankrupt National Steel, Lone Star Company in 2007, and other steel-related companies.[33] Indian giant Mittal Steel entered the US market in 1998 with the acquisition of Inland Steel. In 2006 it merged with another global steel producer, Arcelor, to become ArcelorMittal, which by 2014 controlled 23 percent of the US market, while US Steel controlled another 20 percent or so. These two companies dominate domestic production, but imports, which account for almost a quarter of flat-rolled tons sold in the United States in 2014, along with global overcapacity make this a troubled industry despite large productivity increases.[34]

Industries in the logistics network have also seen consolidation, part of the revolution in "the means of communication and transport," as Marx put it. After years of mergers, five rail freight carriers now employ 80 percent of those working in that industry.[35] UPS and FedEx alone employed 40 percent of the country's 1.7 million trucking and express delivery workers by 2014. If the next five trucking firms are added, the top seven employ almost half the workforce.[36] Airlines have been merging at least since the 1960s, but in the last decade ten majors were reduced to four: Delta, American, United, and Southwest, which now control 80 percent of air passenger traffic. The remaining 20 percent is shared by eight smaller surviving airlines. Not surprisingly, airline employment has fallen from 614,000 in 2000 to 464,000 in 2010.[37] Telecommunications, another key part of the industrial "core," important also to logistics and e-commerce, saw an even more drastic centralization of capital. The 1984 breakup of AT&T created seven regional Bell operating companies plus AT&T in long distance, along with rivals GTE, MCI, and Sprint. By 2014, one industry analysis reported, telecommunications providers, including wired and wireless, had "re-consolidated their industry in the past 10 years to four players, who together control 90% of the market," with further deals being announced "at an unprecedented pace."[38]

Consolidation has also swept many material-producing and -affecting service industries. Today nearly three-quarters of the country's formerly independent community hospitals are in large urban-based corporate systems or chains, where some 4.6 million workers are subject to lean production norms and just-in-time supply chains. Furthermore, as a result of the M&As that have produced these chains and the simultaneous closing of state and local public hospitals, more than eight hundred community hospitals have closed since the early 1980s. At the same time employment in community hospitals rose by about 1.2 million full-time-equivalent workers, meaning that on average hospitals employed more workers by 2009. Similarly, more than half of all nursing care homes are now in mostly urban-based corporate chains.[39]

The hotel industry, too, has gone through a major restructuring. As one study put it in terms of industry restructuring as of 2000, "Most dramatic have been the changes around ownership in the form of widespread consolidation and the growth of publicly held corporations. . . . The consequence is that a few very large corporate chains, each owning a range of brand-name hotels that serve a variety of markets, now dominate an industry once populated by a myriad of small family-owned hotels."[40] More recently real estate income trusts (REITs) and private equity outfits such as the Blackstone Group LP have gobbled up older chains or brands. Between 2000 and 2008 the hotel industry saw 2,266 mergers and acquisitions valued at $391.3 billion.[41]

General retail went through "a big shakeout in the 1990s" in which "Wal-Mart Stores was the engine driving change," for example, forcing Sears and Kmart to merge in 2005. The rise of Amazon.com set off another "huge wave of consolidation in the sector." Indeed, sales from e-commerce increased by almost nine times from 1999 to 2009, growing from 0.5 percent of retail sales to 4 percent in a decade and, by one estimate to 8 percent by 2013—e-commerce firms being at their core warehouse operations employing about a quarter of a million workers by 2009.[42] The retail grocery industry also saw a sweeping consolidation. By the late 1990s the top four supermarket chains controlled an average of 72 percent of sales in the one hundred largest metropolitan areas, while the top eight food retailers controlled nearly half of sales nationally by 2009.[43] Wal-Mart appeared here as well, as the leader of the top four grocery chains followed by Kroger, with Safeway and Publix replacing Costco and Supervalu in the top four by 2013.[44]

Indeed, according to one study, by 2000, "All segments of the food industry have experienced significant consolidation." In addition to meatpacking and grocery mentioned above, "Consolidation among broad-line food distributors (those supplying a wide variety of products) is particularly noteworthy . . . the share of the top three (Sysco, Alliant, and US Foods) grew from 32 percent in 1995 to 43 percent in 2000." In 2001 US Foods acquired Alliant, so that two companies controlled almost half the market.[45] In 2014 Sysco attempted to buy US Foods for $8.2 billion but was stopped by a court injunction in June 2015 at the behest of the Federal Trade Commission. Nevertheless, Sysco continued buying up smaller food distribution firms, spending $116 million in acquisitions in fiscal 2015.[46]

Greater Capital Intensity

It might be added to this picture that not only are millions more workers employed by bigger, mostly urban-based national concentrations of capital, on average today's workers also toil under increased capital-labor ratios on the job. After all, in the Marxist view of competition the continual advance in technology and, hence, accumulated capital is central as each firm attempts to become or compete with the most efficient firm in their industry, what Botwinick calls the "regulating capital."[47] In the case of M&As this is compounded. As firms buy up other firms to expand market share through expanded production, they necessarily combine units with varying degrees of capital intensity, efficiency, and profit rates. Since competition pushes a firm to attempt to achieve the highest level of efficiency in the industry, the newly combined company must bring the least efficient units up to the highest standard possible. Some of this can be done by closing or selling off less efficient units, but since the purpose of the merger or acquisition is to increase productive capacity and market share, there is clearly a limit to this strategy. Instead firms will attempt to improve the efficiency of all units through the application of the latest technology, thus increasing capital intensity. Indeed, this is just what many firms have done, resulting in increasing the amount of capital per worker.

From 1992 to 2012, the real net private stock of fixed assets per production and nonsupervisory worker rose from $1,432,845 to $2,382,390 or by 66.3 percent. In manufacturing, it rose from $98,828 to $247,138 or 151.1 percent over these years. For those in information industries it grew by 81.6 percent, while the real net stock of assets per employee in hospitals grew by 92.2 percent. The increase in net "equipment," that is, technology, in hospitals grew by an amazing 175 percent over those twenty years. These are substantial annual growth rates ranging from 3.3 percent for the private sector as a whole to 7.6 percent for manufacturing. Only transportation and warehousing, where the increase in total assets per worker was 23.8 percent, at 1.2 percent a year, appears well below average.[48] This is most likely because a good deal of what actually goes into the expansion of the underlying infrastructure of the logistics network as a whole, such as roads, tunnels, bridges, harbors, sewage, utility conduits, and so on, are counted as public expenditures. For example, state and local capital budgets, which cover many of these functions and provide the bulk of funds, grew from $123.1 billion in 1990 to $348.8 billion in 2008. Much of this is funded by bond issues to the private sector, which grew from $97.9 billion in 1990 to $284.7 billion in 2008 for capital projects in transportation, utilities, and industrial aid, among others. While not all of this went to logistics infrastructure, state and local governments play a big role in the development of new logistics locations and clusters. For example, one logistics park in Chicago's huge cluster was built with $150 million in public funds. It is clear that the BEA figures for transportation and warehousing underestimate the increase in capital expenditure for the expanding logistics sector as a whole.[49]

Although investment, like GDP, grew more slowly than during US capitalism's heyday, annual fixed nonresidential investment has actually formed a larger percentage of GDP during non-recession years of the neoliberal era than in the 1960s: averaging 11.7 percent from 1982 until 2015, compared to 10 percent during the 1960s. At the same time the mass of fixed investment is much larger than in the 1960s. Indicative of this increase generally, both the industrial capacity index and the capital-labor ratio grew from the mid-1980s and then took off during the 1990s just as the wave of mergers and acquisitions also accelerated. These increases point to the fact that mergers alone were not sufficient to meet competition and that capital investment also increased, as noted above. After 2000, the capital-labor ratio leveled off due to the recessions of 2000 and 2008 and then began to grow again around 2012.[50] That the merger movement and related investment have made a difference in the overall size of manufacturing firms can be seen in how those corporations with assets valued at over $1 billion rose from 71 percent of total assets in 1990 to 87 percent in 2010.[51] Competition was engendering not only mergers but increased capital accumulation and technology as well.

Like the formation of larger firms along definite industrial lines, greater capital intensity offers expanded opportunities for successful direct action and increased power in collective bargaining. As political economist Anwar Shaikh argues: "Capital-intensive industries will also tend to have high levels of fixed costs which will make them more susceptible to the effects of slowdowns and strikes. At the same time, because labor costs are likely to be a smaller portion of their total costs, such industries are more able to tolerate wage increases."[52] This potential, of course, depends on workers and their unions using the implied power. And, as we will see below, higher wages alone do not disqualify these workers from Marx's warning that increased accumulation also means worsening conditions as capital struggles to extract more surplus value. It will take strong workplace organization to resist this tendency.

On average, the nation's workplaces are not getting smaller measured by the average number of workers. Although the number and proportion of workers employed in manufacturing workplaces has shrunk significantly, for the economy as a whole, levels of employment concentration have gone up in terms of numbers and remained about the same as proportions of the workforce. In 2008 altogether 24.7 million workers were employed in workplaces of five hundred or more, or 20 percent of the employed workforce, compared to 16.5 million, also 20 percent, in 1986. Those employed in workplaces of a thousand or more rose to 16.5 million, or 14 percent, of the total workforce in 2008, from 10.7 million, or 13 percent, in 1986. What these figures reveal is that, first of all, the majority of workers in the United States have always worked in relatively small workplaces—a fact that did not prevent working-class upsurges in the past. More importantly, over eight million more workers are employed in relatively large workplaces than was the case when lean production and globalization took off. One of the big gainers in those employing a thousand or more workers has been in health and social services, with hospitals almost certainly accounting for much of the increase in workers in larger workplaces, from 3.6 million in 1999 to 4.4 million in 2008.[53]

"It follows therefore that in proportion as capital accumulates, the situation of the worker, be his payment high or low, must grow worse," wrote Marx in *Capital*.[54] And so it is that the capital that employs many of these workers is bigger, the capital-labor ratio greater, and the condition of the majority grown worse. The enormous gap between productivity growth and wage stagnation along with the falling of interest rates was, as political economist Shaikh put it, "the secret of the great boom that began in the 1980s."[55] At the same time, it is a major source of the increased inequality that affects the entire working class and those on its periphery in the United States—indeed, throughout the developed industrial economies.[56] Furthermore, this "Gilded Age" level of inequality has finally entered the political awareness of the country, at least in part due to the Occupy Wall Street movement. A 2015 New York Times/CBS News poll, for example, showed that 67 percent of those surveyed believed the gap between rich and poor was "getting larger," while 65 percent said this gap needed to be "addressed now," and 57 percent thought the government should do more to "reduce the gap."[57]

Here it is important to state that what has emerged or is emerging in the consolidation trend is not "monopoly capital" based on some neoclassical quantity theory of competition in which fewer capitals compete less. Quite the opposite, concentration and centralization are functions of competition, the effort to capture more profit by capturing more market share—in this case partly by absorbing the competition as well as increasing fixed capital. As Howard Botwinick put it, "Within the context of large-scale enterprise, the relentless drive to expand capital value is necessarily accompanied by a growing struggle over market shares. These two dynamics, accumulation and rivalry, are inextricably bound up with one another." The "battle of competition" doesn't end as larger capitals defeat or absorb smaller ones. On the contrary, it pushes each firm to compete more effectively by increasing "the productive force of labor as much as possible." Competing firms, in effect, leapfrog as each attempts to become more efficient through the application of still more capital, and competition tends to increase in intensity as the stakes grow greater. As capital accumulates and greater sales are required to recover costs, "The old struggle must begin again, and it is all the more violent the more powerful the means of production already invested are," writes Marx.[58] As a consequence, the pressure on the workforce will continue. So competition, consolidation or centralization, and the push for greater productivity are all of a piece in the reality of contemporary capital accumulation.

Similarly, increased competition and centralization via accumulation in no way eliminate the certainty of future crises on the scale of the Great Recession or greater. Indeed, the recent rise in the capital-labor ratio since the recession most likely points to a future falling rate of profit and subsequent slump. In other words, consolidation does not solve all problems. Nevertheless, the fact that the new structure of US capitalism has not been displaced by the Great Recession gives reason to believe that what has emerged and is still taking shape will be with us for some time.

CHAPTER FIVE

Logistics: Capital's Supply Chain Gang

Even as capital in the United States was consolidating in industry after industry, the ties that bind the production of goods and services together, whether locally or across space, were tightening in new and important ways. As Marx noted, "The revolution in the modes of production of industry and agriculture made necessary a revolution in the general conditions of the social process of production, i.e., in the means of communications and transport."[1] This is, of course, an ongoing process, and one of the outstanding features of the restructuring of the production of goods and services in the era of lean production and new technology has been the reorganization of supply chains—the so-called "logistics revolution." Supply chains have long been part of the production of goods and services. The rise of global value or supply chains and the geographic relocation of domestic production and suppliers first experienced as fragmentation, however, have, like consolidation in business organization, brought about their opposite in a dramatic geographic and technological reorganization of supply chains, a "revolution" in "the means of communication and transport," as Marx put it.

One of the most important changes in the reorganization of supply chains is their geography, the concentration of workers in key "nodes" or "clusters," along with their technological drivers and linkages. If suppliers have relocated to lower-cost areas within the United States or even offshore, bringing about a degree of vertical "dis-integration," the sinews of transportation that move both intermediate and final products (including imports) within the

United States have been reconfigured into enormous "logistics clusters" of transportation hubs, massive warehouses and distribution centers, "aerotropolises," sea-ports, intermodal yards, and sophisticated technology that bring tens of thousands of workers into finite geographic concentrations, mostly in or adjacent to large urban metropolitan areas. While there are about sixty such clusters in the United States, the biggest of these are found around Chicago, Los Angeles, and along the New Jersey Turnpike in the New York–New Jersey port area, each concentrating at least 100,000 workers. Chicago's metropolitan area is said to have 150,000 to 200,000 warehouse workers alone, and, according to one study, warehouse workers compose only about 20 percent of the total logistics industry in the United States. More recently the giant UPS "Worldport" superhub in Louisville "provides 55,000 jobs," while that of FedEx in Memphis employs 15,000 workers directly so far. The Memphis airport in which FedEx is based is the "largest cargo airport in the world," and Memphis is also a rail and trucking hub employing 220,000 workers.[2] Describing the workforce in the most modern of these clusters, the "distribution cities," one group of scholars noted that they contained "a small percentage of professional, managerial and technical occupations and a high proportion of working-class occupations."[3]

The location of these major logistics clusters in metropolitan areas is often explained simply by the fact that all of these urban locations are in large degree ports and centers of air, rail, and highway intersection. As important as these factors are, there is something more to it. As Marx noted in *Capital*, volume 3, "The shorter the turnover time (of capital), the smaller the idle portion of capital compared with the whole; the greater therefore is the surplus value appropriated, other conditions being equal."[4] Conversely, the longer the turnover time, the less surplus value is appropriated. "Physical infrastructure dominates logistics investment," Sheffi argues.[5] While a good deal of infrastructure is publicly funded, as we saw above, most of it comes from state and local capital budgets, which are, in turn, largely funded through state and local debt, that is, bond issues underwritten and marketed by private financial institutions.

For example, state and local long-term debt for 2008 amounted to $2.5 trillion. Most of the state and local bonds are held by private investors, either individuals or financial institutions, and hence enter the circuits of capital mediated by government priorities, which these days are "entrepreneurial" and oriented toward "public-private partnerships" such as logistics parks.[6] These investors, however, must wait years before receiving returns on their investments. Because the turnover times of sunk capital that characterize logistics clusters and their internal infrastructure are long and profits slow in coming, there is enormous pressure on both owners and users of this infrastructure to seek out relatively cheap labor compared to that employed in the movable aspects of logistics: trucks, trains, planes, ships, and the like.

All the metropolitan sites of the major logistics clusters are also homes to large "ghettos" and "barrios" housing huge numbers of unemployed and underemployed working-class people who are to a large extent "enclosed," both spatially and occupationally, by racial segregation and discrimination, the disappearance or drastic shrinking of previous employment possibilities in manufacturing or the public sector, and the diminution of state benefits— they are the quintessential reserve army of labor. As such, the workers that maintain the internal infrastructure, fill the warehouses, and move things around within the cluster are paid poorly and treated as dispensable. On the other hand, the existence of this large reserve army of low-paid labor limits the locations of the biggest logistics hubs to large metropolitan areas that house these workers. This is the unspoken locational "metric" that makes the Los Angeles, Chicago, and the New York–New Jersey metropolitan areas, the country's three largest metropolitan statistical areas with their millions of low-income Black and Latino people and relatively high poverty and unemployment rates, the biggest logistics clusters of all.[7]

The Case of Chicago

As one study of logistics agglomerations says of Chicago:

> Chicago is a major industrial center and one of the world's leading shipping and distribution hubs. It is the focal point of all U.S. railroads. In addition, Chicago's trading tradition, access to the Great Lakes routes inland waterways, connectivity to major highways, four airports and large logistics parks (such as Elwood, Joliet, Logistics Park Chicago) make it an important logistics hub.[8]

The Chicago metropolitan area logistics cluster contains a major seaport on the St. Lawrence Seaway–Great Lakes system, which employs 2,711 workers directly and another 4,000 indirectly.[9] It is the largest rail center in the United States and the only one in which six Class I rail systems meet. Some five hundred freight trains pass through the Chicago area every day. It is also the juncture of major interstate highways, and its main airport, O'Hare, is the second busiest in the country. Its inland "Midwest Empire" in the Chicago–Joliet–Naperville metro area is home to a typical example of the "public-private partnership" in the Centerpoint Intermodal Complex, built on a former US Army munitions plant site, partly funded by state and local governments, spanning 6,000 acres, and owned by "the largest industrial real estate developer in metropolitan Chicago." The entire metro area Inland Empire employs some 200,000 workers in the top five warehouse occupations in about 200 to 300 warehouses, as well as 39,410 heavy tractor-trailer truck drivers, 23,990 light truck and delivery drivers, and 17,550 industrial truck and tractor operators, to mention a few other occupations. While not all of these workers are necessarily employed within the cluster, many are, and many others move in and out of it and beyond to the manufacturing firms along the interstate highways of the Midwest.[10]

A 2010 survey of warehouse workers in Will County in the heart of the Chicago metro area conducted by Warehouse Workers for Justice found that 48 percent of warehouse workers were African American, 38 percent Latino, 11 percent white non-Latino, and the rest a mixture of Asians, Arabs, Native Americans, and "others." Women compose about a quarter of the warehouse workforce. In addition, there are truck, rail, and communications workers in large numbers passing through this massive agglomeration of capital and labor. For the thousands of warehouse workers, wages are low and employment insecure. The pay of the major warehouse occupations in Will County ranged from $9.28 an hour to $14.55 in 2010, almost two-thirds are paid below the poverty level, and all are below the government's low-wage level. As a result, 37 percent hold second jobs and 25 percent rely on government benefits of one sort or another. Some 63 percent are employed by temporary agencies rather than by warehouse outfits, third party logistics (3PL) firms, or retail giants such as Wal-Mart that own or use the warehouses, and receive little in the way of benefits.[11] If one were looking for both employment and economic precariousness, this would be the place.

As one study noted with academic understatement, "Populated centers offer availability of labor and proximity for logistics companies."[12] At the core of the metro area, the city of Chicago with its 2.7 million people is obviously such a center. With a poverty rate of 23 percent, compared to that of 14 percent for the nation in 2010, and an unemployment rate of 25 percent among the city's 888,000 African Americans and 12 percent among its 780,000 Latinos, Chicago was an ideal location for one the nation's largest logistics clusters.[13]

Altogether, according to one academic study, the logistics industry in the United States employs 3.2 million workers, 85 percent of them located within metropolitan areas.[14] This figure doesn't include all those engaged in transportation and is focused on those directly serving logistics clusters. For example, this count failed to include the 185,000 railroad workers employed by the major freight carriers. Thus, the total is probably closer to 3.5 or even 4 million.[15] Marx was clear that transportation workers who move commodities produce surplus value. Since commodities must change location both during production and to reach the market, he wrote in the *Grundrisse*, "Economically considered, the spatial condition, the bringing the product to the market belongs to the production process itself."[16] In volume II of *Capital* he concluded, "The productive capital invested in this industry [transportation] thus adds value to the products transported, partly through the value carried over from the means of transport, partly through the value added by the work of transport."[17]

Marx, like today's logistics gurus, considered storage as dead time that only added costs and produced no value. Today, however, as one warehouse management textbook put it, "Companies are continually looking to minimize the amount of stock held and speed up throughput." Almost a third of warehouse companies in the United States practice "cross-docking," in which "Same-day receipt and dispatch is the target," and this is expected to rise to 45 percent by 2018. As Bonacich and Wilson state, "A single state-of-the-art cross-docking facility for a retailer can handle up to seventy thousand containers and pallets each day of varying size, weight, and fragility." Even in more conventional warehouses, where stock may remain in place for a while, the object is to move it as quickly as possible. A growing number of warehouses also perform final steps in manufacturing, often to "customize" a product, including many imports.[18]

In other words, most warehouse labor today involves the movement, relocation, and additional manufacture of goods and is more akin to transportation or even manufacturing labor than that of mere storage. Indeed, following Marx's definition of transportation as part of the overall production process, most of the workers in these giant clusters are engaged in goods production despite being classified as something else by the Bureau of Labor Statistics. Furthermore, contemporary warehouses, like other production facilities, are high-tech operations. While in real terms warehousing net assets in structures grew by 45 percent from 1982 to 2009, the value of equipment increased by 187 percent, compared to only 56 percent in manufacturing.[19] Thus, the

more than 3.5 million workers in logistics, many once considered service producers, are in fact a central part of the industrial core of the working class
identified by Hal Draper.[20] The supply chain, from raw materials to the very
doors of Wal-Mart is, in the Marxist view, a production assembly line—one
that is tightly controlled by just-in-time systems operating through logistics.
Logistics clusters are, therefore, *value-producing agglomerations* at the center of
today's broader production processes, much as the clusters of auto assembly
plants of yesteryear in Detroit or the steel mills in Gary were at the center of
their supply chains of parts, raw materials, and so on.

The workers in both the clusters and broader production systems are not
only tied together by urban-based concentration and intermodal transportation but also by the advanced technology that drives, tracks, pulls, and pushes
the modern just-in-time supply (production) chain. As a result, competition,
both domestic and international, has become increasingly "time-based competition." As one expert put it succinctly concerning product delivery, "Time
has become a far more critical element in the competitive process."[21] Marx
made the broader point that in the circuits of capital, as capital moves from
its money form to commodities and then to market to become money again,
"even spatial distance reduces itself to time; the important thing, e.g., is not
the market's distance in space, but the speed—the amount of time—with
which it can be reached."[22] Since the actual speed at which trucks, trains,
planes, and ships move things has not changed much in the last thirty years,
the object of the "logistics revolution" has been, along with bigger ships and
longer trains and truck trailers that carry more, to move more things as
quickly as possible with minimal storage time at the points where products
change modes of transport, through the warehouse or distribution center, and
all along the supply chain to the final market. They must aspire to, as Marx
famously put it, "the annihilation of space by time."[23]

This requires advanced information technology. As one expert put it, "An
information supply chain parallels every physical supply chain."[24] Information technologies such as RFID, GPS, barcoding, electronic data interchange
(EDI), and so on are employed to keep just-in-time delivery as tight as possible at each and every point. Developed by Wal-Mart, RFID not only tracks
goods. As Bonacich and Wilson point out, "A more sinister side of this new
technology is that it enables employers to keep closer track of what employees
are doing."[25] The tightening of movement applies not only between logistics
centers but within them as well. For example: "The advanced scheduling technology employed in the new (as of 2011) Union Pacific intermodal yard in

Joliet Logistics Park coordinates all movement of rail cars, trucks, trailers, and containers throughout the facility. The system cut truck-processing time by an average of 75 percent."[26] This constant push for speed, like "management by stress" in the immediate production process, puts enormous external pressure on workers all along the supply chain and within the logistics clusters. With increased competition, advanced technology, and the logistics revolution, more and more workers have found themselves locked into what amounts to a global supply chain gang. These chains, however, can be broken. Along with their interconnectivity, their very time-bound tension makes them extremely vulnerable to worker action.

The vulnerability of logistics systems and supply chains is increased by the fact that for the most part their reorganization and tightening has meant that on average each supply chain employed in the production of a final commodity has seen a reduction in the number of suppliers, making the task of organizing them somewhat simpler and the impact of direct action in any one "node" in the chain more effective. In the US automobile industry this development has been spectacular, with the number of firms supplying the major assemblers, both US- and foreign-owned, dropping from an average of a thousand to three to six hundred over the last two decades.[27] As one logistics guru summarized the trend generally, "A further prevailing trend over the last decade or so has been the dramatic reduction in the number of suppliers from which organizations typically will procure materials, components, services, etc."[28] This reduction in the number of suppliers is in part a consequence of the general consolidation of firms in industry after industry. That is, suppliers like any capitalist must compete by increasing technology and the scale of production. At the same time, the reduction in suppliers indicates the limits of geographically extended outsourcing—the previous and still current "spatial fix" of many firms that has failed to protect them from the impact of at least the last two recessions.

In addition, there is the fact that all these changes in the concentration and centralization of capital and the rise of huge logistics clusters represent an enormous amount of fixed and sunk capital. It's all very fine that due to "financialization," capital in its money form flies around the earth at the speed of light, spreading investment wherever it touches down, but once the "buck" has landed and is transformed into roads, rails, ports, warehouses, factories, communications systems, equipment, and the like, these investments don't just get up and walk away. As Marx pointed out in volume 3 of *Capital*, "The transfer of capital from one sector to another presents significant difficulties, particularly on account of the fixed capital involved."[29] The same is true in terms of geographic shifts, whether at home or abroad. From 1998 to 2014 new capital investments in structures amounted to $658 billion in manufacturing, just over $200 billion in warehouses, and $150 billion in transportation. According to the BEA, the average life of a manufacturing facility is thirty-one years, while that of a warehouse is forty years and that for air and "other" transportation structures thirty-eight years.[30] The infrastructure on which they rest and function (land, roads, rails, ports, wires, utility conduits, etc.) is certain to last even longer and cost more.

As David Harvey put it succinctly, "The spatial mobility of commodities depends upon the creation of a transport network that is immobile in space."[31] The logistics networks are tied together by the nation's highways, where trucks move 8.8 trillion tons of goods a year, the 200,000 miles of freight-carrying railroads that move about 1.9 trillion tons of freight each year, inland waterways carrying 404 billion tons, and aircraft moving about 4 billion tons.[32] Trucks, however, must have roads; trains, rails; planes, airports; and the biggest container ships or super-tankers, ports. In addition, they must have terminals, fueling stations, and communications systems that guide them, all of which are also chokepoints in the system. The embedded contours of industry, logistics, communications, and commerce that have taken shape in the last couple of decades are not likely to decompose or relocate much for some time—and their centers in major metropolitan population concentrations make much of this complex a more or less stationary target for unionization and collective action.

To put this most recent transformation in historical context, the recent restructuring of goods production in the United States is the third geographic reorganization of production in the post–World War II era—the third attempt at what David Harvey calls a "spatial fix" to the problems of falling profit rates. The first came following World War II with the partial movement of major assembly as well as parts manufacturing out of many northern urban industrial centers into rural or semirural areas of the South and to a lesser extent the West. This was enabled by the construction of the interstate highway system in the 1950s and 1960s. From 1947 to 1972, valued added in manufacturing in the South grew by four times, compared to twice for the nation as a whole. After this it continued to increase, but at a slower rate.[33]

The second geographic shift followed the 1974–75 recession and, even more, the one in 1980–82 with its massive destruction of capital and jobs. This involved further relocation of some assembly production but especially the production of intermediate inputs (outsourcing) out of northern urban areas, this time into rural areas of the Midwest and to a lesser extent the South. While this trend has continued to some extent, the major features of the third and current geographic reorganization involve the concentration and centralization of both those capitals producing the final goods and services as well as the production of intermediate inputs, North and South, and the insertion of the contemporary urban-based logistics clusters into the overall production process of more and more industries. What is clear from the failure of the first two attempts at a "spatial fix" to stave off crises, along with US capital's efforts at a "global fix" through accelerated trade and overseas investment, is that ultimately the new geographic configuration will be no more successful. As Harvey puts it, "There is, in short, no 'spatial fix' that can contain the contradictions of capitalism in the long run."[34] But as the persistence of many of the production sites of the previous reorganizations show, these investments are either prisoners of their embedded fixed capital or they face the firing squad of devaluation. The survivors, of course, become linked to the just-in-time logistics networks. Thus the deep embeddedness of the third and most recent geographic reorganization indicates that it will be around for some time.

The overall picture of the context in which the US working class has taken shape since the early 1980s began as one of decentralized production via outsourcing, increased precarious work, and the experience of fragmentation. As is so often the case in the expansion of capital accumulation, however, the reality of competition has produced an opposite tendency in the increased concentration and centralization of capital in almost every realm of the production of goods and services. As part of this process, more and more aspects of production are tied together in just-in-time supply chains that have reproduced the vulnerability that capital sought to escape through lean production methods and relocation. This is so despite the fact that outsourcing continues because the firms that do the outsourced or contracted work must themselves become bigger in order to compete, on the one hand, and are utterly dependent on the logistics network in order to attract business, on the other hand, whether they are located in the North, South, East, or West.

This emerging reorganization of US capitalism, of course, exists in a global context, and many of the competitive forces driving these changes are international in nature. The logistics clusters, in particular, are not only at the center of production systems within the United States but are also nodes in the global systems of production, commerce, and trade. As we have seen, these hubs in the supply chains of industry and commerce move and sometimes contribute to the manufacture of imported goods as well as those produced domestically. For some goods produced abroad, they are part of the intermodal "land bridge" that moves them coast to coast across the United States, from Asia to Europe, or the reverse so that the realization of their value, like their production, is achieved outside the US economy, though their transport across the United States adds to their value.

To a certain extent, logistics clusters compete with one another at home and abroad. The US coastal ports and intermodal "land bridge," for example compete with the Panama Canal and the clusters around it. But each cluster also competes for the business of transport, third party logistics (3PLs), communications, warehouse, manufacturing, and retail firms. Thus, the clusters and the firms that work in them are subject to the same pressures as any capitalist operation—the need to grow and reduce costs through low wages, work intensification, and new technology in order to remain competitive. Their ability to attract huge concentrations of labor despite the low wages of many of their workers lies in what has been said above about the reserve armies of labor that live in nearby urban concentrations. At the same time, a significant proportion of this adjacent labor force has been drawn from around the world. In this aspect, the rise of logistics has made a significant contribution not only to the shifts in the occupational and geographic structure of the US workforce but also to the changing ethno-racial composition of the US working class and its economic deterioration.

A New Phase of Capitalism?

The convergence of lean production norms, electronic and biometric surveillance, digital technology, business consolidation, increased capital intensity, and the "logistics revolution" has certainly altered the shape of accumulation, the integrated contours of the production of goods and services, and, perhaps most importantly, the terrain of class conflict. While this convergence and the emerging field of struggle appear most developed in the United States, the trends are common to much of the industrial and industrializing world, including China. Does the capitalist development that has taken shape over the last three decades—especially since the turn of the twenty-first century—represent a new phase? I would argue that it does but at the same time caution that we resist the temptation to give it a simple name. Labels like "Fordism," for example, never captured the totality of the era of mass production. Nor for that matter has mass production ceased to be a common feature of manufacturing despite customized frills or "batches" that are often based on the same platforms, sometimes labeled, for lack of a better term, "post-Fordism." Indeed, the use of such prefixes "post" or "neo" doesn't really tell us anything about capitalist development. Nor did Harvey's clumsy addition of "flexible" to accumulation to describe the early years of lean production and vertical disintegration of production or the "postmodern condition" tell us much about what was actually new.[35] Least useful of all are neologisms like "gig economy" or "sharing economy" that trivialize the deeper reality of capitalism, its dynamics, and the altered state of working-class life.

Nevertheless, a new terrain of class struggle has emerged from the convergence of the trends analyzed above, which in many ways is more favorable to working-class initiatives than either the last period of labor and social upsurge in the 1960s and 1970s or the transition period of the 1980s and 1990s that preceded the new phase of consolidation and integration. Furthermore, the Great Recession that began in 2007 has, if anything, only continued the trends that produced this new situation. Will these conditions produce the sort of social upsurges we saw in the 1930s or the 1960s and 1970s?

CHAPTER SIX

The Coming Upsurge?

L abor movements seldom grow significantly by increments over extend-ed periods. The British labor historian Eric Hobsbawm argued that the growth of unions and other social movements cannot be measured by "a mere rising slope."[1] Rather they to tend grow rapidly in the midst of explosive and usually unpredictable strike "waves" or "leaps" as Hobsbawm (1964), Ernest Mandel (1995), John Kelly (1998), Leopold Haimson and Charles Tilly (2002), and Beverly Silver (2003), among others, have argued. Since the 1870s, these worker upsurges have been international, at least among the developed indus-trial nations. For the twentieth century there is general agreement that major upsurges in the industrial countries occurred in the years just before and after World War I, following World War II, and from the mid-1960s to the mid- or late 1970s. There is disagreement over the 1930s. Kelly sees only a minor up-surge in the second half of the 1930s, Silver sees a more substantial upsurge in the "metropolitan" countries also in the second half of the 1930s, while Mandel shows a dramatic upswing beginning around 1933.[2] The basis for the different calculations is not clear, but since Mandel's version is closer to the experience of the United States on which this study is focused we will use his estimates for the 1930s. There is general agreement on the other twentieth-century labor upsurges. More controversial are the causes of these strike waves.

What is it that causes masses of workers to initiate and join in rising lev-els of strike action and union growth? Are there specific conditions that send hundreds of thousands or even millions of workers into the streets within a period of a few years? This has been debated by academics and activists in the neoliberal era as strike activity and union membership have declined across much of the industrialized world. Economists have long argued that the level of strikes is influenced by the ups and downs of the business cycle—workers are more likely to strike during economic upswings, less likely in recessions. Even to the extent that this is sometimes the case, it is clear that not every upswing of the nine- or ten-year business cycle brings anything like a labor upsurge. Indeed, the economic recoveries of the 1980s and 1990s only brought a decline in strikes and union membership.

A more sophisticated effort to pin strike waves on economic trends has been the efforts to associate the major labor upheavals since the 1870s with "long waves" of economic growth and decline. Long waves are generally associated with the work of Russian economist Nicolai Kondratieff who documented long waves in price movements in the 1920s. Each long wave lasts about fifty years, with waves of growth or decline said to be about twenty to twenty-five years in length, allowing for some ups and downs of the business cycle within each long wave. Others have extended these waves up to the present using profit rates, GDP, or industrial output as well as prices. Using the calculations of the three authors cited in table IV below with some modifications, we can construct a rough table of the global long waves and their up-and-down swings over the past 120 years.

Table IV: Long Waves in the World Economy, 1890–2010

Long Wave	Upswing	Downswing
1893–1945	1893–1914	1914–1940
1945–1982	1945–1975	1975–1982
1982–present	1982–2007	2007–?

Sources: Mandel, 1995, 82; Kelly, 1998, 85; Shaikh, 2016, 727.

Since the simple movement of the economy either up or down does not by itself imply any causal relationship, Mandel and Kelly attempt to correlate the cycles of labor upsurge with Kondratieff long waves, arguing that the big upheavals tend to come toward the end of the long upswing as profit rates fall and capital attempts to restrain or cut real wages and intensify work in one way or another. If we now construct a table for strike waves in the twentieth century, measured somewhat differently by Mandel, Kelly, Silver, and the BLS, some problems arise. For one thing, the strike waves often overlap with up and down swings. The 1930s are a particular problem for this theory not only because some see an upsurge, while others don't, but also because the 1930s are part of a long downward wave when major upsurges in strikes are not supposed to happen, even during short-term upswings in the business cycle. The strike wave that most historians peg to the years 1966–74 actually lasted until 1978 in the United States and United Kingdom, at least as measured by the number of strikes and strikers. Table V shows the major international strike waves that would have affected the United States.

Table V: Strike Waves, 1900–1975

Years	Upsurge	Decline	Upsurge
1900–1945	1910–1920	1920–1932	1933–1937
1945–1982	1945–1949	1953–1965	1966–1978
1982–2007	none	1982–now	none

Sources: Mandel, 1995, 39; Kelly, 1998, 87; Silver, 2003, 126–27; Moody, 2007a, 99.

In addition to the problems mentioned above, the biggest difficulty in correlating long waves and strike waves, let alone proving causation, comes with the latest "Kondratieff" upswing from 1982 to 2007. Mandel allows that the cycle of class struggle "is relatively independent of the long waves of more rapid accumulation and slower accumulation, although to some extent interwoven with them."[3] Kelly, apparently more sure of his theory, writing in the mid- to late 1990s, predicted, "Contrary to postmodernist claims that the classical labour movement is in terminal decline, long wave theory suggests that it is more likely to be on the threshold of resurgence."[4] As much as one might agree with Kelly's critique of the postmodernists' prophesy of doom, it is all too clear that there was no resurgence or upsurge of labor anywhere in the developed industrial countries in the latest long upswing of capitalism.

While for whatever reasons Kondratieff long waves no longer correlate with labor upsurges, if this ever was actually valid, all is not lost. While they don't develop the observation, both Mandel and Kelly note that capital will attempt to restore falling profit rates through the "reorganization of the labour process at plant level" or more broadly "impinge either directly on workers' living standards (through wage controls or wage cuts, intensification of labour or labour shedding)."[5] While both see this as happening toward the end of the long economic upswing, it is the notion of attacks on living standards and particularly on working conditions through changes in the labor process that offers us a closer approximation of the *causes* of working-class upheavals. It is this underlying cause of increased class conflict that we now examine in more detail.

The causes of working-class upsurges and even of revolutions rooted in changes in the labor process have been examined and analyzed in detail in some twenty-four essays in a remarkable collection edited by Leopold Haimson and Charles Tilly entitled *Strikes, Wars and Revolution in International Perspective: Strike Waves in the Late Nineteenth and Early Twentieth Centuries.* This volume looks at strike waves in several European countries and the United States up to the years following World War I. Most of the authors in this collection reject or minimize the movements of economic cycles as a cause of major strike waves. The two introductions to the collection note the trends that were part of the "shared experience" of European industrial workers in the early twentieth century: urbanization, business consolidation, and "changes in the character and organization of work processes."[6] Wars and the subsequent weakening of the old regimes, of course, played an important role in those countries where the post–World War I strike wave took on a revolutionary character, as in Russia, Germany, and Italy. But most of the essays cite the enormous change in the organization of work, including the introduction of Taylorism or scientific management, in the years leading up to World War I as a source of worker discontent *and* action before, during, and after the war.

The introduction of various forms of "management reform" and "scientific management," including Taylor's version, in the years before and during World War I and worker resistance to them in the metal-working industries that were at the center of strike waves in those years are documented for the United States, Germany, Russia, and Britain.[7] In each case, these pushes for work reorganization and intensification played a direct role in fostering both workplace organization and the upsurges of that era. In Britain this became the shop stewards' movement, in Germany the Berlin-based Revolutionary Shop Stewards, and in Italy the factory councils.[8] In the United States, workplace-based delegate systems also emerged in these years in a number of industries.[9] Nevertheless, these attacks on working conditions were meant to and did create an "imbalance" in the power relations between capital and labor, particularly in the workplace. A number of these studies also reveal rising rank-and-file opposition to union leaders who failed to respond to the new situation.

An outstanding example of this is found in Richard Müller, leader of the Revolutionary Shop Stewards in Berlin, who played a central role in strike actions during the war and the revolutionary upsurge that followed. Müller and the Revolutionary Shop Stewards began resistance to the intensification of work in the German metal-working industry during the war by studying and analyzing Taylorism. Müller wrote popular pamphlets for workers, explaining scientific management. Müller and the shop stewards also opposed the pro-war and pro-management policies of the leaders of the metalworkers' unions, the DMV (Deutscher Metallarbeiter-Verband). Although the German Revolution of 1918–21 failed, the shop stewards played a key role in the upsurge.[10]

One of the two introductions to the Haimson-Tilly collection summarizes a major theme in explaining the strike waves of that era:

> Indeed, in the view of many of the contributors, by the eve of the war, all of the major, established, organized collective actors implicated in labor conflicts—employers, agencies of the state, and in many instances also the leaders of trade unions and of existing political parties—displayed a growing unwillingness, or inability, to recognize the legitimacy, if not apprehend the very nature, of the grievances and aspirations of the workers who were drawn into these conflicts.[11]

Thus, not only did the reorganization of work along "scientific management" lines produce organization and rebellion, but also the inability of employers, politicians, and even union leaders to understand how this affected the workers led to the rank-and-file character of that upsurge. This is a situation that describes the conditions prevailing before and during the upsurge of 1966–79 as well as those that have converged on working-class life in the United States in the last decade or so.

Eric Hobsbawm described the sort of conditions that led to what he calls "leaps" or "explosions" of strike activity and union growth as "accumulations of inflammable materials which only ignite periodically, as it were under compressions."[12] This, too, describes well the conditions that have accumulated in stages over the past three decades: lean production, electronic and biometric forms of work measurement and monitoring, the new contours of just-in-time supply chains, and the "logistics revolution"—each adding to time pressures and work intensification. None of these changes by themselves produced sufficient "compression" or the spark that could ignite a new labor upsurge, but in the last decade or so, perhaps delayed by the dislocations of the Great Recession, the convergence of these changes has embraced more and more sections of the US working class. On top of this has come the increasing decline in living standards as real incomes shrink, "the social wage" fades, and political attacks on workers and unions increase—this in a rich country where billionaires grow like weeds.

We cannot know when, or perhaps even if, this convergence will produce a conflagration. Mass production and "scientific management" took shape almost two decades before the upsurge of the 1930s. The management offensive of the 1950s preceded the highly visible 1966 five-week strike of thirty thousand airline mechanics that halted 60 percent of the nation's air traffic and announced the era of rank-and-file rebellion that would accelerate in the early 1970s.[13] The "accumulations of inflammable materials" that underlay these waves of strikes and union growth had to become generalized and widely experienced before an "explosion" was likely. Although we can see plenty of signs of resistance and the feelings of "injustice" that mobilization theory tells us precedes any upsurge, it is impossible to fully gauge the subjective factor needed to set things in motion. And, of course, there are other intervening social, economic, and political conditions that can suppress militancy and rebellion for a time. Predictions of an upsurge are almost always a futile pursuit, as Kelly's suggestion that in the late 1990s labor was "likely to be on the threshold of resurgence" reminds us.[14] What is needed now is not crystal ball gazing but preparation.

A "Militant Minority"

The strength, durability, and outcomes of these periodic upsurges depend to a large degree on the formation and development of the activist layer of the labor movement. It is this layer that not only supports the unions during good times and bad but also plays a key role in the upsurge. To the degree that there is a core within the activist layer that is class conscious and politically aware, the activist layer is strengthened and the force of the upsurge and, hence, its outcomes stronger and more durable. Labor historian David Montgomery noted the importance of this active core of the class in understanding the course of class struggle. He wrote, "Both 'history from the bottom up' and the common fixation on great leaders have obscured the decisive role of those whom twentieth-century syndicalists called the 'militant minority': the men and women who endeavoured to weld their workmates and neighbours into a self-aware working class."[15] The socialist and syndicalist leaders of the shop stewards' movement in Britain or the revolutionary shop stewards in Germany during and after the First World War mentioned above are examples of this.

Such a layer existed in the US working class in the early 1930s that made the upheaval that produced the industrial unions of the Congress of Industrial Organizations (CIO) both powerful and durable. These were mostly radicals, members of the Socialist Party, Communist Party, Trotskyists, Musteites, and veterans of the IWW (the Industrial Workers of the World). The activists from these and similar groups organized the first major strikes in 1933 and on a grander scale in 1934 with the strikes of Toledo auto parts workers, Minneapolis Teamsters, and San Francisco longshore workers.[16] They played a central role in crucial actions such as the sit-down strike at General Motors in Flint, Michigan, in 1937.[17] Their understanding of capitalism and their organizational know-how helped launch this upsurge despite the fact that they also often fought each other. It was these working-class radicals that formed the backbone of the new stewards' organizations at the heart of industry, provided information and analysis within and across union lines, and, when necessary forced upon often reluctant officials both elements of democracy and the broader mobilizations that gave the CIO upsurge its power and durability.

In contrast, the "rank-and-file" upsurge from the mid-1960s to the late 1970s lacked a strong "militant minority" at the core of the broader activist layer. The working-class Left in the labor movement had been decimated after the war. As Paul Le Blanc, who writes of a somewhat broader concept of a "radical labor subculture," summarized the roots of this change, "There was a dramatic break in the continuity of this labor-radical tradition in the U.S. after 1945, because of the realities that resulted from the Second World War, and the social, economic, political and cultural transformations of the 1950s and 1960s."[18] These included among other factors, McCarthyism, the Cold War, suburbanization, and the relative prosperity of much of the working class. Here is how I summarized this several years ago:

> Unlike the other social movements of the 1960s and 1970s, there were no nationally recognized leaders or organizations that straddled the movement as a whole. Nor was there the sort of radical core of organized leftists that has provided so much of the indispensable grassroots leadership, at the shop floor level and across the movement as a whole, as there had been in earlier labor upheavals. Socialists and other radicals played important roles in some rank-and-file organizations—in the Teamsters, the UAW, Steelworkers, and a few others—but their numbers were few, and none of their organizations were strong enough to provide anything like national leadership and direction to the movement as a whole, with perhaps the exception of TDU (Teamsters for a Democratic Union) in the IBT.[19]

The efforts of the socialists and others to play this role in the 1970s came too little and too late. The result was that most of the strikes and rank-and-file movements of that era remained politically rudimentary and isolated from one another. This inability to become a self-conscious national phenomenon meant this upsurge left little in the way of a durable grassroots leadership for labor when the neoliberal era emerged, with its demands for concessions from the unions, the introduction of lean production, labor-management cooperation schemes, anti-union consultants, and so on.

This raises the question as to whether there exists such a "militant minority" today large enough to help shape and strengthen the next upsurge when and if it arrives. This isn't just a matter of making a head count of the Left in the labor movement. As always, part of the answer lies in the self-activity of the working class itself. It is through their own activity that working-class people begin to see the real nature of their relationship to capital and to develop the "militant minority" that is always the backbone of the waves of insurgency that characterize the rhythms of intense class conflict. My own view is that there is such a layer in the making in the various union-based rank-and-file reform movements that have been arising in the last several years, as well as in other grassroots working-class organizations and campaigns. While this layer does not yet form a coherent "militant minority," it nonetheless has a center that was entirely absent in the last upsurge in the United States in the *Labor Notes* project briefly discussed below. First, however, I look at the weak state of the labor movement and possible ways to take advantage of the new terrain of class conflict in order to reverse organized labor's decline.

Official Strategies That Failed

Because the period of consolidation was also one of continuous disruption of old patterns of work and organization, as well as of the workforce itself, workers and their unions have been disoriented and, as often as not, defeated. Pulling out of this tailspin has proved difficult, with union membership in the private sector down to 6.6 percent in 2014 and up only 1 percent in 2015 despite a small gain of 195,000, that in the public sector falling to 35.2 percent, and strikes still at all-time lows, averaging 147 a year from 2010 to 2015, during which there were only 111 strikes.[20] As a result of this decline, many labor leaders began looking for new ways to stem the downward tide. The four main tactics they settled on were inward-looking: union mergers to boost membership, contract concessions to try to save jobs, labor-management cooperation schemes, and "neutrality" and card-check agreements as a way to increase organizing.

The number of union mergers rose from thirty-one in the 1970s to thirty-five in the 1980s and forty-two in the 1990s, the bulk of them led by just five unions. While this produced some giant conglomerate unions like the Service Employees International Union (SEIU), the United Food and Commercial Workers (UFCW), and the United Steel Workers (with about two dozen jurisdictions in which steel workers were a tiny minority), it brought no real gains to the movement as a whole.[21] Contract concessions and labor-management cooperation simply enabled the move to lean production, the flattening of wages, and the massive loss of manufacturing jobs discussed in chapter 1. Decline continued apace.

In 1995, the complacent Cold Warriors who had run the AFL-CIO since its founding forty years earlier faced the first open challenge for the top leadership in the labor federation's history. Calling themselves the New Voice, the challengers promised change: more organizing, independence in foreign policy positions, and greater racial and gender diversity in both leadership and membership—in short, a renewed labor movement. The three leaders who composed the New Voice slate had some credentials for the job. John Sweeney, SEIU president and the ticket's presidential candidate, could take some credit for the inspiring 1990 victory of SEIU's Justice for Janitors campaign in Los Angeles, which brought thousands of building service workers into the union. Richard Trumka, head of the United Mine Workers (UMW) and vice presidential candidate, had led the successful no-holds-barred strike and occupation against Pittston in 1989. And Linda Chavez-Thompson of the American Federation of State, Municipal, and County Employees (AFSCME), vying for the AFL-CIO executive vice presidency, was one of the first Latinas to achieve a high position in a major US union. In contrast, John Sweeney, who as president of the federation held the real power, was in many ways an unlikely reformer. In his many years as SEIU president, he tolerated double-dip salaries and shared leadership with people like New York's Gus Bevona and Detroit's Richard Cordtz, who were known to be corrupt. And he hired the American Management Association to train his growing SEIU staff, with the *Harvard Business Review* at the top of the curriculum, according to a sympathetic study by Michael Piore.[22]

This contradictory cocktail—toleration of the old and dubious, progressive experiments, and business methods—goes some way toward explaining just what the New Voice put in place and why revitalization was an elusive goal. As Jeremy Brecher and Tim Costello remarked at the time, the approach of "the New Voice program was essentially to build a new AFL-CIO staff structure that largely bypassed the existing officers and departments."[23] A new bureaucracy was to be added to—or in some cases, replace—an older one, hopefully circumventing the conservative structure of the federation. As a longtime labor observer described the new changes in *Labor Notes*, "For every union problem there's a new Washington solution."[24]

Perhaps the biggest disappointment was in the area of new organizing, the New Voice reformers' top priority. Despite the refashioned Organizing Institute, the number of workers organized through the NLRB (National Labor Relations Board) fell from an average of over a million in the 1980s to 934,000 in the 1990s and to just over 900,000 in the first nine years of the 2000s when Sweeney was still in charge. To be sure, with the encouragement of the New Voice leaders, reliance on the NLRB gave way to "neutrality" agreements, in which willing employers allowed a simple majority show of support or an expedited election to bring union recognition. The problem was that most employers weren't willing. The unions that embraced the neutrality agreement tactic did better on average for each campaign, but in the face of recalcitrant employers the number of such accords remained low. It worked best with employers with which the union already had a bargaining relationship. The Communication Workers of America (CWA), which termed this "bargaining to organize," had some success. As measured by the Federal Mediation and Conciliation Service (FMCS), such "voluntary" recognition campaigns rose from a mere 227 in 1998 to 420 in 2001 before falling back to 258 in 2004, the last year the FMCS recorded them. This never constituted more than 10 percent of NLRB elections. The SEIU grew mostly among home health care workers. One of the few areas of growth was among nurses, who belonged to several unions but saw the formation of the growing National Nurses United in 2009.[25]

The problem was that neither the New Voice leaders nor even the most promising programs they set up could change the essentially conservative culture of the unions. More often than not, new organizers found themselves locked in the union hierarchy, still deploying old methods of organizing. Many simply dropped out. Nor was there anything in the New Voice program that proposed to mount the sort of assault on America's unwilling employers that could begin to alter the balance of social power in the US economy. Organizing without a shift in power was not going to work. What was missing in all these changes and innovations was anything directed at activating or mobilizing labor's ultimate source of power: its membership. Here, still in the millions, were workers with their hands on the levers of production of societies' goods and services who might actually challenge corporate America if mobilized. It was as though the idea of rank-and-file "involvement" had just appeared on the horizon. Herman Benson, whose Association for Union Democracy had been supporting union members fighting for participatory unionism for decades, wrote of the New Voice leadership, "They look everywhere except to what is most effective: the free independent democratic activity of union members inside their own unions."[26] So, over the long run, organizing never outstripped member losses for all but a few unions.

In 2005, frustrated at how little reform efforts were yielding, the AFL-CIO split, with Sweeney's own SEIU, now helmed by Andy Stern, leading five other unions out of the federation to organize the Change to Win (CtW) federation and the next round of top-down reform. Far from the tidal wave of new organizing and membership predicted by CtW, the new federation saw its ranks drop from 5.5 million in 2006 to 4.8 million in 2008, losing 458,083 in that year alone, even before the Great Recession hit full force. Between 2005 and 2010 organized labor engaged in its own top-down civil war, with the SEIU alone raiding some seven unions. By 2015 CtW was down to 3.7 million members after two of its major affiliates left to return to the AFL-CIO. By 2010, the SEIU's growth machine ground to a virtual halt in terms of actual dues-paying members and fell slightly by 2015. The AFL-CIO, for its part, had grown by three-quarters of a million members from 2010 to 2015 to 12.5 million, partly due to the return of two CtW unions to the AFL-CIO fold.[27]

Rich Trumka took over from Sweeney as AFL-CIO president in September 2009. As *Labor Notes* put it at the time, "Rich Trumka . . . inherits a world of hurt."[28] Labor's civil war, however, began to de-escalate in 2010 when SEIU's Andy Stern resigned in semi-disgrace, soon becoming a director of the private firm SIGA Technologies.[29] At its 2013 convention the federation took a step toward alliances with nontraditional labor organizations, such as the New York Taxi Workers Alliance and various workers' centers. The New York City taxi drivers are an important example of workers who are labeled "independent contractors" but who nevertheless managed to organize a majority of New York City's 35,000 taxi drivers, strike twice, and force gains from the city. With help from AFL-CIO unions they have formed a national union and have been elected to a seat on the AFL-CIO's executive council. Not all affiliated unions welcomed this step.[30] Despite this largely symbolic gesture and a good deal of resistance in the ranks, from 2005 to 2015 union membership fell by more than a million. The idea that a change at the pinnacle of labor's bureaucratic hierarchy could save the unions from capital's multisided attacks and the great economic shifts of the times was always an illusion.

Striking Back?

One of the casualties and most likely causes of labor's continuing decline was the near abandonment of the strike as a weapon against capital. If surges in strikes come in waves, so do their decline. In the United States the downward trend began with a steep drop during the deep recession of 1980–82. But it became a victim of the "strategies" of concessions and labor-management co-operation even when the economy grew again in the 1980s. The trend, however, was an international one. An ILO study of strikes in thirty-eight nations, measured by the number of days on strike, showed that strike activity had fallen by 80 percent from the 1970s to the early 2000s.[31] Research for the European Trade Union Institute covering both manufacturing and service work in the fifteen core countries of the European Union calculated that strike levels had dropped by 40 percent from the 1990s to the 2000s.[32] The drop in the number of strikes in the United States from the 1970s to the first decade of the twenty-first century was even larger than that in Europe, falling a huge 95 percent. Nor was it simply a function of lost union membership, which declined by 45 percent over those years.[33] Appendix F shows the number of strikes and worker hours on strike from 2002 through 2015 as tracked by the Federal Mediation and Conciliation Service (FMCS). They show that while strike activity was already at an all-time low, the Great Recession that began in 2007 had a further impact, with the number of strikes per year falling from 268 in 2006 to 108 in 2014 and then going up slightly to 111 in 2015.

Yet in 2015 the number of worker hours on strike rose dramatically, from a low of 6.8 million hours in 2014 and an average of 13.3 million hours a year from 2008 through 2014 to just over 39 million hours on strike in 2015 (see appendix F). It is possible this is only a blip, but the incidence of long strikes during 2015 and 2016 indicates that more workers are going on strike for longer and winning at least partial defensive victories. One contributor to this rise in hours on strike in 2015 was the escalating strikes of oil refinery workers who are members of the United Steelworkers. These eventually brought out 6,500 workers in February and March of 2015. In the end they won advances on health and safety and hiring issues.[34] Other candidates were the 1,700 call center and telecom workers at FairPoint, a spinoff from Verizon in New England, who struck for eighteen weeks from October 2014 through late February 2015. These members of the International Brotherhood of Electrical Workers (IBEW) and CWA won protections on subcontracting, layoffs, and work transfers.[35] The FMCS strike figures used here are for the federal government's fiscal years that begin on October 1, so that all eighteen weeks of this strike fall within FY 2015. Others included 16,900 Washington State teachers who struck from March 22 to June 23, the 2,100 members of the UAW Local 833 who struck the Kohler company for most of that year, and the 3,500 members of the National Union of Healthcare Workers (NUHW) at Kaiser Permanente in California who struck for a week, among others.[36]

The year 2016 promised to continue this trend. The biggest and longest strike of 2016 was that of 39,000 members of the CWA and the IBEW against Verizon, which began on April 13 and lasted for forty-five days. Although the unions made some concessions prior to the strike, notably on health care costs, the strike was a highly active one and on balance considered a victory on important questions of outsourcing, transfers, and job security.[37] Ten thousand members of four affiliates of the militant National Nurses United (NNU) struck in June 2016. The longest was that of five thousand nurses in Minneapolis/St. Paul who struck for over a month. Suggesting that the Verizon strike may have emboldened others to take direct action, CWA locals conducted a number of shorter grievance strikes at AT&T locations in California and Nevada. The significance of this is that permanent replacements cannot be used by the company in strikes over grievances.[38] As in many of the 2015 strikes, those in 2016 were typically characterized by high levels of active rank-and-file involvement.

There were non-strike actions that brought partial victories through mass actions in a period where even those have been rare. Chrysler workers rejected their national contract, as did Teamster car haulers. Teamster pensioners mounted a two-year campaign that prevented the Central States Pension Fund from cutting their benefits by 50 to 60 percent. As Jane Slaughter summarized some of the recent partial victories: "The three cases share one common characteristic: grassroots action by tens of thousands of rank-and-file members. Not clever PR campaigns, not pounding the bargaining table or lobbying, not photo ops, but getting in someone's face, in numbers."[39] If all of this is more than just another slight uptick, much of the credit must go to the Chicago Teachers Union for its successful and highly visible 2012 nine-day strike that taught others that strong preparation and grassroots organization can win.[40] So much so that when it threatened to strike again in 2016, "Mayor 1%" Rahm Emanuel gave in before the threat turned into another embarrassing victory of that city's teachers, parents, and students.[41]

It is too soon to say whether or not these actions point to an upturn in working-class rebellion. One thing is clear, however. Grassroots organization, preparation, and active involvement by union members can make a difference. Furthermore, some of the best-organized strikes and actions have found their inspiration in unions where rank-and-file reform movements were present, such as in CWA Local 1101, which was at the center of the action in New York during the Verizon strike, or the Teamster victories supported by Teamsters for a Democratic Union (TDU) and, of course, the Chicago Teachers Union. Similarly, newly formed unions such as the NNU and NUHW have chosen a militant course in the heart of America's private health care industry. To this list must be added the unprecedented nationwide strike of prisoners against the forced labor they are required to perform and its coordination by the Incarcerated Workers Organizing Committee of the IWW. The many difficulties of fighting back in the neoliberal era do not form an absolute barrier to action, while the new terrain of class conflict can open new paths to power.

"Don't Mourn [or Wait], Organize!"

The new and emerging shape of capitalism offers opportunities, not certainties. It does, however, point to some broad strategic directions and possibilities. There are three dimensions that offer some promise: the larger size of national or regional corporations in many industries; the huge concentrations of workers, particularly Blacks and Latinos, in urban areas; and the fragility of the whole just-in-time logistics supply chain system. In most of the industries described above, one or more unions already have a foothold. Worker-to-worker organizing in those industries along the lines of the national corporations or chains can use the stronger union presence in urban concentrations much like Farrell Dobbs's approach to organizing midwestern truckers and dockworkers in the 1930s. Then Dobbs and the Teamsters used truckers in the urban union stronghold of Minneapolis to "reach outward" to over-the-road truckers, warehouse workers, and local drivers in the Midwest.[42] Today this can mean using the urban base to reach out to the adjacent huge logistics clusters and manufacturing "out on the interstate" as well as local services.

A routinely underused source of power in this regard is the large concentration of union members in the nation's largest metropolitan areas. Once a year, in some cities, union leaders and activists manage to gather thousands of union members for a symbolic parade on Labor Day—and usually that's it. Yet the Chicago metropolitan statistical area (MSA) had over 618,000 union members in 2014, Metro Detroit still had 261,000 members, San Francisco–Oakland 259,000, and New York City's five boroughs 877,000, while in the New York–Northern New Jersey MSA there are 1.7 million, and so on.[43] If even a fraction of these union members can be recruited to worker-to-worker organizing in their area, to rebuild workplace organization—the stewards' army cum militant minority that is the backbone of the labor movement—and mobilized as mass "street heat" to back up organizing, strikes, and other workplace actions, the conditions of the working class and its presence as a movement can make this part of the answer to gaping inequality. If this is to work, it cannot be yet another attempt at bureaucratic top-down mobilization that can be demobilized at the will of union officials. Leadership is important, but it must involve the activist layer, tomorrow's militant minority, seeking coordination across union lines. The big question here, of course, is who will take the initiative? Big urban local unions of teachers in the process of changing their union and fighting to defend public education might be highly visible candidates to initiate such coordinated self-activity. Or perhaps nurses building a new unionism? Or reform Teamster locals? Or transit workers? There are no limits to the potential candidates. What about the Central Labor Councils? Most of these are sunk in decades of inertia and may well form a barrier to citywide multi-union organizing. Not all are so moribund. The Lorain County AFL-CIO, whose unique political course is discussed below, has been an active force in defense of working-class interests for decades, and certainly there are more like it. Where they can be a center for organizing they should be used. Where they can't, ways will have to be found to bypass them.

Basic to this coordinated self-activity should be the strategic use of the enormous vulnerability of most supply chains that exist throughout the re-structured systems of production and circulation, not only of goods but of many services as well. Strategic actions, whether strikes or workplace actions, can have far-reaching effects. While it is possible that the Trump administration will find a way to cancel some recent NLRB decisions, some of the legal barriers to "inside strategies" that can have an immediate impact on just-in-time systems have been recently removed by the NLRB, so that, when a contract has expired or there is no contract, grievance strikes, work-to-rule, and overtime bans are legal.[44] Another leg up for organizing in industries where temporary agencies play a substantial role, such as in warehousing, is the recent NLRB ruling that facilities owners and temp agencies are "joint employers" and must bargain over wages and conditions.[45] At the same time, it appears that after several years of sliding public support for unions, to the point where only 48 percent of those surveyed in 2009 approved of them, their approval rate has risen to 58 percent as of August 2015.[46]

Some of the general strategic directions mentioned above have been proposed in one form or another in recent years but have faced barriers to their implementation. Peter Olney's Los Angeles Manufacturing Action Project (LAMAP) proposal for a multi-union campaign to organize the manufacturing outfits along LA's Almeida Corridor, which fell apart due to the short-sighted cost-benefit analysis of some union leaders, comes to mind.[47] Prominent among these barriers is the structure and culture of many unions themselves. A serious chicken-and-egg question remains as to whether today's level of organizing and resistance can break through the decades of bureaucratic inertia or whether the unions must change to make these kinds of actions possible. It is easy to say some of both, but if the unions and the labor movement as a whole aren't changing, all the opportunities offered by consolidating, just-in-time capitalism can be lost.

Fortunately there are thousands of union activists already attempting to change their unions into democratic organizations committed to strong workplace organization, member involvement, racial and gender inclusion, the rejection of labor-management cooperation in its many forms, and direct action when possible—in short, a rejection of the norms of bureaucratic business unionism. To a greater extent than in the rank-and-file upsurge of the 1960s and 1970s, today's movements for change in the unions share these ideas and goals as something of a common program. This is a wave of rank-and-file rebellion that has taken hold among teachers, teamsters, transit workers, nurses, flight attendants, telecommunications workers, public employees, machinists, and railroad workers, to mention a few. In the case of the teachers, what began with the election of the Caucus of Rank and File Educators (CORE) in Chicago was followed by similar victories of teacher rank-and-file movements in Massachusetts, Newark, Minneapolis, and Los Angeles. This was followed by the formation of a national teachers rank and file, United Caucuses of Rank-and-File Educators (UCORE).[48] In 2016, the rank-and-file opposition slate in the Teamsters, Teamsters United, came close to electing Fred Zuckerman for president, sweeping the central and southern regions, winning the US vote, but losing in Canada. Nevertheless, Teamster United elected six international vice presidents.[49] For the most part, these rank-and-file movements are more than mere electoral slates. Most began by fighting around the issues that affect their work and lives only to discover that their incumbent leaders were incapable of waging such a fight. And so, as Labor Notes director Mark Brenner estimated, there are perhaps half a million or more union members in locals and national unions where the rebels have taken charge—with many more pushing at the doors. The activists that lead and fill the ranks of these movements are the potential material for the sort of "militant minority" that has always led change, growth, and confrontations with capital. Over two thousand activists from these rank-and-file movements, along with those from immigrants' rights groups, workers' centers, and other representatives of "alt labor," gathered in Chicago in April 2016 at the eighteenth biannual Labor Notes conference to exchange ideas, get inspiration, and perhaps create a shared identity. Whether the sorts of activists represented at Labor Notes conferences will constitute an effective militant minority over time, of course, remains to be seen.

Most labor and social movement activism for the immediate future will be and should be focused on the many issues that affect the working class and its various sectors. It should be a period of movement building through direct action and organizing. Few political breakthroughs are likely without a significant expansion of mass action and working-class organization. History has shown us this again and again. There is plenty of reason to believe that building on existing resistance and movements can begin to shift the potential for change, both objectively and in the minds of more and more working-class people. We know the anger and frustration are there, even if it sometimes expresses itself in reactionary ways, but it needs organized direction and grassroots leadership to realize the sort of ferment that will make greater things possible. One example of how direct action can have an impact on consciousness and even public opinion was the 1997 Teamster strike against UPS. Because this involved a high level of rank-and-file participation and issues that addressed conditions faced by many working-class people, specifically the rise of part-time employment, this strike caught the imagination of many, with the public supporting the strikers over UPS management by two to one.[50]

A more recent striking example of how a progressive alternative can appeal to the same people who were often attracted to Trump during the 2016 presidential primaries was the fact that many of these voted for Bernie Sanders in the Democratic primaries. Anti-elite ideas demagogically sounded by right-wingers like Trump can be put in a radical Left context to win workers away from the Right. As we will see below, many of those who don't vote share ideas to the left of those who do. If they were organized, either in unions or politically, they could be a major force for change. While the priority has to be on direct action and organizing, it is also necessary to understand the political changes that have accompanied the enormous changes in the organization of capital in the United States.

PART III

The Changing Political Terrain

CHAPTER SEVEN

Capital and the Return of the States

The election of Donald Trump as president in 2016 came as a shock to many, but the fact is, aside from the uniquely idiosyncratic personality politics of the candidate, the underlying economic and political forces that led to this outcome had been long in the making. Taking advantage of the devastation of so many industrial communities, the Republicans long ago learned how to appeal to the conservative social views and racial prejudices of many white working- and middle-class voters, as well as to their legitimate economic plight, and to successfully tag the Democratic Party establishment as part of the nation's political and social elite out of touch with globalization's victims. Both aspects of this demagogic appeal being grounded in reality, the Republicans increased their electoral support among these two groups to the point where 40 percent of white union household members were more or less consistently voting Republican in national elections by 2000. This proportion held even in the 2012 election, when Romney received 40 percent of the vote.[1]

The other side of this tarnished coin is the fact that the Democrats long ago abandoned the "lunch pail" politics and whatever slight policy preferences for working-class people or unions they once had, embracing free trade, cutting aid to the cities, as we will see below, and putting the unions at arms' length insofar as legislation was concerned. It is important to understand that the Democratic Party, with rare personal exceptions, turned its back on the entire working class, not just the white industrial workers in the Rust Belt who got so much media attention in 2016. The difference, of course, is that

African Americans and Latinos, much less immigrants, were significantly less susceptible to Republican appeals to racial prejudice and/or nostalgia for a real or imagined more prosperous or ethnically homogeneous past. Instead, perhaps uninspired, African Americans, Latinos, and the young stayed home in greater numbers than expected. African Americans did not vote in the proportions needed for a Democratic victory, and the share of Black voters fell from 13 percent of all those who voted in 2012 to 12 percent in 2016, while the Latino vote failed to grow as fast as expected, according to CNN's exit polls. In addition, Democrat Hillary Clinton actually got smaller proportions of the Black and Latino vote than did Obama in 2012.[2]

The Obama administration's adherence to neoliberal priorities, promotion of free trade, and its failure to address the very real plight of working-class people in the inner cities, the Rust Belt, and elsewhere, saw the results of this sordid history come home. As *Jacobin* magazine pointed out in its morning-after editorial, "Under President Obama, Democrats have lost almost a thousand state-legislature seats, a dozen gubernatorial races, sixty-nine House seats and thirteen in the Senate."[3] As much of the public turned against the effects of neoliberalism, the Democrats clung to it and committed political suicide in race after race. While Trump himself may not have been the inevitable outcome, the growing likelihood of the defeat of yet one more neoliberal, establishment Democratic candidate was.

Once the Left populism of Bernie Sanders, which did appeal to many white working-class voters as well as young people in general, had been defeated and the Democratic candidate became the quintessential representative of the out-of-touch neoliberal elite and arch free trader Hillary Clinton, the ability to win back white working-class voters, including many who had voted for Obama in 2012, in the key "battleground" states evaporated. As did the much-needed high voter turnout of African Americans and the assumed near total support among Latinos, 29 percent of whom went for Trump, along with a majority of white women, who voted for Trump by 53 percent. According to the CNN exit poll, in the 2016 election, union households voted 43 percent for Trump, indicating a significant shift for the worse. The biggest shift, however, was in the virtual collapse of the Democratic vote among all groups in key "battleground" states, as we will see in the postscript below.[4]

All of this led to the loss of Ohio, Wisconsin, Pennsylvania, Florida, Michigan, and, therefore, the election despite Clinton's significant "win" in the popular vote nationally. It was not that Trump's voting coalition was in its majority composed of white working-class voters. Trump garnered almost half of all voters earning $100,000 or more, $200,000 or more, and $250,000 or more. Furthermore, many of those "less educated" supporters the media focused on were among the seventeen million disproportionately conservative and Republican small business owners who lack a college degree, not the proletariat.[5] Nevertheless, the shift of white, blue-collar workers to the Republicans in 2016 and before was enough to tilt the election to Trump in the Rust Belt states where their numbers counted. Despite the demographic trends that were supposed to save the Democrats, therefore, their abandonment of the entire working class opened the door to a victory of an extreme and dangerous demagogue. Part of the Republicans' ability to take advantage of the Democrats' self-inflicted weakness lay in their earlier turn toward improved organization at the state level—an arena long ignored by Democratic strategists, labor leaders, and, indeed, many traditionally Democratic voters. We turn now to an examination of the changing structure of the state that this shift has brought about before analyzing the alterations in the Democratic Party itself.

It should be fairly obvious that the rhythms of profitability, recurring crises, facility relocations, and subsequent decline in and restructuring of manufacturing would produce both an economic impact on the state and an accelerated political intervention from capital and its representatives in government. Yet the role of the state in capitalism is necessarily a contradictory one. For capital, it is, on the one hand, a necessity for social order, the protection of private property and accumulation, defense in a competitive and violent world, negotiator of the terms of globalization, instrument of imperial expansion, and subsidizer, and, on the other hand, it is ultimately a drain on surplus value via taxation even if much of this comes from the wages of workers. The whole program of neoliberalism, of course, is meant to resolve this seeming conflict by redistributing the costs of the state from capital to the middle and working classes by tax reductions on business and the wealthy, shifting the burden downward and increasing the flow of the nation's surplus value to capital.

Things are rendered even more complicated by the multilayered nature of the American state, with its federal government, 50 states, 3,000 counties, nearly 20,000 municipalities, and 16,500 townships.[6] No level of government, however, has been exempt from the attack on the state as a cost to capital or perceived barrier to accumulation that has characterized the neoliberal era. In fact, this plethora of governments has become a source of massive tax relief and government subsidy for corporate America. As location, relocation, and outsourcing became means of escaping unions and lowering labor costs in the era of lean production, corporations played one city, county, or state against others in order to receive the tax breaks, subsidies, land deals, and other incentives that looted the public treasury in return for the promise, not always fulfilled, of jobs.

The capitalist state possesses a certain "relative autonomy" by virtue of the need to reconcile from time to time the demands of the various factions within the capitalist class as well as those flowing from conflict between social classes and other social divisions—for example, race, gender, and so on. Engels described the basis for this relative independence from capital as the state developed historically:

> It is the interaction of two unequal forces: on the one hand, the economic movement, on the other, the new political power, which strives for as much independence as possible, and which, having once been established, is endowed with a movement of its own. On the whole, the economic movement gets its way, but it has also to suffer reactions from the political movement which is itself established and endowed with relative independence.[7]

This relative independence is reinforced in the United States by the fact that the capitalist factions have long outsourced political rule to professional politicians of the two major parties who develop interests (and often wealth) of their own. This historic process of seeking autonomy has often been expressed by the increase in executive power and the growth of bureaucracy to administer and enforce it.[8]

State formation, however, like class formation, is an ongoing, complex process shaped to a large degree by class and other social conflict as well as by the influence, direct and indirect, of capital and periodically by social movements "from below." On the one hand, in the late nineteenth century it was the individual states that played the dominant role in such social legislation as there was—with the exception of the federally funded Civil War Union veterans' pension scheme.[9] It was in this period that racial segregation and "Jim Crow" laws took shape in the southern states. The development of the American state for most of the twentieth century, on the other hand, was characterized by the increased dominance of the central government, itself in part a response to the rise of the giant business corporation and the integration of the national economy. The Progressive era, the New Deal, and the civil rights era of the 1950s and 1960s saw the federal government take center stage in social policy as it already had in foreign policy. The recessions of 1974–75 and 1980–82 announced the end of the Keynesian era, as capital looked for and adopted neoliberal approaches to state policy.[10]

At the level of the federal government, capital's political effort to reshape the function of the national state from its Keynesian regulatory operation to what became its neoliberal direction goes back to the 1970s and the work of the Business Roundtable and others in formulating and lobbying for the neoliberal agenda.[11] To a considerable extent during the Reagan years and followed in the 1990s by Clinton's ending of "welfare as we know it" and his declaration that "the age of big government is over," the federal government increasingly got out of or deemphasized the business of social support as much as was feasible while still maintaining social order—this latter goal being accomplished by the increasing militarization of the police and the expansion of the racialized "carceral state."[12]

Increasingly, however, this is not just a matter of cuts, austerity, deregulation, privatization, and so on but of the growing political polarization and paralysis of the federal government in domestic affairs combined with almost total autonomy in international affairs by the executive branch, that is, its endless wars and aggressions. This latter autonomy is the historical result of America's more than a century as a world imperialist power that has become built into the structure of the US economy and the psychology of the ruling class and, indeed, much of the population. Politically the paralysis of domestic politics at the national level is largely a consequence of the rise of the Right with a rhetorically populist appeal and backing from considerable factions of capital, first in the rise of the "new Right," then as the Tea Party, and most recently, with perhaps less enthusiasm from even conservative capitalists, Donald Trump, on the one hand, and the continuing decades' old retreat of capital's liberal factions (mostly represented by the Democratic Party) into neoliberalism, on the other. This, in turn, precludes real resistance to the Right at the level of politics, even where many within society's capitalist elite find the Right's extremes distasteful—Trump being only the bitterest pill. Simultaneously, with significant success in shifting the federal state's function from industry regulation and social support, and its increased paralysis, corporations, the wealthy, and political conservatives turned their guns (and campaign money) on state and local governments.

As sites of economic and political change, the states' increased role was facilitated by efforts to reform and reshape state legislatures that began in the 1960s and accelerated in the 1970s, much of it funded by the Ford Foundation, so that by the 1980s legislatures in many states became full-time or nearly full-time lawmaking institutions, in which paid professional legislators replaced part-time amateurs. Most remaining part-time state legislatures are found in low-population states in the West. Along with these changes, as the office of state legislator became professionalized and better paid, came the rise of political action committees and other sources of funds for candidates organized by party leaders in state legislatures, who, as a result, increased their ability to discipline their party members.[13] Not surprisingly, the lobbyists soon followed: "Currently, about 40,000 lobbyists are working in state capitals, and the number of associations and related groups has quintupled over the past 50 years. Lobbying in the states is now a billion-dollar business every year."[14] As states became an increasing target of business interests, they also faced growing financial problems.

The roots of the recent escalation of the fiscal crisis of state and local governments in the United States lie in the demands of capital on these governments in the corporate-initiated game of locational competition for the past three decades or so, as capital itself relocated and reorganized. Cities and states desperate for new investment or even to stave off plant closings, as older industries withered or moved and new ones scanned the field of spatial possibilities, have offered businesses a variety of tax breaks, exemptions, subsidies, and incentives that cost states and cities at least $50 billion a year by the early 2000s.[15] By 2012 a *New York Times* exposé reported that "states, counties and cities are giving up more than $80 billion each year to companies" in incentives alone. Interestingly, the biggest share of these giveaways went to manufacturing, which *Times* reporter Louise Story estimated at $25.5 billion a year. Among the chief beneficiaries were outsourcing, tax-dodging champions Ford and General Motors.[16] (Did you really think these remnants of the "old" economy didn't count anymore?)

This practice is often dated to the 1970s, but it accelerated in the 1980s and after with the wave of restructuring, plant closings, and outsourcing that was a consequence of lean production and the merger movements. In particular, in manufacturing this trend saw a move away from inner cities, with businesses seeking "subsidies for jobs out by the interstate," as Greg LeRoy put it in his study, *The Great American Jobs Scam*. A major player in this game of highway robbery was, once again, General Motors, which played thirty states against one another over the location of its new super lean, "team concept" Saturn plant in 1985. The "transplants" that moved into the South in the 1990s simply followed suit.[17] Not only was capital restructuring itself, it was also restructuring the state at every level.

Having learned that states would modify taxes and offer incentives on an ad hoc basis, capital simply turned the pressure up for permanent tax relief.

Politically this was accomplished mainly through the rise of the Republican Right and its focus on state-level organization and power—including new state-level think tanks, fundamentalist big-box churches, deepened grass-roots party organization, and the shift of campaign contributions to state politics. Consequently, many states have lowered their corporation tax rates to 6.7 percent, compared to nearly 10 percent in 1980. A study found, however, that by the early 2000s over half the Fortune 500 companies were paying much less than the official rate—by 2003 an average of 3.35 percent, compared to the official 6.8 percent rate at that time. Furthermore, in recent years more and more states have cut the personal income tax and relied more on regressive sales and property taxes, while federal aid to states has been inadequate to address budget deficits. Nevertheless, the big cuts came in corporate taxes. From 2007 to 2012 corporate tax revenues to state and local governments fell by 19.6 percent, from $61 billion to $49 billion.[18] With the tax base of the states already undermined, the Great Recession rapidly turned budget surpluses in forty out of fifty states into deficits everywhere.[19]

The 2010 Republican sweep of eleven state legislatures and governors brought accelerated attacks on public workers, beginning in Wisconsin, as these states passed laws undermining not only public worker bargaining rights but conditions for all state and local workers, while simultaneously cutting public services. Standing behind these successful attacks, as well as scores of less successful ones, were huge corporate backers, including Wal-Mart, Coca-Cola, FedEx, and Exxon Mobil, all affiliated with the Koch brothers' American Legislative Exchange Council (ALEC), along with the more mainstream corporate representatives, the US Chamber of Commerce and National Association of Manufacturers. Their shared goal was a permanent reduction in state and local public services and employment—a restructuring of the state at its most basic levels.[20] Budget cutting was not the monopoly of Republicans, however. Democratic governors in Massachusetts, Iowa, and Pennsylvania are among those "who have wielded the budget axe against public employees."[21]

Those who have paid the price for all this corporate largess are, of course, the public employees and the working-class people who depend on public services. The federal government cut 285,124 jobs between 1990 and 2010, 173,466 or 60 percent from the US Postal Service, which also faces the threat of privatization. This hit workers of color, who compose over half the mail sorting and processing staff, the hardest. From 2009 through late 2015, state governments lost 68,000 jobs, while local governments cut 418,000.[22] Particularly hard hit were teachers, as states cut school aid to cities, which on average accounts for about 46 percent of local school budgets. While between 2008 and 2015 the number of students rose by 804,000, the number of teachers fell by 297,000—with women accounting for the majority of these workers.[23] Up to 2009, state and local employment provided over half the country's union members, but by 2015 they had fallen behind private-sector members. From 2009 through 2015, the number of local government union members dropped by 684,000.[24] This was, of course, a consequence of the political attack on these workers and their unions that accelerated after the 2010 elections.

Emboldened by their successes in state antilabor legislation, Republicans in state after state have proposed "right-to-work" laws, which passed in three traditional strongholds of industrial unionism: Indiana, Michigan, and Wisconsin.[25] Through this intervention at the state level, capital acting through right-wing Republican politicians, sometimes with support from Democrats, has in effect further altered *national* labor policy in a pro-business direction. To many people, state governments appear at best as the training ground and launching pad for career politicians with higher ambitions or as seats of petty claims and corruption with little relevance to major policy formation in comparison to the federal government. As it turns out, corporate America had a more nuanced understanding of the altered role of the states in the US political system, and increasingly the states have become major levers of neoliberal governmental restructuring and corporate power.

As of 2015, Republicans dominated thirty-one state legislatures to the Democrats' eleven, with the remaining eight split between the two parties. In power at the state level, right-wing Republican legislatures have set about crafting a permanent majority for themselves in the US House of Representatives by using the states' constitutional power to redraw congressional districts and disenfranchise significant numbers of people of color. This turn toward the states by the Republican Right has been financed by an equally large redirection of campaign donations from corporations and the wealthy to state-level elections. The 2010 *Citizens United v. FEC* Supreme Court decision freed corporate and individual "independent" campaign contributions, as a result of which those for both parties in some states targeted by the Republican Right rose significantly, as table VI shows. Insofar as this is successful, it not only reinforces their control of the state government but also boosts their chances of holding on to a majority in the House of Representatives—despite the demographic trends that point toward a growing proportion of voters of color. Whether this strategy works or not remains to be seen, but reliance on the Democrats to undermine or halt this right-wing, racist steamroller is bound to fail, due to the Democrats' adoption of much of the neoliberal agenda and their stance as the party of compromise.[26]

Table VI: Campaign Contributions to State-Level Elections, 2008–2014 (in millions)

State	2008	2010	2014
Wisconsin	$17	$42	$78
Michigan	$43	$84	$75
Illinois	$92	$187	$252
Texas	$118	$251	$263
Total US	**$1,600**	**$2,500**	**$2,200**

Source: National Institute on Money in State Politics. "2014 Candidate Elections Overview," 2015, www.followthemoney.org.

If anything, it seems that in the United States the state as a whole has become less relatively autonomous from capital. This is not only because of the vast and increasing amounts of money that pour into the election campaigns and infrastructure of both parties at all levels of the political system, and the legions of corporate and right-wing lobbyists that infest Congress and state legislatures. As a result of the removal of more and more barriers to and imposed costs upon capital, it has accrued the freedom to move, merge, and mutate into today's new giants of accumulation, many of which are global actors as well. These giants *are* "the economy" and as such have both explicit and implicit power and influence over politicians, who accept the rules of the game (domestic and global), as well as over the state they administer. Arthur Lipow explained this well when he wrote: "When the representatives of the big national corporations speak they are listened to because they do so in the name of jobs and the health of the economy, with the premise, stated or not, that what is good for their company or industry is good for the economy or the nation. This is a powerful argument, and it is one which the legislators and the executive basically accept because they genuinely agree with it."[27] As Engels put it in the simplest of terms, "the economic movement gets its way," particularly when those in charge act as its willing, if sometimes unconscious, servants. The role of wealth and the wealthy, especially the activists of the capitalist class, in the operations of mainstream electoral and legislative politics has become far more visible, as has the staggering inequality they are defending and advancing.

Toward a Police State?

As the states and their governments became more important in the overall focus and outcomes of politics, three other related changes occurred that have further altered social relations and political power in the United States: the astronomical rise of incarceration and "stop and search" operations even as crime rates dropped; the increase in the killing of Black men by police officers; and the militarization of state and local police forces. All three were related to the "war on drugs" declared by Nixon in June 1971 and accelerated under Reagan in the 1980s.[28] To a large extent, however, it was the state and local governments that implemented this "war," passing tougher sentencing laws, accelerating "stop and search" actions, increasing and militarizing their police forces, and escalating killings by the police, above all of African American men.

The rate of incarceration (prisoners per 100,000 population), which had remained steady from the 1940s through the 1950s, actually fell during the 1960s. In the 1970s, however, it began to rise, and then in the 1980s, like so many measures of the neoliberal era, it soared until the Great Recession in 2008. Although the rate of violent crimes began to fall rapidly after 1992, there was no letup in the rise of the federal and state prison population, which rose by nearly five times, from 329,821 in 1980 to 1,610,446 in 2008. Only with the increased fiscal crisis of the states did the prison population fall slightly, to 1,561,500 in 2014. The proportion of Black and Latino prisoners rose from 52 percent in 1980 to a high of 60 percent in 1993 and then leveled off at 56 percent—still over twice their combined percentage of the population. The incarceration rate for Black men was over six-and-a-half times that of white men.[29]

The astronomical incarceration rate has its legal basis in "tough-on-crime" laws passed mainly by states beginning in the 1980s. As Human Rights Watch summarized this in its 2014 report *Nation Behind Bars*, "Law-makers have criminalized minor misconduct, instituted mandatory prison sentences even for low-level crimes, and established "three-strikes-and-you're-out laws for recidivists."[30] And, as one study noted, "The more black residents a state has, the tougher its laws tend to be."[31] At least 85 percent of prisoners are in state institutions. State-level spending on prisons also increased from about $5 billion in 1967 to $44 billion in 2007 before the recession forced some reductions. Like other aspects of the rightward move of politics in the United States, particularly at the state level, "'tough-on-crime' has remained a default approach for all too many politicians."[32] This was by no means just a Republican obsession. Democratic governor of California Jerry Brown, for example, vetoed a measure to reduce simple possession of a drug from a felony and then increased state spending to build more prisons in 2014.[33]

Then, to the surprise of many, on September 9, 2016, the forty-fifth anniversary of the Attica prison uprising, thousands of prisoners in as many as twenty-four states went on strike, led by the prisoners' solidarity group Free Alabama Movement (FAM) and apparently coordinated by the Incarcerated Workers Organizing Committee, an affiliate of the IWW. Prisoners are forced to work at various jobs for pay that ranges from 40 cents an hour to nothing. This they called slavery, and they proposed ending it "by refusing to be slaves any longer."[34] As of this writing there is no news of the outcomes of these strikes.

The war on the Black community goes beyond incarceration to everyday harassment and victimization. The primary tactic in this war is the "stop and frisk" operation, whereby police are allowed to stop and search anyone for any reason if they claim "reasonable suspicion." The 1968 Supreme Court ruling in *Terry v. Ohio* reversed the court's civil libertarian trends in earlier cases like *Miranda* and aided the acceleration of stop-and-frisk in the 1990s across the country.[35] There are no national figures on this, but studies done in a number of cities make it clear that, like incarceration, this practice has become massive and racially targeted.

The *Philadelphia Inquirer* reported in 2015 that police in that city had conducted about 200,000 stop-and-frisk confrontations a year and that, as of 2014, 72 percent were against African Americans.[36] An ACLU study of Boston showed that police had conducted 204,000 "police-civilian encounters," as they were politely called, between 2007 and 2010. Of these, 63 percent were against African Americans, although Blacks are only 24 percent of the city's population.[37] In New York City, stop-and-frisk encounters reached 685,000 a year in 2011. According to the Center for Constitutional Rights, some 85 percent or nearly 600,000 of those stopped were Black or Latino. This was up from 1997–98, when 45,000 stop-and-frisk encounters occurred and two-thirds of those frisked were Black or Latino.[38] By 2012 stop-and-frisk operations had risen to 16,000 a week or over 800,000 a year and become so outrageously racist that in 2013 a federal judge in New York ruled that they amounted to "a policy of indirect racial profiling" and violated the constitutional rights of minorities in New York. After that they fell to about 2,000 a week. The outgoing police commissioner, Ray Kelly, argued that crimes would increase. In fact they dropped by late 2013.[39] What didn't decline was the outright killing of Black men by police.

Until very recently, the federal government made no attempt to keep thorough records of the killings of civilians by the nation's 18,000 police departments. Fortunately, the project Mapping Police Violence, the *Washington Post*, and Britain's *Guardian* newspaper have recently instituted databases to keep track of police shootings. All three place the number of police killings in 2015 at around a thousand. The *Guardian*'s "The Count" puts it at a total of 1,146, while the *Washington Post* recorded 990 killings. Mapping Police Violence's website shows an upward trend from January 2013 through January 2016. The *Guardian* counts shows 598 shootings during the first half of 2016, above the rate for half of 2015. The *Washington Post* also shows a gain in 2016, with 533 killings in the first half of 2016, again more than the 495 for half of the 2015 count.[40]

As is by now common knowledge, a disproportionate number of those killed are Black or Latino. Of those in the *Guardian* count for 2015 who were identified by race or ethnicity, 27 percent were Black, over twice their proportion of the US population, and fully 48 percent were people of color. For the first half of 2016, Blacks were 26 percent and all people of color 47 percent, scarcely an improvement. The *Washington Post*'s proportions were virtually identical.[41] All of this despite increased national attention to this issue and the rise of the Black Lives Matter movement since the killing of Michael Brown in Ferguson, Missouri, on August 9, 2014. As there were only two convictions of police for shootings out of the hundreds of such killings in 2015, it is clear that police departments across the country feel no need to restrain their officers.[42] Racism, as well as a "shoot first, ask questions later" culture, pervades American law enforcement. And it is a culture that is far more heavily armed than it was half a century ago.

Just as the shooting of Michael Brown by police in Ferguson focused the nation's belated attention on the epidemic of police killings of Black men, so the presence of armored vehicles, sniper riflemen, and police in body armor and battle fatigues, some carrying assault rifles, and aggressively facing down peaceful protestors in Ferguson a couple of days later highlighted the militarization of the police across the United States. For decades the US military has been supplying the country's police forces with equipment, arms, technology, and training acquired through a century or more of counterinsurgency, low-intensity conflict, and full-scale war the world around. The ACLU calls it the "war comes home." It might also be called the "empire strikes back as the surplus from one war after another finds its way to the streets of America."[43] The escalation of this "war" began with President Reagan and was accelerated by President Clinton. It is a bipartisan war.

Most of the recent police hardware and weapons technology was transferred under the Department of Defense's 1033 program, initiated by Clinton in 1997, which authorized providing surplus military-grade weapons and equipment for the war on drugs and then the war on terrorism—all for no more than the cost of transportation. Under this program an estimated $4.3 billion worth of military equipment has been transferred to state, county, and local police forces. The annual value of these deadly gifts to state and local police rose steadily from $1 million in the 1990s to $450 million in 2013. To this has been added training funded by the Department of Homeland Security (DHS). As the ACLU report argued, "It is clear that local law enforcement agencies use DHS funds ostensibly obtained for the purpose of fighting terrorism to conduct ordinary law enforcement activities."[44] Except that increasingly they are less "ordinary."

The evolution of the SWAT (Special Weapons and Tactics) teams is a clear example. As the ACLU reports: "SWAT was created to deal with emergency situations such as hostage, barricade and active shooter scenarios. Over time, however, law enforcement agencies have moved away from this original purpose and are increasingly using these paramilitary squads to search people's home for drugs.[45] The number of SWAT teams has grown by four times since the mid-1980s, while their deployment has risen from three thousand a year in 1980 to fifty thousand a year recently. It is no longer unusual for police to "respond to protests with tear gas, carrying automatic weapons and sniper rifles, and riding in vehicles that would not look out of place in Bagdad or Aleppo."[46]

Like incarceration and stop-and-search operations, which disproportionately impact African Americans and their communities, the ACLU report concluded, "Our findings add the unfair and disproportionate use of paramilitary home raids to this shameful list of racially biased drug enforcement." Their study of eight hundred incidents of SWAT raids on people's homes shows that 39 percent impacted Black individuals, 11 percent Latinos, and 20 percent whites, the rest were not identified by race or ethnicity due largely to poor record keeping of state and local law enforcement agencies.[47] This only covers SWAT raids. How many more have died as a result of the shootings discussed above due to the use of advanced weapons? What about a modernized Spartan-like phalanx confronting assembled unarmed citizens? What is apparent is that however developed the police state is in the United States as a whole, in African American inner-city communities it is already a reality.

The growth of state government in the legislative and "law enforcement" fields has visibly shifted the effective center of political activity away from the federal government's paralyzed legislative and executive branches for the foreseeable future. Yet the federal government remains the dominant institution of the state. In 2016, despite all the efforts by conservatives and neoliberals to reduce the role of the central government, it still commands enormous powers over state and local government and, more importantly, over the economy, foreign policy, and the military. In nominal terms its budget has grown by three times since 1990, to $3.9 trillion in 2016. This compares to the $3.4 trillion spent by all state and local governments in that year, which must be divided between fifty states and thousands of local governments.[48] The American central state, however, is far more than the three branches of government spelled out in the Constitution.

The rise of the national security state and of a massive permanent military since World War II has changed the political landscape in a number of ways. Through the use of military contracts and purchases, as well as the construction of military bases in the United States, the federal government contributed the population shift toward the Sun Belt in the South and West, which strengthened the rise of the New Right as well as reinforcing the shift of industry from the Northeast and Midwest.[49] Perhaps even more important for the long run has been the implantation of the national security state, with its huge permanent military establishment, into the very core of US politics as well as the economy. While the "defense" budget now amounts to about 15 percent of the federal budget, of the total of the 3.9 million people employed by the federal government as of 2010, 47 percent, or almost half, worked for the defense establishment, either as serving military personnel or in a civilian capacity. This does not include those who work for agencies such as the FBI, CIA, NSA, DEA, Department of Homeland Security, or the National Guard. The concept of the state as a coercive apparatus in defense of capitalism as a system at home and abroad is alive and well. Furthermore, it is one whose imperial reach is global. Susan Watkins of *New Left Review* offers a summary of this when she writes that the United States not only commands a vast military but "an estimated 900 military bases, including transit and refuelling stations; huge garrisons in Europe, East Asia, Central Asia and the Middle East; and armed presence in over 130 countries."[50]

It is obvious that the current state of politics in the civilian branches of national government offers no real challenge to this. Conservatives, neoconservatives, and Tea Party militants who claim to seek to get "government off our backs" are, of course, among the most enthusiastic supporters of today's militarized governments at all levels. As Gary Gerstle puts it, "The national security state, militarization and federalization of crime fighting, and building of business and personal fortunes via central state contracts were a form of big government endorsed by conservative, antigovernment leaders and their followers."[51] The Democratic Party was not some junior partner in the formation and conduct of US foreign policy and international economic affairs. Its politicians, allied academics, and elites have been the major framers of America's imperial role in the world, possibly since Woodrow Wilson led the United States into the World War I and certainly since Franklin D. Roosevelt and his aides shaped the entire post–World War II role of the country as the major military and economic power in the world. While this imperial role and its policies have been bipartisan, all of this has been mostly crafted, expanded, amended, and vigorously supported by Democratic presidents from Truman through Johnson, Clinton, and Obama and ratified by bipartisan congressional majorities. As one mainstream political scientist points out, concerning the US entrance into World War II and the international order that followed, the United States "was to be the principal architect of the succeeding international environment. Both tasks would belong largely to the Democratic Party."[52] It is blindingly obvious that this role did not change under the Obama administration, nor would a Hillary Clinton administration have shifted or reduced the imperial stance or militarist preoccupation of the United States. As Joanne Landy writes about Hillary Clinton's international outlook, "Hillary Clinton stands squarely within the longstanding bipartisan consensus on foreign policy, and, indeed, along with many Republican politicians, is on the more aggressive end of the consensus."[53]

Nevertheless, there has been a significant shift in public dissatisfaction with the domestic impact of war, the rise of a police state, and the impact of austerity on the working class and its various sectors. While the Right has had the initiative for some time, resistance on the Left is growing. The rise of the Black Lives Matter movement, the movement for immigrant workers' rights, and the potential of an insurgent labor movement raises once again the question of electoral politics. These movements come up against a state that at all levels is not only thwarting their demands but also, with rare exceptions, actively aiding capital in the destruction of living and working standards and the undermining of organized resistance through legislation, court rulings, and just plain force. The electoral upsurge of 2016, which centered on the Sanders campaign for the presidential nomination, its ability to rally millions to a genuinely left-wing alternative, and near success in terms of elected delegates, points to renewed efforts to move the Democratic Party in a progressive direction or in some way use it to create a new political force in the United States. The election of Trump will most likely accelerate this as many on the left run for cover in hopes that the Democrats can be pushed to the left and save the day. Given the record of past attempts to move this party to the left or reform it, what are the chances of those on the left who choose to work inside the Democratic Party's state-mandated institutions succeeding this time?

CHAPTER EIGHT

Prisoners
of the American Scheme

The American electoral system is rigged against third parties, despite the fact that third parties are a regular feature of US elections. This we call the American Scheme, the political setup that always delays the arrival of the famous American Dream for millions but delivers regularly for the notorious "1%." That the American Scheme of electoral politics strongly favors a two-party system is beyond doubt. So the more practically minded leaders of various social movements and politically left currents have often tended to orient in one way or another to the Democratic Party. Populists in the 1890s, organized labor in the 1930s, the civil rights movement in the 1960s, women's and gay rights movement in the 1970s, and the movement against the Vietnam War of that era, all tried to shape this "party of the people" to their goals—with at best only episodic and partial success.

Sometimes giving analytical and even some organizational coherence to these efforts have been important figures on the left such as publicly acknowledged democratic socialists Bayard Rustin and Michael Harrington in the 1960s and 1970s. These Left-led efforts to influence, reform, or realign the Democratic Party have usually come in the wake of social upheavals—sometimes at their height, as with the CIO in 1936 or the Populists in 1896, and at other times when the movement has passed its active, disruptive peak and actual influence on political outcomes has waned, as with the civil rights movement by the mid-1960s. The idea is that the movements must move from "protest to politics," to cite Bayard Rustin's influential 1965 essay.[1] The underlying assumptions of these organized efforts were, first, the fact that over time the Democratic Party, and for that matter its Republican rival, was susceptible to change, and was indeed changing in the 1960s and 1970s. Second is the analysis that the Democratic Party is not really a party at all but rather a loose electoral coalition of social and political elements with little organizational coherence and, hence, permeable and changeable.

Over the course of the twentieth century, the Democratic Party did indeed change: from the party of white supremacy and state's rights to that of modern liberalism, with its greater emphasis on welfare provision and the central role of the federal government. In the broadest sense it followed the major changes in liberal capitalist politics across the developed world—from simple laissez-faire liberalism to the rising role of the state during the twentieth century in dealing with the system's recurrent crises, episodes of intensified class conflict, and increasingly large corporate forms. These have been political changes imposed by transformations in the system itself, along with its crises, producing one or another form of state intervention, mostly enacted by opponents of socialism, much as Karl Polanyi analyzed at mid-century.[2] That is, the rise of economic regulation and the welfare state are not anomalies of capitalism but aspects or phases required by the turbulence of the system itself. This more statist phase of capitalism, not only in the United States but internationally, would itself falter on the deepening of the crisis of profitability of the 1970s and the organization of capital into powerful pressure groups, leading to the rise of neoliberalism globally and within the Democratic Party. Of course, these changes came about through human agency and conflict, demographic and social changes in the country, and economic developments, but the history of the Democratic Party follows that of the changing needs of the system as defined by one or more sections of capital with remarkable consistency.

The transition of the Democratic Party to the New Deal, for example, required social upheaval, but it also involved the support and cooperation of large sections of capital. Thomas Ferguson and Joel Rogers demonstrated that "at the center of that [New Deal] coalition" were not just labor and poor farmers "but something else—a new power bloc of capital-intensive industries, investment banks, and internationally oriented commercial banks."[3] As historian Gary Gerstle has argued more recently, "Business interests shaped the politics of the Democratic Party coalition throughout the New Deal Era."[4] Shawn Gude adds to this analysis a list of such business interests as "Shell and IBM and General Electric, Lehman Brothers and Goldman Sachs and Bank of America." Major financial figures such as John D. Rockefeller Jr. helped draft major New Deal social legislation. In the Great Society era, business made sure that the new benefits for the poor were paid for out of payroll taxes, not from profits.[5] Indeed, as Ferguson and Rogers argue, "It is worth noting explicitly that it was the leaders of business groups . . . who arrayed in almost wall-to-wall support of LBJ's prodigious fund-raising efforts in the 1964 elections and the promotion of a Great Society. They also staffed the upper tiers of LBJ's administration, dominated most of its important commissions, panels, and informal circles around the President."[6] This, as well as the opposition of other sections of capital, limited the working-class gains of both these reform eras—and capital did this in part by being central to the Democratic Party itself.

Capital as a class is never a political monolith. It responds as a class to its own crises through internal conflict, as well as interclass conflict, which is why virtually every capitalist nation with an ostensibly democratic electoral system has more than one explicitly pro-capitalist party, or, lacking that, major internal factions within the party, as well as, with the exception of the United States, labor, socialist, social democratic, or communist parties. As a class driven by competition, capital has no inherent way of reaching consensus other than through organization, debate, and political conflict. Parties are one such organization, but there are many others, such as think tanks, pressure groups, trade associations, and organizations specifically meant to influence government policy, such as the Business Roundtable or the hundreds of lobbying firms clustered along Washington's K Street.

Some of the time, as during periods of social upsurge such as the 1930s or the civil rights era of the 1950s and 1960s, these organizations of capital must take into consideration the sentiments and actions, real and potential, of the party's mass base—not only to win elections but also to stave off deeper social turbulence. So the Democratic Party and indeed US politics as a whole changed over time, sometimes in a direction more beneficial to the working class, African Americans, Latinos, or women when they asserted themselves in ways and to a degree that could not be ignored. If that is the case, why cannot the mass base of that party that is heavily working class, Black, and Latino, in cooperation with the party's more left-wing forces, transform the party into a genuinely progressive force for real social change? The answer to that lies not in abstract theory alone—the proposition that it is a capitalist party by virtue of funding, business participation, leading personnel, ideology, and practice—or even in the unbroken series of failures to do this but in the structure of that party seen as a whole. But first let us look at one of the better-organized efforts by the Left to bring about just such a transformation—the realignment strategy of the 1960s and 1970s.

From the early through mid-twentieth century, the institutional basis of the Democratic Party had been the coalition of conservative and racist southern Democrats politicians (the Dixiecrats) and northern political machines with organized labor as a junior partner, supported more or less behind the scenes by various sectors of capital. In Congress, an alliance of Dixiecrats and conservative Republicans had tied up progressive legislation. The basic idea behind the realignment strategy was to drive the Dixiecrats out of the Democratic Party, thus breaking up the congressional alliance of Dixiecrats and conservative Republicans, while making the party's "liberal-labor coalition" along with the rising Black vote dominant and the party more consistently liberal or even social democratic. The idea was endorsed by the Socialist Party in a 1960 pamphlet entitled *A Way Forward: Political Realignment in America* and appeared in 1962 in Students for a Democratic Society's *Port Huron Statement* and in Bayard Rustin's call for the civil rights movement to move from "protest to politics" cited above.[7] It was hinted at in Michael Harrington's popular exposé of poverty in the United States, *The Other America*, and became a major theme in his subsequent writings.[8] As leader of the Democratic Socialist Organizing Committee (DSOC) in the 1970s, Harrington worked to influence labor leaders and liberal politicians in order to build the liberal-labor coalition, a "party within the party," he saw as central to both the party as a whole and to driving the Dixiecrats from the Democratic Party.

In one sense, the period from the mid-1960s to the late 1970s appeared as an opportune time to realign the party. On the one hand, the urban political machines, one of the two major institutional pillars of the Democratic Party, were in deep decline. Some lasted longer than others, but virtually none survived the 1970s.[9] As one study stated, "The last of the old-style machines, presided over by Chicago's Mayor Richard J. Daley, died along with him in 1976."[10] On the other hand, the Dixiecrats were, indeed, beginning their exit toward the Republican Party due in large part to the passage of the civil rights acts of 1964 and 1965. Furthermore, party loyalty was on the decline, with many voters splitting their votes between candidates of the two major parties. As Walter Dean Burnham pointed out in his classic study of realignment via "critical elections," straight party ticket voting had declined from 74 percent of voters in 1952 to 50 percent by 1966.[11] Similarly, "party unity" voting in Congress, that is, disciplined floor votes along strict partisan lines on important legislation, fell from around 70 percent of floor votes in both houses during the 1950s to 58 percent in the House and 51 percent in the Senate by the early 1970s.[12] In short, the party and its voter base were in flux. Yet, while the machines faded and Dixiecrats began their exit, the Democratic Party began its trek to the right even as the realignment forces appeared to gain influence through the DSOC-backed Democratic Agenda. Why?

For one thing, the "liberal-labor coalition," in which liberalism was understood as a power bloc, was an illusion. This type of "coalition" analysis was supported by much of academic pluralist political science at the time, which for decades focused on voter behavior rather than underlying conditions, institutions, group pressure, and party and legislative organization, much less social class as anything more than a correlation of income and education. Explaining some of the problems of political science as a discipline, Burnham wrote in 1970, "The behavioral revolution in political science drew very heavily from psychology in its early stages, rather than from sociology, economics, or history."[13] Voter coalitions were understood as a result of subjective preferences, which explained voting and, supposedly, party behavior. When looking at the 1984 election as political scientist Samuel P. Huntington described it, Ferguson and Rogers sarcastically wrote, "One might think, too, that the Democratic slate in 1984 was determined by groups of women, blacks, and Hispanics, who flew Democratic presidential hopefuls around to their respective headquarters to decide whom they would name to head the ticket. Such conclusions bear little relation to reality."[14] As a constituency of the Democratic electorate, to an even greater degree than the groups Ferguson and Rogers describe, liberalism was at best a strain of sentiment and a cluster of pressure groups without the power to realign US politics.

Modern liberalism, after all, was and is a class ideology that accepts the most basic premises of capitalism concerning private property and the market—albeit with some limitations and, when necessary, reforms. While it proposes social reforms, such as the New Deal or the Great Society, in line with its acceptance of private property and the market, its goals are almost always limited to "equality of opportunity" rather than equality of results. This ideology and its various versions, along with the party's more conservative political tendencies, is one aspect of what makes the Democratic Party a capitalist party. Post–World War II liberalism, although embraced by much of the union leadership, was mostly a middle-class phenomenon, which meant it lacked the potential social, occupational, or economic cohesion of either capital or the organized working class. As a political current it never challenged the corporate or private form of property in the means of production, while it rapidly abandoned such New

Deal—expanding programs as a national health care system by the early 1950s.

In addition, the reform proclivities of modern liberalism were subdued by the Cold War, its ranks divided over the war in Vietnam, its ideology dependent on a body of economic theory (Keynesianism) that would be discredited in the 1970s, its social vision limited by a pluralist method that denied class as agent of change or conflict inherent to the system, and, despite early sympathy for the civil rights movement ("equality of opportunity"), its leaders frightened by the uprising of Black America that took shape by the late 1960s. It was another irony of the period that the civil rights and Great Society legislation that came at the climax of the civil rights movement in the mid-1960s were carried out not by the great names of liberalism. Once elected, John F. Kennedy deemphasized civil rights. As longtime Democratic pollster Stanley Greenberg reported, "Kennedy proposed tax cuts, which were his highest priority in 1963, not the civil rights bill."[15] It was the "born-again" liberal Texas party "regular," pragmatist, warmonger, and ruthless congressional leader Lyndon Johnson who pushed though the Civil Rights Act of 1964, the Voting Rights Act of 1965, and affirmative action policies. The names of liberalism's best-known leaders of that era, such as Hubert Humphrey, Jimmy Carter, and Walter Mondale, were synonymous with compromise and retreat.

To be sure, there were always decent, occasionally even heroic liberals, but as a political movement or bloc attached to the Democratic Party it was never a coherent or dependable force for social change. For a brief moment the liberals seemed to grab control of the party during George McGovern's 1972 antiwar presidential campaign. But getting the party nomination and controlling the party were never the same thing. By the mid-1970s McGovern and his supporters were on the sidelines, and the mainstream "liberals" were back on top with Jimmy Carter and a new generation of what would later be known as neoliberals in Congress.

In practice, labor, the other side of this coalition, meant not even the organized working class, much less the class in its diverse reality, but the labor bureaucracy of the period. Perhaps above all this meant the United Auto Workers (UAW) and its president, Walter Reuther, until his death in a plane crash in 1970. Even before his death, however, as Reuther's biographer Nelson Lichtenstein wrote, "Reuther had wedded himself to Lyndon Johnson, subordinating both a breakthrough at General Motors and a realignment of the Democrats to LBJ's presidential agenda."[16] Kevin Boyle, in his largely sympathetic account of the role of the UAW in the Democratic Party, notes the change in that role: "Liberalism's defeat in 1968 transformed the context in which the UAW promoted its political agenda. No longer did the UAW try to push the dominant political ideology to the left."[17] He argued that the UAW's post-Reuther efforts on a behalf of McGovern in 1972 and the Progressive Alliance in the late 1970s "were little more than hollow gestures, symbolic actions."[18]

The 1977 formation of the Progressive Alliance by UAW president Doug Fraser was one of the last attempts to give organizational coherence to the "liberal-labor coalition." This came shortly after Fraser resigned from Carter's Labor-Management Group and made his famous statement to the effect that management had "chosen to wage a one-sided class war today in this country." The founding meeting of the Progressive Alliance at Cobo Hall in Detroit on October 17, 1977, brought together many of the leaders of this coalition, from Fraser himself to Michael Harrington. But it was, in Fraser's own words, a "coalition from the top." It was not meant to be the other side in the "one-sided class war." As socialist union activist Stan Weir, who reported on it in detail, observed, "The atmosphere during the Cobo Hall coalition meeting was without the excitement of new ideas because of the isolation of union officials, liberals, and socialists from the ranks of labor."[19]

It could hardly have been otherwise as the UAW leadership of those years, like much of the labor bureaucracy, was in a posture of retreat before capital and in a struggle with its own membership, which, from the mid-1960s through the 1970s, had been rebelling against both employers and the very leaders who were to be the vanguard of realignment.[20] After 1970, the labor side of the illusory "liberal-labor coalition" fell to George Meany, who had little interest in broad social reform. The realignment strategy was a top-down one dependent on office holders and high-level political and union "influentials" who invariably ended up supporting the very top-level, rightward-moving politicians who thwarted the whole project.[21] The "liberal-labor coalition" was a chimera.

Ironically, perhaps, the Democratic Agenda and the realignment forces reached their peak of influence at exactly the moment when the Democrats launched their historic turn to the right during the Carter administration in 1977–80. Carter and Congress with an overwhelming Democratic majority advanced the neoliberal agenda through cuts in social services well before Reagan, reduction of corporation taxes, increases in defense spending, and the introduction of deregulation in air transport, trucking, and, most disastrously, finance. The new generation of Democrats entering Congress supported this agenda. In 1977, one hundred House Democrats also supported, and Carter refused to veto, the Hyde Amendment, which excluded abortion from free health care to women on welfare.[22] Labor's two major legislative proposals, labor law reform and *common situs* picketing, although allegedly supported by Carter, went down to defeat in Congress. In 1977, an AFL-CIO Committee on Political Education (COPE) memo noted that "the 2-1 Democratic majority in the U.S. House is pure illusion," as many Northern Democrats voted against labor's proposals. Two years later, AFL-CIO legislative director Kenneth Young complained with considerable restraint in the *American Federationist* that "the 95th Congress compiled a record that was a disappointment to labor and its allies."[23]

The problem was that a majority of those northern Democrats elected to Congress since 1974, as the *American Federationist* article cited above stated, "are more apt to be upper income, professional people, businessmen and businesswomen." This post-Watergate generation of Democratic politicians' "reforms" of federal election laws opened the door to the corporate political action committee (PAC) (see below), and these politicians were the first to benefit from the growth of business PACs. It was these new Democrats who were responsible for the failure of labor's main demands. Some 60 percent of newly elected Democratic representatives, for example, voted against the proposed consumer protection agency.[24]

Carter also attempted to break one of the last mass strikes of the 1970s, that by the United Mine Workers, by invoking the Taft-Hartley Act. The striking miners ignored the president and adopted the slogan "Taft can mine it, Hartley can haul it, and Carter can shove it."[25] The neoliberal agenda, however, rolled on as the Joint Economic Committee of Congress, with a Democratic majority and the endorsement of the liberal's liberal Ted Kennedy, reported in 1979 "that the major challenges today and for the foreseeable future are on the supply-side of the economy."[26] For the Democrats, the Keynesian foundation of post–World War II liberalism was a thing of the past. As Paul Heideman put it in his analysis of the realignment strategy in *Jacobin*, "The window for realignment had closed."[27] As loyal Democrats, however, Harrington and the realigners went on to support Carter in 1980 once Ted Kennedy's primary challenge was defeated, and Walter Mondale in 1984 as the party moved to the right.

If the correlation of political changes with developments in business attitudes, organization, and practice is often difficult to document, this one isn't. After a general rise in profit rates from the mid-1950s, the high point of the postwar boom, this key measure of capitalist prosperity virtually collapsed

from the mid-1960s until the early 1980s.[28] Up to this point, the command-
ing heights of US capital, the large industrial, commercial, and financial corporations, had tolerated or even supported America's comparatively limited
welfare state, and to a lesser extent the businesslike collective bargaining that
had evolved in the years following World War II, so long as control over the
workplace was ceded to management. The collapse of profitability, however,
ended this toleration as business sought to roll back what it now saw as the
costs of the Keynesian era. As we have seen above, in the realm of production
this meant the introduction and spread of lean production and concessions
from the unions. In the field of politics and economic policy it meant a sharp
turn toward what would become neoliberalism.

As Thomas Byrne Edsall described this turn, "During the 1970s, business
refined its ability to act as a class, submerging competitive instincts in favour
of joint, cooperative action in the legislative arena."[29] The leader of this cru-
sade was the Business Roundtable, founded in 1973 and representing most of
the major industrial, commercial, and financial corporations in the United
States, and whose connections with the Carter administration were direct.
The roundtable developed the roster of deregulation, tax reductions, welfare
cuts, privatization, and so on that have been the neoliberal agenda up to this
day. It was soon followed in its activist course by the broader US Chamber of
Commerce and the National Association of Manufacturers. The Trilateral
Commission, also founded in 1973 by top business leaders, refined the international free trade dimension of the developing neoliberal agenda—with
connections to the Carter White House and other Democrats. At the same
time, post-Watergate reforms opened the door to corporate PACs, which proliferated from 89 in 1974 to 784 in 1978 and 1,467 in 1982. Corporate and trade
association PAC campaign contributions rose from a mere $8 million in 1972
to $84.9 million in 1982, much of it going to the new generation of Democrats
mentioned above as well as to Democratic incumbents.[30]

In the 1980s, partly as a response to Reagan's election, the party took a further step toward neoliberalism when Charles Manatt, a lawyer and banker from
California, became chair of the Democratic National Committee (DNC). As
Ferguson and Rogers succinctly describe his role, "Manatt swiftly embarked
on a sweeping reorganization of the party," sprucing up its direct mail and
computer operations and orienting party organizations toward even greater dependence on business money. Manatt, for example, was instrumental in
founding the Democratic Business Council, which was specifically organized
to "reform the party's finances" and grant business leaders direct access to "task

forces and study groups to develop party policies." As the deep recession of 1980–83 disillusioned some business leaders with the Reagan administration, and the Democrats did well in congressional elections, Manatt sponsored a series of dinners and meetings with top business leaders to swing them, or at least their money, to the Democrats. In 1981 the DNC-appointed Hunt Commission was set up to rationalize the presidential nomination system. Its main "reforms" were the establishment of the notorious "super delegates" and the frontloading of the primary season "designed to advantage the early front-running candidates and ensure that party insiders would be 'heard' at the convention."[31] And that was only the beginning.

It was this changed situation that Jesse Jackson and the Rainbow Coalition confronted in 1984 and 1988. By this time the myth of a "liberal-labor coalition" was truly dead. The labor leadership and the realigners were supporting the likes of Mondale and Dukakis, old liberals were converting step by step to the new ideology and to the demands of capital, while a new generation of Democratic politicians arrived in Congress and lesser offices fully attuned to the business agenda and the funding requirements created by the rising costs of elections. For its part, the labor movement as a whole was in retreat, its numbers cut drastically after 1980, its leaders making concessions and more often than not succumbing to the charms of labor-management cooperation and the requirements of lean production. The temptation of an alliance with internal forces seeking progressive change was simply not there. Although African Americans were winning elected office at most levels, they did not yet form the sort of internal bloc that the old machines, the Dixiecrats, or even organized labor once had. In fact, some Black Democratic political officials were originally opposed to running a Black person for president on the grounds, so fundamental to the "American Scheme," that it would mean the reelection of Reagan (the "greater evil"), while some refused to back Jackson in 1984.[32]

To make an impact and rally the discontent that was real among African Americans and many white working-class voters, Jackson and the Rainbow Coalition forces assaulted the Democratic Party at its most permeable national level—the presidential primaries. The Rainbow campaign was an activist one, with Jackson visiting union picket lines as well as rallying the Black vote. He did remarkably well, particularly in 1988, gaining surprising victories in Michigan and elsewhere.[33] But in the end, the Rainbow Coalition faded, and the rightward march of the Democrats continued, symbolized by the formation of the Democratic Leadership Council (DLC) in 1985, appropriately dubbed by Jackson "Democrats for the Leisure Class."[34] It would be further solidified at the highest level in Bill Clinton's two terms as president. In the wake of the 1984 election, the process by which younger neoliberal Democrats replaced older liberals, as well as conservative southern Democrats, "at all levels of the Democratic Party," accelerated.[35] It is obvious that an assault from the left on the presidency not accompanied by one across the board on Congress cannot change the shape or direction of national politics even if it is relatively successful in gaining votes, as the Jackson challenge was. Jackson and many of his supporters backed Mondale in 1984 and Michael Dukakis in 1988, inadvertently contributing to the rightward shift of the party. He virtually blessed the dominant neoliberal faction with his injunction that the Democrats "need two wings to fly."[36]

The party would continue its trek to the right with the formation of the DLC in 1985. Its trajectory was not only political, moving toward fiscal moderation, deemphasis on the state and welfare provision, free trade, greater emphasis on "law and order," and strong national defense, but a geographic and demographic shift as well. As one study described the DLC view even before Clinton ran for president in 1992: "The party needed to escape the geographic locus of its reliable strength, the Northeast and industrial Midwest, for the growing West and South. It needed to escape the spatial locus of its reliable strength, urban America, for the growing suburbs. And it needed to escape the social locus of its reliable strength, the working class and the poor, for the growing middle class."[37] This was just what happened. As Democratic strategists targeted middle- and upper-income voters, "The rate at which the Democratic Party reached out to high-income Americans increased nearly four-fold between 1980 and 2004."[38] This reprioritization was reflected in Democratic policy changes: when Clinton had a majority in both Houses of Congress during his first two years, he chose to put the passage of the North American Free Trade Agreement, which labor opposed, over health care reform, which labor generally supported. And when health care reform came it would be based on "managed competition" and the central role of the insurance industry.[39] By this time, the Democratic Party was already implementing further changes in the structure and operation of this "Big Tent" party that would make anything like a takeover far more difficult.

CHAPTER NINE

The Democratic
Party Cul-de-sac

While for obvious reasons few on the left today advocate realignment per se, many still argue that the Democratic Party can be "moved" to the left by working in it to elect progressive candidates at various levels—or at the very least that it can serve as a platform for a future split to the left. It is not really a "party" at all, goes the argument, in that it is not a membership organization like Canada's New Democratic Party or the British Labour Party. Rather it is just a collection of shifting electoral coalitions. Elections these days are "candidate-centered," meaning the candidates run and shape their own campaigns, as any number of political science books will tell you. Anyone can run for office on the party's state-mandated primary ballot line, and there is little discipline in its legislative or congressional bodies to prevent one from advocating for change and voting one's conscience, and so on.[1] It is permeable.

To some extent, of course, the Democratic Party *is* permeable. It could not play its role in the great American Scheme if it weren't. It is precisely its ability to attract and absorb the leaders and activists of social movements and organized labor that makes it, as some of us still insist, "the graveyard of social movements." When positive changes came, as argued above and again below, it was due to mass social upheaval. The absorption into Democratic Party politics came mostly as the movements' leaders sought gains through the traditional political process—even if sometimes in nontraditional ways, like via the Rainbow Coalition. The party they attempted to influence, however,

119

never fulfilled the demands or hopes of the movement leaders and activists it absorbed. From the populists to the CIO to the civil rights movement this "non-party" succeeded in incorporating such leaders and activists—sometimes including token representation on the Democratic National Committee. While the upheavals brought some reforms, and the incorporated leaders were cheered for such achievements, their absorption was accompanied by the increasing move to the center-right.

For organized blocs involved in trying to influence this "party of the people" from within, politics are reduced to pressure tactics. For organized labor, in particular, attempts to influence the policies and practices of elected Democratic officials are reduced to financial donations (which often pale in comparison to those from capital), endorsements, and get-out-the-vote efforts on behalf of favored individual candidates. This is followed by lobbying in hopes of getting them to actually support labor's goals—mostly directed from the top of the unions. The process is, in practice, analogous to the collective bargaining with which these leaders are familiar. It involves negotiation, occasional temporary mobilization, and compromise. The difference is that in collective bargaining, the mobilization phase can involve the withdrawal of labor, which can temporarily cripple the employer. There is no such force available in conventional politics other than the idle threat to withdraw labor's votes. All of this contrasts sharply with the older practice of labor seeking direct representation through its own party, something, with the brief and partial exception of the Labor Party in the late 1990s (see below), US labor has not attempted for generations, but which socialists might want to put back on the agenda.

Consider the fact that, as a result of its practice in the "permeable" corridors of the Democratic Party, organized labor, still the largest organized social group in the United States, has won only one of its major legislative demands since World War II—the establishment of OSHA (Occupational Safety and Health Administration) covering workplace health and safety under Nixon—even when the Democrats controlled Congress and the presidency, even during the "Keynesian" era, even before labor's rapid decline as well as during the neoliberal era. This record goes right up to the Obama administration and the 111th Congress with its Democratic majority in both houses. Labor's main goal at that time was the passage of the Employee Free Choice Act (EFCA), which would have made organizing easier. Here, not only did five Democratic senators refuse to support the EFCA, opening it to a Republican filibuster, but as *Forbes* reported favorably at the time, "President Obama

… has maintained a wise and judicious silence on the EFCA."[2] In fact, Obama pushed it out of the way in favor of his health care bill. As AFL-CIO president Richard Trumka observed then, "The President and (Rahm) Emanuel have both said they don't intend to bring Employee Free Choice Act up until Health Insurance Reform is done."[3] Nor, to put it mildly, has the Democratic Party become the party of Black liberation despite the loyalty of the official African American leadership, including Jesse Jackson, and of most Black voters—or the election of a Black president.

Permeable at the edges, the hierarchical conglomerate that is today's Democratic Party is far more organized, professionally managed, and well funded than in the era of realignment or even during the Jackson challenge. It is, again, not a membership organization. Its millions of voters have no direct influence over its candidates, organizations, or policies—or in reality over how their elected officials behave once elected. There is nothing remotely democratic about either its state-mandated or real structures. As Arthur Lipow pointed out, "Only in America is it true that direct membership participation in the parties does not exist except in the sense that individuals register their party preference with an official agency of the state or are habitual voters for one or another party." This, he argues, makes the party "the creature of professional politicians," which is profoundly undemocratic.[4] This means, among other things, that anything like the election of left-winger Jeremy Corbyn to Labour Party leader in Britain in 2015 by 60 percent and again in 2016 by 62 percent in a membership vote, limited as that victory is vis-à-vis the opposition of the Parliamentary Labour Party, is something that could never happen in the United States.[5]

The permeability of the Democratic Party exists only indirectly in pressure politics or more immediately in the direct primary system of candidate selection, which as we will see is not a neutral space. In the name of fighting corruption, the reforms of the progressive era were meant to undermine party organization—not just the machines but also the mass populist, labor, and socialist parties arising in the late nineteenth and early twentieth century. Marco d'Eramo in his history of Chicago points out that the reforms of that era were meant to "limit the domain of politics." As he argues: "It is in the name of the battle against corruption that an attempt is made to reduce the public sphere to the private sector's gain and advantage. It is in the name of the battle against corruption that the most antidemocratic counter-revolutions in America's history have succeeded."[6]

The introduction of the direct primary that replaced the selection of candidates by party members, Lipow wrote, "undermined representative institutions, made political parties—even the capitalist political parties—less responsible and less representative as organizations." Furthermore, the direct primary individualizes and atomizes political participation, whether that of a candidate or a voter. As Lipow states, "Individuals can be powerful in modern society only through organization."[7] The primary reduces "organization" to a one-shot, "candidate-centered," professionally run campaign over which the atomized voters have no say. It seems strange that those who argue for working "within" the Democratic Party cite this individualizing, undemocratic characteristic of the American Scheme as something good for the Left.

The temptation to enter the party primary as a means of moving politics in a more progressive direction is aided by the illusion of "hollow" organization at the precinct or district level. That this level of organization has been weakened and reduced in importance in election campaigns with the rise of purchased, professional forms of campaigning, discussed below, seems to increase its permeability. But there is an often-unnoticed price for entry—namely, loyalty to the party's ticket. Those active at the lowest level of electoral functioning, as well as its higher levels for any period of time, are expected to support the party's candidates, including the "regulars" when the progressive challenger loses. Since the chances of winning a primary are stacked against outsiders due to incumbency, money, and preexisting local leadership, this is a dilemma facing those who wish to "storm" the primary. In any case, the local level exists within an institutional and socioeconomic context that has increased in power in the last few decades.

The actual centers of power of this party exist in the elevated spaces of its structure, the congressional and state legislative organizations, and the invisible class forces supporting these, all of which are accessible only to higher-level office holders, party apparatchiks, big funders, and a tiny number of highly influential individuals. In a formal sense, as the party describes its structure, it is composed, in descending order, of the Democratic National Committee (DNC), Democratic Governors Association (DGA), Democratic Senatorial Campaign Committee (DSCC), Democratic Congressional Campaign Committee (DCCC), Democratic Legislative Campaign Committee (DLCC), Association of State Democratic Chairs (ASDC), and state Democratic Parties. The DLCC, which raises money for state legislative candidates, is relatively new, having been formed in 1994, and reflects the shift to state legislative activity discussed above.

The key institutional centers are really in the DNC, DSCC, and DCCC, on the one hand, and the state parties, on the other. These organizations are filled by party apparatchiks and office holders. In the case of the DNC there are a token number of labor, African American, Latino, and women members, but the core remains the state party chairs and vice chairs, elected officials, and national apparatchiks. In real power terms, it is its state leaders, elected officials, and full-timers who fill these committees who are "the party." For the most part they are responsible only to each other and, of course, their major donors, who compose the invisible elite class forces behind the institutions.

In the self-description of the Democratic Party's formal structure, while most levels now provide election services and engage in candidate selection, fundraising is central to all of these organizations. As the party's website describes the functions of the DNC, "The DNC also raises money, hires staff, and coordinates strategy to support candidates throughout the country for local, state, and national office."[8] The DNC, DSCC, DCCC, and DLCC all raise huge sums in campaign contributions. Since there are no membership dues, other than what elected officials and staffers are expected to contribute, each level of party organization must raise funds from outside its structure. As we will see in detail below, by far the largest proportion of the funds they raise come from business and the wealthy—that is, the capitalist class. Thus, capital, in additions to all its external forms of influence or its contributions to individual campaigns, is directly connected to the party's entire structure through personal donations and business and trade association PACs, which supply the lion's share of the budgets and the funds dispensed by the DNC, DSCC, DCCC, and DLCC. This is one aspect of the capitalist nature of this party.

While money has long played an important role in US politics, the redistribution of wealth upward in the United States in the last four decades, the enormous consolidation of capital in the last twenty years, and the increased importance of the states in the legislative field described at various points above have all contributed to changes in party organization, above all its increased dependence on donations from business and the wealthy, and the way elections are conducted at every level of American politics. This represents a qualitative change from the New Deal, civil rights, and realignment eras. Particularly crucial has been the turn away from the old neighborhood-based machines and county organizations that turned out the vote to *purchased* forms of voter turnout and campaigning, such as TV and other media time or space, direct mail appeals, professional campaign consultants, pollsters, legal advisers, computer experts, providers of digitally targeted voter information, and so on. While some argue that TV is ineffective in reaching young people who use social media, it nevertheless remains a major form of campaign communication for statewide, congressional district, and even local elections—possibly because older people are more likely to vote. All of this has increased the cost of elections far beyond the era of radios, newspapers, and political machines. It is above all capital that has funded this change and the acceleration of its costs.

By the early 2000's, mass media spending absorbed about 45 percent of national-level campaign budgets. In the 2014 congressional elections expenditures on TV time reached an all-time high of $814 million. In New York's 2013 election for mayor and city council, "independent" spending—that is, spending not by the candidates' campaigns but by groups such as the real estate interest, businesses, and various unions—amounted to almost $16 million, about two-thirds of it on mass mailings and TV ads.[9] One consequence of this is that the old neighborhood-based precinct organizations often seem "hollow" because they have lost their importance as a means of reaching voters. Thus, the most obvious, but by no means the only change, has been the enormous increase in the role of money and for-profit firms providing campaign services of various sorts in elections—a change that virtually by definition favors capital and the wealthy.

The total cost of presidential elections rose from $161 million in 1980 to $2.6 billion in 2012 and is projected to reach $5 billion by the end of the 2016 election cycle. The cost of presidential primaries alone rose from $94.2 million in 1980 to $1.4 billion in 2016, or by fifteen times.[10] Adjusted for inflation it still rose by five times across the neoliberal era. These increases are not just a matter of inflation or population growth. They are the result, first of all, of the "direct primary" system of selecting candidates which has more than doubled the cost of presidential elections and increases them at all levels. For example, candidates in the Democratic primary that chose Bill de Blasio as the party's mayoral candidate in 2013 spent a combined $29.1 million, while in the general election that made de Blasio mayor of New York, the two major candidates spent $9.4 million.[11] While not all primaries are this expensive, they unquestionably contribute to the need to raise ever-increasing amounts of money. Also contributing mightily to this financial arms race are the changes in how elections are run: the costly "air war" of TV, mass mailings, and targeted online messaging via the digital massing of demographic and personal voter data; the elaboration of elite party organizations; the rise of the pollsters; the invasion of consultants; and the new fundraising techniques (from mass mailings to crowdfunding). And there are new costs already taking shape in the air waves and wires of the digital universe.

Election Cost Inflation and the Digital Death of Democracy

As most of us know by now, information about you and just about every-thing you've done that involves the Internet, the state, or a commercial transaction is now "public" (in private hands) and for sale. If you ever made an online purchase or bank transaction, bought anything on a credit card anywhere, had a coffee at Starbucks, possessed a driver's license or voter registration with your address and phone number (land or wireless), had your fingerprints taken, or had your gender, ethnic, and assorted biometric details recorded; all this personal data has been uploaded and downloaded, gathered and sorted, correlated and coded, encrypted and de-encrypted, *and sold.* Among the purchasers and resellers are firms specializing in voter targeting, such as Artistole, Xaxis, Voter Contact Services, and DSPolitical, the latter of which specifically serves Democratic campaigns.[12] According to John Aristotle Phillips, the CEO of Aristotle, they can provide customers with "up to 500 different data points on each individual."[13]

Among the purchasers of these services are political parties, election campaigns, and candidates at all levels. From this assembled data an algorithm can be created that allows a political campaign to target and contact those most likely to vote for their candidate. The parties or campaigns that purchase this service, in turn, use it to spread targeted messages to specific groups or even individual voters mostly via the Internet through various platforms, including Facebook, which apparently made a bundle off the 2016 election.[14] All of this is, of course, the application of advanced marketing techniques to what was once thought of as a fairly direct if often corrupt form of human interaction, organization, and intellectual exchange in determining who will run the various levels of government. You know: politics.

Digitalized politics cost more and more money. As one recent academic study of voter mobilization said of these new techniques, "Campaign consultants have a business interest in deploying these kinds of tactics and the fact that no one knows for sure whether such tactics generate votes allows sub-optimal campaign tactics to persist."[15] The low levels of voter turnout in most elections and the declining Democratic vote indicate just how "sub-optimal" these tactics are. Nevertheless, spending on digital political ads rose from $22 million in 2008 to $158 million in 2012 and is expected to hit $1 billion for the 2016 election and over $3 billion by the 2020 elections.[16] No doubt they will continue to soar as they are increasingly available for elections way down the ballot to the local level, according to the Democratic digital outfit DSPolitical.[17] Aside from the soaring costs this invasive digital targeting adds to US elections and the continued erosion of our privacy, it further removes political campaigning from any direct human contact. As reporters for the *Guardian* put it, "Campaigns of the future will depend as much on being able to track people across screens and apps as knocking on doors or sending out flyers."[18] It's not that no doors are knocked on or no phone calls are made, but it is the algorithm that decides the limited number of actual voters to be visited or called to turn out the vote. In practice this has meant identifying those most likely to vote; that is, the better-off part of the population. Most of the persuasion side of campaigning is done online through ads on Facebook, YouTube, your smartphone, and so on. The knowledge about local voters once in the head of the precinct captain is no longer needed as far more data are fed through an algorithm that has your number. The campaign "air war" has taken on a new dimension in the digital ether. The "ground war" is increasingly the "waves and wires war," with such door-knocking as is done is targeted to those most likely to vote.

More importantly, the shaping of the political process, already an auction, will be even further outsourced to the profit-making "expert" firms that provide this service. Whatever is left even of limited "bourgeois" democracy in the United States faces death by digitalization, execution by experts, and profits for the pundits. Along with its unappealing message of austerity and neoliberal inevitability, the elevation of Democratic Party election strategy and practice to elite/expert levels, from Clinton-style "triangulation" and the mass media binge of the 2000s to today's algorithmic campaigning, are a major cause in the electoral failure of the Democrats at almost every level as the turnout for Democratic candidates falls. This is discussed in more detail in the postscript following the conclusion.

The antidote lies in the activation and organization of large numbers of people to talk to, persuade, mobilize, and organize even more people to impose a measure of democracy on the elites that no longer have any use for it. This is not something that can be accomplished in the institutions and socioeconomic milieu of the Democratic Party. As the Trump era unfolds, a grassroots approach becomes all the more important.

It is well known that both corporate and wealthy political donors frequently give to the election campaigns of both parties. Recently, writing in *Jacobin*, Corey Robin made the point that wealthy donors who give to both parties "can expect their material interests will be fulfilled. Not because of bribery, simple quid pro quos, access, or influence, but simply because both parties are so ideologically amenable to meeting the needs and interests of wealthy donors."[19] That is, the politicians of both parties accept capital's argument cited by Lipow above that "what is good for their company or industry is good for the economy or the nation."[20] At the same time, in terms of Congress or state legislatures, these business and wealthy donors, not satisfied with mere ideological hegemony, do in fact expect and receive "access" to legislators of the majority party. This includes the drafting of legislation by corporate lawyers and lobbyists in contact with congressional staffers. For this reason, there is a certain rhythm to where contributions of business and the wealthy to congressional candidates go. In years when the Democrats control one or another chamber of Congress, corporate money is more or less evenly divided between the two parties. For example, when the Democrats controlled the House in the 110th Congress (2007–2008) Democrats received $56.7 million from corporate PACs and $47.6 million from trade associations, while Republicans got $51.3 million and $38 million, respectively.[21] Today, with the Republicans dominant in both houses, they receive far more than congressional Democrats. For the congressional election cycle of 2014, Republicans received 65 percent of business PAC money, almost two-to-one to Democrats.

Table VII shows this pattern for the entire neoliberal period. Off-year elections are used to avoid the impact of presidential contests on funding. Three things are obvious. First, the Democrats did proportionately much better in corporate and trade association contributions when they controlled the House and, therefore, the committees of the Congress in session at the time of the election—money flows to the incumbents in control of the legislative process. Second, even when the Republicans do significantly better, the amount going to Democrats is far from trivial. Third, the total amount spent on campaigns of both parties by business PACs has gone up over time. There is no slacking in this financial arms race.

Table VII: Corporate and Trade Association PAC Contributions to Off-Year House Campaigns ($ million)

Election Cycle	Majority Party*	Democrats	Republicans
1981–82	Democrats	$14.2	$21.7
1985–86	Democrats	$24.3	$25.2
1989–90	Democrats	$38.0	$30.0
1993–94	Democrats	$45.7	$36.5
1997–98	Republicans	$33.7	$62.9
2001–2	Republicans	$46.6	$78.8
2005–6	Republicans	$62.0	$113.7
2009–10	Democrats	$141.4	$142.1
2013–14	Republicans	$105.3	$193.0

*In the Congress in session at the time of the election.

Sources: US Census Bureau, *Statistical Abstract of the United States*, 1990, 269; 1992, 275; 1994, 292; 1996, 291; 2000, 296; 2004–5, 260; 2008, 260; OpenSecrets, 2010, 2016, "PAC Contributions to Federal Candidates," www.opensecrets.org/pacs/sector.php?cycle=2010&txt=P01.

Some see a ray of hope with the increased importance of crowdfunding that Bernie Sanders's campaign perfected, but the fact is that even this more broadly based way of raising money only upped the bidding in the auction that is American politics. More will be said about this relatively new phenomenon below. Looking at what presidential campaigns spent in the primaries, not including federal funds, Sanders's $227.4 million disbursements for the 2016 pre-nomination period exceeded Obama's $211.7 in 2012. Total pre-nomination spending by candidates for 2016 amounted to $849.1 million, compared to $496.7 million in 2012 and $611.6 in 2008, when there were a similar number of primary candidates and the hard-fought contest between Obama and Hillary Clinton. Since the 2000 election, also with a large number of primary candidates, pre-nomination spending has grown by over two and a half times in nominal terms and doubled in real terms.[22] Crowdfunding accounts for a good deal of this escalation. But these figures only scan the surface of the changes brought about by the interaction of changed business attitudes and organizations, functional changes in party organization, and the vast and growing sums of money that fund them.

In most states the structure of the two parties that make up the American Scheme are state-mandated hierarchies of state and county organizations. In the era of urban machines, northern city-based county organizations were dominated by the machine, while most county organizations in the South were run by a "courthouse gang." State party organizations, like the state legislatures of that time, were weak and counted for little. Increasingly in the 1960s and 1970s, though people often still use the term, the urban machines lost patronage and faded due to civil service reforms, the rise of federal programs that replaced patronage, court cases banning patronage, white flight, suburbanization, and the increased presence and political role of African Americans and Latinos in the cities.[23] At the same time, state party organizations became more professional and well-funded as state legislatures became more important in terms of legislation, tax incentives, and in the administering of federal programs and funds. With the machines gone, county organizations, sometimes still dubbed "machines" even though they lost power, became more dependent on or subordinate to the state party. By the turn of the twenty-first century one study described the emerging state party organizations as follows: "They have larger, more complex organizational structures. They have different functions to perform, with much emphasis on serving the needs of candidates and raising money. . . . They operate in a more partisan and competitive environment." The increased costs of TV ads, the "air war" in campaigns, "led to restored strength for state and national parties."[24]

Today, reports a more recent study of state politics, "Every Democratic and Republican state party now has a full-time chair or executive director. Most have other professional staffers as well, who handle fundraising, communications, field operations, and campaigns."[25] These "services" extend to state and local campaigns, including primaries. While some legislative and local districts are small and elections can be conducted almost on a door-to-door basis, "a large proportion of statewide, legislative, and local candidates—particularly non-incumbents—need the kinds of help that they may not be able to afford but that a state party organization can provide, such as political consultants and computer resources."[26] With these changes, of course, came a certain amount of control as the state party sought a majority in the state legislature and attempted to run it, like Congress, as we will see below, on a more disciplined basis.

By the 2000 election cycle, election spending on all state offices had hit the $1 billion mark, and by 2014 it had more than doubled to $2.2 billion.[27] State parties not only helped fund these elections but contributed more to congressional and presidential elections as well. The rising strength and importance of state party organization was reflected in the growing amounts of state party spending by the Democrats on federal elections that rose from an insignificant $8 million in 1980 to $295 million in 2012.[28] Thus, the various levels of party organization were increasingly interdependent. They now help in candidate selection, funding, and campaign advice in local, state, and national elections. To run for state or congressional office as a Democrat often means clearing or overcoming the actions of today's more powerful state party organizations.

At the local level, as one writer who favors working in the Democratic Party notes, "In city and county politics, real estate and banking interests dominate the local councils."[29] Indeed, in New York City's 2013 city council elections, the real estate industry's front group "Jobs for New York" contributed 78 percent of "Independent" spending in what the city's Campaign Finance Board called "an unprecedented $6.3 million to support or oppose City Council candidates in 2013." This real estate group focused on Democratic primaries in sixteen open seat contests for an average of $251,000 per candidates.[30] More broadly, today, as candidates have turned from the old machine and party "reform" groups' "ground war" in the neighborhoods to the media "air war" in city elections, campaign funds came from financial services, lawyers, the hospitality industry, convention and tourism, and advertising, as well as real estate, while modern "pinstripe" patronage has returned to pretty much the same crew.[31]

This more recent shift in the way elections are conducted is a reflection of the deeper transformation of the Democratic Party from a bourgeois party organizationally rooted in mostly corrupt grassroots organizations—machines and courthouse gangs—to a professionalized, well-funded, and elite-run multitiered conglomerate with a permanent bureaucracy at its core. The Democratic Party and the Republican Party, are, of course, not national membership organizations. One is a Democrat by virtue of registering with the state as one or simply imagining oneself a Democrat. This imaginary or registered "membership," the party's core electorate, has no power or influence over the real party structure. When state parties were weak, the national structure of the party amounted to little more than smoke-filled rooms and the quadrennial convention. Today, however, the national Democratic Party has a year-round existence in the much improved and well-funded Democratic National Committee. State party leaders, themselves more powerful, make up the core of the DNC. While the DNC is not a center of philosophical debate, it is a center of fundraising, campaign coordination, and influence. It also organizes and rigs the quadrennial national party convention that nominates the presidential candidate, spells out the largely meaningless party platform, and sets the slightly more meaningful party rules. As with other aspects of party organization, one measure is the amount the DNC spends on election campaigns.

In 1980 the DNC spent only $14.8 million on campaigns, but by 2000 this had risen to $122 million and by 2012 to $292.3 million.[32] As of August 2016 it had raised $98.9 million in that year's election cycle. Some of this went to state Democratic Parties, further tying them to the national leadership. Florida got the biggest contribution, $572,651, and Alabama the smallest, $7,173. A huge proportion of this campaign money as well as its operating budget comes from big business. Among the DNC's biggest funders in 2016 were Microsoft, Pritzker, Time Warner, the private equity Blackstone Group, and several investment firms, such as the $65 billion Renaissance Technologies, which gave $881,450 in 2016, the largest donation in that cycle. Of the $98.9 million the DNC had raised by August 2016 in that election cycle, $50 million came from business, $7.1 million from lawyers and lobbyists, $1.6 million from ideological or issue groups, and a mere $66,500 from labor.[33] The balance of contributions to these committees not mentioned comes from individual donors. Many of these are wealthy or well-to-do people with enough money to gain access. Many are just individuals who have no say in anything the party apparatus does. While the DNC may not equal the power of the Central Committee of the German Social Democratic Party, it clearly has more to say about candidate selection and funding than it did in the days of realignment. The DNC, however, is only part of the national apparatus of the Democratic Party.

The Democratic Party in Congress also forms in different ways part of the actual hierarchy and structure of the party when it comes to candidate selection and campaign funding, as well as, of course, legislation. The internal party structure of Congress will be discussed below; here we are concerned with the role of the congressional Democratic Party in elections. The congressional Democratic Party is not composed of the humble of the earth and does not reflect the US population in terms of income or wealth. Most are lawyers, many are rich—the median wealth of congressional Democrats in 2014 was $1.1 million, compared to a median of about $81,000 for all US families. Thus, more than half the Democrats in Congress are millionaires.[34] Comparing the average net worth of senators and representatives from the two parties we see that as of 2012 Democratic senators were worth an average of $13,566,333 to a mere $6,956,438 for Republicans. Republican representatives did somewhat better than Democrats at $7,614,097 to $5,700,168, but House Democrats still held ten times the national average (mean) of $534,000.[35] (Is it any wonder that demagogic right-wingers can label the Democrats part of the out-of-touch elite?) Both major parties have congressional campaign committees that help select candidates and/or determine which ones will succeed by directing funds toward favored candidates, over which the congressional millionaires—who are mostly incumbent representatives or senators—have much to say.

According to a textbook published by the *Congressional Quarterly*, while congressional aspirants may nominate themselves in primaries, they "quickly encounter national networks of party committees and their allied interest groups. At the heart of these networks are the two major parties' House and Senate campaign committees, now active in nearly all phases of congressional elections." This includes candidate recruitment.[36] As with the DNC, campaign expenditures from the Democratic Senate Campaign Committee (DSCC) and the Democratic Congressional Campaign Committee (DCCC) have risen enormously. The DSCC campaign expenditures rose from $1.6 million in 1980 to $169.2 million in 2014, by one hundred times, while those from the DCCC increased from $2 million to $206.1 million over those years for a similar increase.[37] Altogether, campaign money that came directly from the party at the national level amounted to $536 million during the 2014 off-year election cycle, out of a total of $734 million spent on House and Senate elections, including primaries. State Democratic Parties contributed another $182.6 million, which means that party money plays a big role in congressional elections that are supposedly "candidate-centered." But doesn't much of this money come from organized labor?

A significant proportion of the money that is funneled through the national-level and state party committees, of course, comes from PACs. Looking at the 2014 off-year election cycle, the last one for which there is complete information as of this writing, as noted above the Democrats spent $734 million on congressional campaigns. Of that, according to OpenSecrets, $205.3 million, or 28 percent, came from PACs. Of that 23 percent, less than a quarter came from unions, while 57 percent came from business—almost two and a half times as much. Lawyer, lobbyist, and issue PACs also contributed to the Democrats, further diluting the influence of the unions.[38]

Funds contributed to the DCCC and DSCC come heavily from business and very lightly from labor. For the 2016 cycle, of the $55.6 million raised by the DCCC as of August 2016, $22.2 million came from business, $3.8 million from lawyers and lobbyists, $2.9 from ideological or issue groups, and a tiny $175,000 from labor. In the off-year cycle of 2014, business gave the DCCC $31.3 million, compared to $1.2 million for labor. Of the total of $41.3 million raised by the Senate Campaign Committee as of August 2016, $17.5 million came from business, $869,300 from ideological and issue committees, and

$117,900 from labor, while in the 2014 cycle it was $26.5 million from business to labor's $910,600.[39] Money for these committees also comes from individuals, including a good deal from wealthy individuals. Around 2010 the DSCC compared its 200,000 donor list to a database of the nation's richest 5 percent and discovered that a quarter of the names matched.[40]

"Follow the money," Deep Throat told Woodward and Bernstein as they investigated the Watergate break-in. Looking at the flow of money into and out of the DNC, DSCC, and DCCC it is clear that to a very large extent, the national committees of the Democratic Party are conduits for business money going to congressional, state, and local party committees and campaigns. At the same time, this money supports these elements of the permanent structure of the party, giving them organizational stability and, no doubt, influencing how DNC, DSCC, and DCCC members see things. No other source of funds for these committees comes close to that derived from business and the wealthy. They, and thus the national Democratic Party structure as a whole, are institutionally tied to the PACs and large contributions of America's capitalist class. Labor money, by contrast, is miniscule as a source of support for the Democratic Party's national infrastructure. Both business and labor PACs, of course, contribute directly to many individual candidates' campaigns at all levels, where sometimes labor's support is proportionately larger, but the backbone of the "party of the people," like its rival, is formed by the largess of capital—whose influence can hardly be trivial. Obviously, all of this makes winning both the primary and general election extremely difficult for an "outsider."

Winning a seat in Congress is not a simple matter in any case. Democratic and Republican office holders like to keep their jobs, and for the most part they do. According to one study, from 1946 to 2002 only 1.7 percent of congressional incumbents lost a primary contest.[41] From 2000 through the 2012 election cycle, fewer than 1 percent of incumbents lost primaries. The figure went up somewhat in the 2014 election, when 2 percent lost their seats in the primary. In elections for the House of Representatives, incumbents retain their seats 93 percent of the time, a percentage that has held from the 1950s through the 2014 election cycle, while Senate incumbents now win 85 percent of contests—up from about 77 percent in the 1950s.[42] The reasons that incumbents win include name recognition, possible favors or "case work" done for constituents, bringing "pork" to the district or state, and so on. But it is money that makes the big difference here, as in so many aspects of the American Scheme.

In the 2014 election cycle, the average cost of a race for the House was $1 million and that for the Senate $7 million.[43] As one study of congressional elections put it, "Potential donors try to avoid wasting their money on hopeless causes. The better the candidate's prospects, the more contributors of all kinds are willing to invest in the campaign."[44] So money flows to incumbents in far greater amounts than to challengers. In the 2014 House elections, incumbents spent three times what challengers were able to raise. Part of this is "pre-emptive fundraising" aimed "at dissuading serious opponents" from entering the primaries in the first place or, barring that, pushing them to drop out early. This is what happened in Elizabeth Warren's incredibly expensive 2012 Senate primary contest (see below). This funding gap has been growing since the 1970s.[45] Incumbents are much more likely to get funds from the DCCC or DSCC, as well as directly from business.

Incumbents also benefit from endorsements by party organizations, politicians, labor unions, and various issue-based groups. A good example of this is the 2016 Florida primary election between incumbent Debbie Wasserman Schultz and Sanders-backed insurgent Tim Canova. Wasserman Schultz is the former DNC chair and member of the "pro-growth, fiscally responsible" New Democrat Coalition spinoff of the now defunct Democratic Leadership Council. She supports private for-profit prisons, payday lenders, and fast track for the TPP (Trans-Pacific Partnership), the latter costing her the state AFL-CIO endorsement, though not that of the local central labor council.[46] As DNC chair she plotted to undermine Bernie Sanders's campaign and was forced to resign from the DNC when WikiLeaks revealed her anti-Sanders emails. Nevertheless, when she faced a well-financed challenge from Canova the party came to her rescue in the form of endorsements from President Obama, Vice President Joe Biden, and presidential candidate Hillary Clinton, who attended one of Wasserman Schultz's rallies. It is also more than likely that some of the more than $500,000 from the DNC that went to the Florida Democratic Party before and during the primary election helped her win handily by 57 percent to 43 percent.[47]

The best chance of an outsider winning in a Democratic congressional primary is in an open seat contest, where the incumbent has retired or moved on. However, there are typically only a minority of open seats in each election cycle. In 2014, for example, 47 House seats out of 435 were open, 19 of them previously Democratic. So a little over 10 percent of all seats and less than 5 percent of Democratic seats were open in the House. There were eight open seats in the Senate, five formerly Democratic.[48] Open seat contests, however, are also very expensive because there are certain to be more candidates with more experience in the primary. "Formidable challengers attract campaign resources," as one study put it.[49] The average cost per candidate of an open seat election for the House was $1.4 million in 2014, up from about $100,000 in 1974, and almost three times that of a challenge to an incumbent.

A Senate race, of course, is even more expensive. The average cost of an open seat campaign for the Senate in 2014 was around $11 million, or more than twice that of a challenge to an incumbent and around twenty times what it cost in 1974.[50] Elizabeth Warren's 2012 election to the Massachusetts Senate seat held by Ted Kennedy until his death in 2009 is said to have been the most expensive congressional race in history. Warren spent $42.2 million, almost four times the cost of an average Senate open seat race, to win the primary and beat her Republican opponent Scott Brown, who spent $35.1 million.[51] The advantages of incumbency, the infrequency of open seat elections, and their expense means that the idea of "progressive" outsiders sweeping the Democratic congressional elections in a short period is a fantasy. Those who wish to "take over" or significantly penetrate the Democratic Party via Congress had better have plenty of cash on hand—along with a lot of digital paraphernalia, many boots on the ground, and a good deal of patience.

The cost of running for state legislative office is much less than that for Congress. A house or assembly seat campaign averaged $60,770 in 2014, while that of a state senate seat was $150,043.[52] The advantages of incumbency, however, hold for state and local elections as well. As one study of city council elections put it, "Incumbency is the 800-pound gorilla in city council elections, as it is in state and national elections."[53] The National Institute on Money in State Politics reported that in recent state legislative elections, "Incumbent legislators were reelected in 2013 and 2014 at the high rate of 91 percent—on par with the average success rate observed since 2001." Despite relatively lower costs than congressional elections, money also matters, and some 84 percent of those who raised the most money won their state election. Those who had the dual advantage of incumbency and spending the most won by an average of 94 percent from 2002 through 2014.[54] The funds going to Democrats from all sources to candidates in state elections also saw business as the largest contributor. In the 2014 races for all state offices, business gave $223.5 million to Democrats, while labor contributed $126.1 million, a better ratio than in national elections but still revealing heavy dependence on business money. In addition, however, the party itself exerted influence through campaign donations from Democratic Party committees, which amounted to $80.3 million in 2014—and, as we saw, much of this money also comes from business. Thus, business influence is greater than the ratio of direct campaign spending indicates.[55]

Business money thus sneaks into the Democratic Party's election campaigns at all levels, through more than one door. Of the $2.6 million raised by the Democratic Legislative Campaign Committee from its top twenty donors for state legislative elections as of August, 2016, $1.6 million or 63 percent came from corporations such as Wal-Mart, AT&T, Comcast, Pfizer, and MillerCoors, compared to $950,000 from unions.[56] Not that labor money always goes to progressives in state elections. Michael J. Madigan, chair of the Illinois Democratic Party and Speaker of the Illinois House of Representatives gets lots of union money. He is known as the "King of Illinois," his leadership in the state house has been described as "absolute," he's been accused of illegal patronage and corruption, and he is a partner in a law firm that specializes in tax breaks for real estate interests.[57] There are plenty more like him. And to perpetuate this, most state parties, particularly those in the East and Midwest, use pre-nominations, that is, primary endorsements, to make sure those who sit in the state legislature are acceptable to party leaders.[58]

Of course, "left liberals and radicals running as Democrats aren't *required* to take any money from those committees," writes Jason Schulman in *New Politics*.[59] True enough, but capital floods the electoral fields through many streams, and it does so even more generously to those of the Republican opponents our left-liberal Democrat must defeat. So even assuming she has passed all the barriers the party will put up in the primary, she had better have the funds from somewhere else. And, of course, the more the party committee's funds flow to incumbents and party "regulars," the more our dissident Democrat must raise from elsewhere. One alternative to party committee money these days is crowdfunding. For Democrats this has come largely from ActBlue, a digital crowdfunding operation formed in 2004. As we will see below, however, it turns out that ActBlue is not really an alternative at all but just another means of keeping the Democratic Party in office. Suppose, despite it all, our left-liberal or socialist rebel Democrat squeaks through all the barriers to win a seat in Congress or the state legislature. Once there, what?

The same *New Politics* article notes that the Democratic Party might be a "political utility of the ruling class" (not the author's term) "if the neoliberal bourgeois leadership of the Democratic Party could impose parliamentary discipline on all elected Democrats, but there is really very little that it can do beyond removing dissidents from congressional committees."[60] Of course, assuming our newly elected left progressive plans to produce more than hot air, being removed from a committee, prevented from ever being a committee chair, or assigned to one irrelevant to her concerns or constituents is political suicide since virtually all meaningful legislative work is done in committees. Since the 1970s, internal party organization, the party caucus, the whips' organization, and leadership have been strengthened.[61]

The idea that the party leadership in Congress or state legislatures can do little to discipline members tends to look back at a time in the 1960s and 1970s when such discipline was relatively lax and only about 58 percent of votes in the House and 51 percent in the Senate were along strict party lines. But this is no longer the case. For the last twenty years or so, disciplined party-line votes in both House and Senate have accounted for 90 percent or more of all floor votes of both parties.[62] There is a great deal the congressional leaders, whips, and party caucuses can do to pressure members to vote the party line, including stripping them of committee seniority or assignments, burying their legislative proposals in committee, denying them "earmarked" funds for their district, and making their re-election more difficult by withholding campaign funds and endorsements and/or funding and endorsing opponents in primaries—and encouraging other loyal Democrats, labor leaders, and other "interest groups" to do the same.

Bowing to party discipline includes the Congressional Progressive Caucus, which passes for the left wing of Congress. Ralph Nader observed in 2013 that under the minority leadership of Nancy Pelosi:

> Over 90 percent of Democrats in the House defer to her and do not press her on such matters as upping the federal minimum wage, controlling corporate crime, reducing corporate welfare giveaways, reasserting full Medicare for all, diminishing a militaristic foreign policy, and other policies reputed to be favored by the party's Progressive Caucus. . . . Instead the Progressive Caucus remains moribund, declining to press their policy demands on leader Pelosi, as the hard core of the Tea Party do with their leaders."[63]

As a 2009 Brookings Institute study of congressional party functioning concluded, "A pattern of tighter, more centralized control—which began more than two decades ago under Democratic rule and then intensified under Republican majorities, especially after the 2000 election—continues unabated."[64] The same has become true in state legislatures. As Smith and Greenblatt recently summarized the change, "In recent years . . . there's been less room for individual legislators to promote their pet causes. State legislative leaders began reclaiming the power they had lost over the preceding decades."[65]

The conformity of most Democratic office holders to party establishment norms and priorities, however, extends beyond parliamentary discipline. If ever there was a test of the relative independence and progressiveness of the political practice of Democrats in office it was Bernie Sanders's campaign for the Democratic presidential nomination in 2016. While millions of Democratic voters flaunted the party establishment by organizing and voting for Sanders, Democratic office holders in their vast majority stood by the party establishment as represented by Hillary Clinton. Of the 232 Democrats in both houses of Congress, 209 endorsed Clinton in the primaries, while only 10 endorsed Sanders.[66] Sanders didn't do much better among his comrades in the Congressional Progressive Caucus (CPC). As of October 2015, despite the fact that Sanders was one of its founders in 1991, forty-five out of seventy-five members of the CPC endorsed Hillary Clinton even before the primaries commenced.[67] In fact, only one senator and nine representatives endorsed Sanders, only five of whom were members of the CPC.[68] Thus, seventy out of seventy-five members of the CPC refused to support an *actual* progressive challenge.

Nor did Sanders do well among the nation's 3,170 Democratic state legislators, of whom ninety-one, less than 3 percent, endorsed Sanders compared to over a thousand, or about a third, for Clinton, at least according to lists compiled for Wikipedia.[69] The self-styled progressives of the "liberal" New York City Council didn't do any better. Only three of its fifty-one members endorsed Sanders, only two of the New York City Council's Progressive Caucus, and one of them, Richie Torres of the Bronx, did so on the day before the primary.[70] The Chicago City Council Progressive Caucus did only slightly better, with three of its eleven endorsing Sanders out of a total of fifty council members.[71] Those hoping to find allies among current "progressives" in the quest to somehow change this party or create a split from are bound to be disappointed.

The growth of the Democratic Party's business-funded bureaucracy over the past half century, the increase in legislative discipline, and the soaring role of money in elections has changed this capitalist party, as well as its rival and the whole political process. The powerful combination of increased business intervention in the political process and party structures, the increased *purchase* of campaign conduct, along with the intensified party competition driven by the rightward-moving polarization of the two major parties has meant an enormous increase in the amount and role of money in elections and legislation since the 1970s. The two-year election cycle for state and federal nonpresidential elections amounted to nearly $4 billion as of the 2014 election cycle and will certainly go up every two years. The presidential election may cost as much as $5 billion in 2016, double that of 2012.[72] In addition to party politics, business has poured billions of dollars into lobbying efforts that have had a substantial impact on legislation at both the state and national levels. In 1996 Washington-based lobbyists spent $400 million, hit a high point in 2010 at $1.8 billion, and then fell slightly to $1.6 billion in 2015, about 85 percent of this coming from business.[73] As we saw earlier, state-level lobbying operations have also expanded enormously. I mention this only to illustrate that business, which accounts for most lobbying expenditures, has been willing to spend generously on political influence despite falling profit rates and repeated recessions. The main concern here, however, is with election spending.

Campaign fundraising, of course, has been changing. Enter the digital crowdfunding platform—above all ActBlue, the leading digital platform for Democratic political fundraising via small contributions. ActBlue and similar outfits such as Crowdpac digitally bundle small contributions made by credit card and earmarked for specific candidates, groups of candidates, committees, or causes.[74] ActBlue reports that, as of September 1, 2016, it has raised "$1,268,294,690 dollars for Democrats and progressive causes in just 12 years." In the 2016 election cycle, up to September, it had distributed over $450 million, about two-thirds of which, or around $300 million, went to election campaigns.[75] Ironically, it was Bernie Sanders's campaign that really put ActBlue on the map. It was his 2.5 million donors who built ActBlue's three-million-plus credit card file.[76] So is this the rebel Democrat's path to campaign funding?

Actually, no. It is any Democrat's path to fundraising and is meant to enhance the party's ability to win office. As of September 2016 it was raising money for Sanders's re-election to the Senate in 2018 but also, on a much larger scale, for Hillary Clinton's race for the presidency, along with scores of run-of-the-mill Democrats. In the 2016 primary mentioned above, Debbie Wasserman Schultz used ActBlue to help her beat Tim Canova, who was backed by Sanders, in the Florida Democratic primary.[77] Of the top fifteen congressional recipients of contributions via ActBlue in recent elections, four were members of the center-right New Democrat Coalition (NDC), one of whom, David Scott of Georgia, was also a conservative Blue Dog, while only two were members of the Congressional Progressive Caucus.[78] A scan of who is raising money via ActBlue in the 2016 race for the House of Representatives shows a few members of the Congressional Progressive Caucus but scores of "regulars" and NDCers as well.

Not only do individual candidates use ActBlue, so does the DCCC. Of hundreds of DCCC expense items reported by OpenSecrets, ActBlue came in sixth at $1.3 million.[79] Party-ActBlue connections are intense. Indeed, while Erin Hill, ActBlue's executive director since 2005, is undoubtedly a liberal, she is also very much a party insider. As her bio for the 2014 Social Enterprise Conference describes her political career: "Erin served on the finances staff of the Kerry '04 presidential campaign and the Democratic National Committee. She's worked in fundraising for scores of congressional and statewide campaigns as well as serving tours of duty on Capitol Hill and in the Massachusetts State House."[80] This is the résumé of an experienced party apparatchik.

ActBlue, despite its liberal origins and while technically independent of the Democratic Party structure, is in fact now part of that party's fundraising apparatus. As the Occupy Wall Street website put it bluntly in 2011, ActBlue is "a Democratic Party front group."[81] It is, in other words, yet one more piece of the multilayered earthworks that keep the party and its establishment in place and safe from assault. ActBlue is no more a vehicle for reform or Left policy influence than the DCCC, DSCC, and DLCC that feed the party's insatiable need for money. Nor is it in any way democratically responsible to the millions of small donors whose contributions it forwards to this broad array of Democratic candidates. It is, rather, the latest and most high-tech development in the history of small donation political funding from the Republican direct mail "revolution" of the 1970s through the professional bundling "wave of the future" of the 1990s and early 2000s and now the digital platform.[82]

As noted above in terms of the 2016 presidential primaries, crowdfunding simply helped up the ante of what is needed to win at every level. Capital will be more than willing to escalate this political arms race as they have for decades. While profit rates have fallen and the recession taken a bite, as we saw in table I above the rate of exploitation has risen over the neoliberal period. As a result, the mass of corporate profits has continued to grow, recently by over two and a half times from $788 billion in 2002 to $2.1 trillion in 2015.[83] On top of that, according to a recent study by Saez and Zucman, the top 1 percent of households in the United States now owns 41.8 percent of the nation's private wealth, which amounts to about $35 trillion as of 2015.[84] It can be safely assumed that these superrich families, like the corporations and industry associations, will continue to be willing to invest some of this outsized accumulated wealth in politics in order to defend their way of life and their class. Even assuming that outfits like ActBlue can double, triple, or even quadruple their funds in the next few election cycles, there is nothing to stop capital from out-bidding them and pushing the costs of elections up even higher. Crowdfunding is, however inadvertently, certain to inflate the costs of winning political office in the already astronomically expensive American Scheme of politics.

From the description of the structure and functioning of the real Democratic Party given above, as well as from its history, it should be clear that the idea of the Left, however broadly defined, "taking over" this political conglomerate is pure fantasy. Not even Bernie Sanders's campaign was ever predicated on such a strategy since it would have required simultaneously sweeping congressional and many state elections as well—something incumbency rates and costs preclude because only marginal gains are possible in each election cycle. The Democratic Party is, after all, a multilayered organization backed by vast amounts of capitalist money, an army of apparatchiks, consultants, digital manipulators, lawyers, and a legion of elected officials desirous of holding on to office who are also heavily dependent of business money.

Bernie Sanders, of course, did extremely well in the primaries, once again raising the idea of an unpredictable "takeover" from the top. Even if he had won a majority of elected delegates, the praetorian guard of "super delegates" could have halted the rebellion. And even if his troops had miraculously broken through their ranks, Sanders would have found himself as a lonely figure at the head of a vast army of apparatchiks, office holders, fundraisers, consultants, and even many voters who were not prepared to follow. However interesting it might be to speculate on what would have happened if he had won or indeed become president, whatever might have followed would not have amounted to a "takeover" of so complex, well-funded, and multilayered a conglomerate as the Democratic Party. Most likely it would have amounted to a permanent state of internal party warfare. In any case, a top-down takeover of the Democratic Party is not only unfeasible but, from the vantage point of building a democratic mass left organization, wrongheaded. As almost everyone on the left agrees, the Democratic Party is in no way a democratic organization. Tinkering with its rules and procedures at the top cannot change a structure and institution that has grown stronger over nearly half a century. Not surprisingly, few of those on the left who advocate working through its electoral and legislative channels today even raise the possibility.

Overall, the Democratic Party is more organized at every level from the states to the Congress to the DNC, more supported by and dependent on (much more) business money and wealthy donors, and more neoliberal than during the era of realignment, McGovern, or the Jackson insurgency. At that time, the illusory "liberal-labor coalition" not only failed to move the party to the left even as the Dixiecrats began their exit but was also unable to stop its lunge toward neoliberalism. In fact, as labor officials complained, the liberals seemed to have gone AWOL certainly on labor issues. Nor could the Rainbow Coalition assault on the top halt its business-driven rightward thrust. How, then, do today's Democratic reformers, progressives, and socialists intend to use this multilayered, professionally run, financially well-greased political conglomerate to create a left-liberal or social democratic party?

The most recent left strategy for work in the Democratic Party appears to be to create a split within the party to the left. Jason Schulman in the *New Politics* article cited several times above, in an argument for why socialists should have been active in the Sanders campaign stated, "The movement to elect Sanders represents the best opportunity to build a much larger socialist movement—and hopefully a split from the Democratic Party that results in an independent leftist party—that I've seen in my lifetime."[85] Certainly, many of the "Bernie or Bust" activists who demonstrated at the Democratic convention in Philadelphia were hoping for just such a split. Undoubtedly too optimistic about the short-term possibility, some nevertheless appear to favor the strategic idea of a split from the Democratic Party as the most likely road to a new party of the Left. Bhaskar Sunkara, editor of *Jacobin* and a leader of the Left Caucus of the Democratic Socialists of America (DSA), also in an article advocating work within the Sanders campaign, talked about tensions within the Democratic Party that "raise the possibility for the realignment of progressive forces on a totally different basis." He goes on, however, to clarify: "This is a different project than the attempts of Michael Harrington (and others) to turn the Democrats into a more traditional social democratic party by pushing it leftward. Our goal must be to transcend the Democratic Party entirely."[86]

Such a perspective shares with the idea of building a new working-class-based party the perception that the Democratic Party as an institution, along with most of its elected officials, is out of step with the anger and political preferences of its major voting blocs—mainly African Americans, Latinos, and working-class people in general as well as a large percentage of young people of both middle- and working-class origin. This, of course, is absolutely true. But even if we assume this political dissonance is as strong or stronger than it was at previous times, such as the civil rights era, there is a good deal of truth in what Paul Heideman writes in *Jacobin*: "The contradiction between the party's base and its investors has existed since the birth of the modern Democratic Party in the New Deal. It has persisted through the Great Society, through the New Politics era, through Carter, all the way up until the present. Again and again, this contradiction alone has proven inert, unable to change the basic structure of power within the party."[87]

It is not that people are inert but that the contradiction itself is because even in periods of social upheaval there is essentially no way for the mass of Democratic voters to impact the party's undemocratic multilayered structure, including its sitting office holders once elected. Trying to make the voices of the unrepresented voters heard by becoming an office holder means overcoming party opposition in the individualized and costly process of the primary, defeating an incumbent in either the primary or general election, attempting to act as a lone or minority force for change once elected by resisting party leaders and discipline, and then getting reelected. All these barriers to making any difference in this rigged setup explain why it never happens, even though many have tried over the decades. Nothing is changed. There is no new democratic political organization among angry working-class voters. The contradiction remains inert. The polarized two-party American Scheme with its "lesser-evil" cul-de-sac means that the disaffected Democrat has no place to go other than the "greater evil" or a faux-populist like Trump, which some have done, or possibly a protest vote for a minor party such as the Greens, precisely because there is no mass alternative. And there is no mass alternative, for one thing, because generations of union officials and activists, civil rights leaders, environmentalists, community organizers, and socialists have squandered their efforts in attempting to realign, reform, and pressure this business-friendly conglomerate behemoth to little effect.

If creating a split among Democrats were just a matter of shifting sections of the electorate, there would have to be something already taking shape outside of the Democratic Party for them to gravitate toward. Alternatively, such a split or transcendence would have to involve a significant number of elected officials. This seems to be the main version of the split perspective. Given the lack of support Sanders received from Democratic politicians and legislators at all levels, including his fellow CPC members, it seems doubtful that these "progressives" have the intestinal fortitude, or the politics, to lead such a development. Particularly since it means legislative limbo for the foreseeable future and a formidable challenge to their seats by the remaining (dominant) forces of the party.

Perhaps then it would be a new wave of leftists and socialists getting elected to important offices, which appears to be at least one part of the strategy of both DSA and Sanders's post-election spinoff, Our Revolution. Given the reality of incumbency, high cost, and, no doubt, bitter resistance from the entire Democratic apparatus, this appears every bit as utopian as the formation of a third party that attempts to be a real national opposition by trying for the same high levels of political office—more on this below. In any case, there is no organization on the horizon with a significant enough social base to be such a center of gravity for a split from the Democrats. Without one, the split perspective lacks credibility. What there is at the moment is an organization dedicated to pointing the forces that made the Sanders campaign the unique political event it was *into* the Democratic Party—it is called Our Revolution.

Revolution by 501(c)(4)?

There is no doubt that the Sanders campaign for the Democratic presidential nomination was one of the most exciting events in US electoral politics in years. It not only drew the support of millions for a self-proclaimed democratic socialist, it activated thousands of those new to politics, introduced radical redistributionist programs, tapped into a huge body of sentiment that favored such programs, attracted significant grassroots labor support, and for a moment pushed the political discourse of the nation to the left. That many of Sanders's supporters wanted the proposed "political revolution" to continue after the Democratic convention was clear, and Bernie himself indicated that it would. The name of that continuation is Our Revolution. Launched on August 24, 2016, on a national webcast that went out to 2,600 local meetings, it seemed an auspicious start.[88]

Even before the launch, however, there was trouble. When longtime Sanders campaign manager Jeff Weaver was appointed president of Our Revolution, eight of fifteen staff members resigned. Partly, they said, it was Weaver's abrasive management style; more importantly it was the decision he made, presumably with Sanders's approval, about the very nature of the organization that was to be at the center of this grassroots revolution. Instead of a democratic membership organization, Our Revolution is to be a 501(c)(4) "social welfare" nonprofit whose activities are defined and limited by the Internal Revenue Service code, that is, the state. Under the IRS code, its activities are limited to fundraising and spending for various purposes. Its spending on political campaigns is limited to under 50 percent of the funds it raises. The rest can go to issue-based campaigns and causes. In addition, it cannot direct or coordinate with election campaigns. It can, however, buy infinite TV and other media time, something the exiting Our Revolution staffers think is a mistaken emphasis for a grassroots movement organization but that Weaver favors. Some even accuse Weaver of wanting to raise money from "billionaires."[89]

While this IRS designation has been around for a long time, 501(c)(4)s became popular as a means for wealthy people and corporations to raise and spend unlimited funds after the 2010 *United Citizens* Supreme Court ruling that political spending was "free speech." It has become the corporate and wealthy person's fundraising conduit de jure because the source of contributions to it, no matter how large, do not need to be publicly disclosed—they are "dark funds," as this undisclosed money is called. Furthermore, the 501(c)(4) can pass on these "dark funds" to the equally trendy and mostly sinister super PACs without reporting where the money came from. Let me repeat, a 501(c)(4) is not a democratic membership organization.[90] Nevertheless, it does play a role in elections.

Initially, Our Revolution endorsed and presumably provided some funds for seventy candidates, most of them running for state or local office. All but two were running as Democrats. The two were running for open seats in the nonpartisan city council elections in Richmond, California, and had the backing of the Richmond Progressive Alliance, which will be discussed below.[91] All the others were officially Democrats, almost all with previous experience as Democratic office holders. In August, Jeff Weaver proudly announced that its "three candidates who won last night . . . join . . . other Our Revolution candidates who have already won their Democratic primaries." Most had run as incumbents, according to *Alternet*.[92] Our Revolution's high-profile non-incumbent challenger, Tim Canova, as we saw above, lost badly to incumbent neoliberal party "regular" Debbie Wasserman Schultz. According to their profiles on Ballotpedia, all of the eleven other endorsed candidates for US Congress who had won their primaries but one were either incumbents or ran for an open seat. The one exception was running in a safe Republican district in Wisconsin with little hope of winning.[93]

By the time of the election Our Revolution had endorsed 105 candidates, most of them for state or local office. Altogether fifty-seven won and forty-eight lost. Of the sixteen candidates for US House of Representative, eight lost and eight won. Five of the winners were incumbents, and the other three ran in open seat races to replace retiring Democrats. None were among the six Democrats who defeated incumbent Republicans. Of the three candidates for US Senate, all lost, including three-term senator Russ Feingold of Wisconsin, who had been ousted by a Republican Tea Party candidate in 2010 and attempted to recapture his Senate seat in 2016.[94] None of the nineteen running for congressional seats endorsed by Our Revolution replaced a sitting Republican. All the candidates endorsed by Our Revolution were already running for office. Our Revolution didn't add anyone to this stream or in any way directly aid or coordinate their campaigns, an activity banned to 501(c)(4)s. It simply endorsed these candidates and possibly defrayed some of their campaign expenses. One has to ask just what difference this 501(c)(4) really makes.

More importantly, is the addition of yet one more big Democratic fundraising operation, let alone one that can raise and channel "dark funds," really what is needed to carry out a "political revolution"? Did Bernie or anyone really think another state-sanctioned and limited bureaucratic fundraising apparatus would energize and mobilize the millions of Sandernistas who made the first foray into a new politics possible? Wouldn't a democratic grassroots organization able to run independent candidates be more to the point?

One "post-Sanders" perspective that appears to be related to the hopes of Our Revolution is to storm the Democratic Party at the precinct- and district-level organizations and primaries in the hopes of gaining office or influence by virtue of sheer numbers. In addition to the facts of incumbency, money, professional and purchased campaign tactics, experience in repelling primary challengers, and prior organization that await such an invasion, there is the additional countervailing fact that those attempting to work at the precinct or district level of the party to elect a left candidate in the primary will be expected to work for the winner, who more often than not, will be the incumbent they tried to defeat. In fact, party activists who plan to stay for any time, of course, will also be expected to work for the entire ticket. Most of these candidates will be the very upholders of the neoliberal or centrist status quo the rebels hoped to dislodge. In this way, the would-be rebels will end up reinforcing the status quo they sought to challenge. Anyone who thinks this party, including its apparatchiks, organizations, and office holders, is up for grabs, on its way to becoming an American social democracy, or on the verge of a split needs to look again.

Overall, the prospects for reforming or splitting from a Democratic Party in serious retreat as the basis for the formation of a truly progressive breakthrough in US politics seem hopeless and the efforts to achieve it pointless or worse—a squandering of the potential of the Sanders challenge. How then to create a mass alternative to the Democrats and the two-party American Scheme?

CHAPTER TEN

Electoral Politics from a Socialist Perspective

Since there are no simple formulas or panaceas, we must return to all that has been said in earlier chapters about the changing terrain of class struggle and of the working class itself. Two points need to be made: 1) as already emphasized, change in the United States has historically come about not through elections or mainstream politics per se but through mass social upsurge and 2) any attempt to build a new party that is not democratic and based on mass labor and social movements, organizations, and actions will fail to have enough strength to defeat the two major parties *and* force concessions from capital, which will stand behind the two old parties. The need for on-the-ground resistance and organization is all the more urgent in the face of a Trump presidency, but it is essential to any effort toward building a credible political Left. Most of the new left social democratic and left populist parties in Europe, even when they originate in mass struggles, such as Spain's Podemos, illustrate this problem despite the electoral advantages they have in parliamentary systems with elements of proportional representation or serial runoffs.[1]

Many social movement activists and socialists in the United States and elsewhere have looked to the formation of these new left parties in Europe in the last several years, but there are crucial differences that need to be examined. For one thing, they are membership organizations, not simply creations of the electoral system. Unlike third parties in the United States, they seem to have found a mass base reflecting the same sort of consciousness underlying movements such as Occupy Wall Street, Black Lives Matter, Fight for

Fifteen, union reform movements, or the Sanders campaign. This new generation of left parties in Europe, however, appears to be stumbling on its lack of emphasis on social struggle on the ground and overemphasis on winning elections. The problem here is not simply the classic problem of "reform or revolution," although that always underlies a socialist perspective. The new left parties in Europe do not propose a socialist transition anywhere in the foreseeable future. They are reformist parties.

Susan Watkins, while warning us that "any characterization of these forces can only be provisional," describes them in *New Left Review*: "Respectful of NATO, anti-austerity, pro-public investment and (more guardedly) ownership, sceptical of 'free trade': as a first approximation, we might call them new, small, weak social democracies."[2] Some, like Podemos and the Parti de Gauche, seem more left-populist but still fit Watkins's basic description. Many of their policies and goals, however, are transitional in nature in that they challenge not only neoliberalism but also the priorities of capital in this era, while at the same time reflecting real popular sentiments. Most of these new parties have been influenced by or even had their origins in the various global justice, occupation, and social movements, although this influence has tended to diminish. Unlike in the United States, where the Democrats remain a major force, the rightward shift and even collapse of the traditional social democratic and communist parties in Mediterranean Europe "opened up a representational vacuum on the left of the political spectrum."[3]

Taking advantage of this vacuum, these new parties attempted to gather in the various forces of opposition that have arisen as a result of austerity, urban housing costs, work intensification, falling wages, unemployment, and the vise the European Union and particularly the Eurozone imposes on the working classes of its member states. As Watkins writes, "In the broadest sense, this is, again, a defence of labour against capital, within the existing system."[4] These are important tasks that, given its small size and fragmentation, the revolutionary Left in Europe, as in the United States to an even greater degree, cannot assume by itself. So socialists of various stripes work within these parties as long as they fulfill this potential. As indicated above, however, these parties invariably run up against a wall precisely because, among other factors, they have in both theory and practice gotten the relationship between mass struggle and electoralism backwards and upside down.

Writing about the development of Podemos in recent years, Luke Stobart notes the influence of Chantal Mouffe and Ernesto Laclau on the leadership of that party and the practice that flows from this essentially left populist politics that emphasizes the leading role of intellectuals. His critique applies as well to the new left social democratic parties such as Germany's Die Linke. He writes, "Left-populism shares with social democracy a fundamentally institutional form of politics; both cast social mobilization in a supporting role at best."[5] Left-populism, he continues, attempts "to build a constituency through conflict," but it is the party organization and its electoral efforts that become central. Ironically, the very social movements that made such parties possible fade in importance in party practice. As a consequence, Podemos has emerged from its grassroots origins "as a top-down party with a monolithic central leadership," while the left-populist electoral approach "encouraged deepening political moderation."[6] To one extent or another this has been the case with other new left parties in Europe. The left-populism of Jean-Luc Mélenchon's Parti de Gauche in France, for example, has moved toward traditional French republicanism and national "sovereignty," which "signals a further shift away from class politics, and a politics of the oppressed more broadly, to a narrow-minded nationalism."[7] Putting electoralism first and relegating mass struggle to a secondary supporting role inevitably leads to moderation of party program and goals, increasingly unaccountable leadership and the loss of party democracy, and ultimately to declining electoral fortunes as well.

Periods of mass upsurge, as we have seen, are relatively rare and unpredictable. Nevertheless, there is always conflict and struggle, particularly in urban areas and in the capital-labor relation itself. In addition to the occasional general strikes that occur in Latin Europe, every major city has seen struggles around housing, education, health care, employment, and racial, gender, and class inequality. There is also the constant struggle over work intensification, casualization, and pay. Indeed, Podemos owes its origins to such urban struggles. Electoralism, however, exerts a powerful pull on resources, activities, and the thinking of leaders. Such has certainly been the case with Pablo Iglesias of Podemos and Mélenchon of the Parti de Gauche. In most of Europe, election to parliament is far easier than election to Congress in the United States due to systems of proportional representation or serial runoffs. So the temptation to focus on such high-level office is greater, and the ability to establish a new party as a presence in parliament, even as a minority, is also greater. This probably adds to the tendency to downplay strikes, occupations, demonstrations, and other forms of mass direct action as pressure tactics or merely supportive of the party's goals. For a new party to gain a foothold in the United States over time, this prioritization must be reversed, both in the elevation of mass action and movement building to a primary position and in the level of political offices a fledgling left party seeks.

By now, the reader may be thinking: aren't all the barriers to running in the Democratic Party, such as the enormous costs and high levels of incumbency, also problems for independent campaigns and third parties? In addition, of course, isn't gaining ballot access also a problem? Not exactly. Some hurdles, such as Democratic primaries, the state parties, and various national committees (DNC, DCCC, DSCC) are specific to running and serving as a Democrat. There are, nevertheless, two aspects to the possibilities of independent political action in the United States: the level at which it is aimed and the necessity of an active mass base discussed above. The two are inextricably intertwined.

Also interrelated is the matter of what, in the long run, we are seeking to build. Certainly it cannot be just an individual or personal campaign, a temporary slate, or PAC, much less a 501(c)(4). The whole point is to create a mass democratic membership organization or party. Whether this new party is initially socialist or simply points in that direction will depend on the consciousness of those willing to take this step, but it must go beyond conventional social democracy. Social democracy either as a historical phase in the development of the workers' movement internationally or as currently practiced wherever it exists has ceased to be an expression, even a reformist one, of the working class. Given all the barriers to effective political action at the national level in the United States, which include not only the well-known problems of the American electoral system but also the rise of the populist Right, on the one hand, and the attitudes and institutional ties of much of the top-level leadership of the unions and various social movement organizations, on the other, it makes the most sense to build from the ground up.

The experience of the Labor Party, launched in 1996 under the leadership of Tony Mazzocchi of the Oil, Chemical, and Atomic Workers, which tried to start a national party based on union affiliation, is relevant in this respect. The neoliberal direction of the Clinton administration provided sufficient frustration to push many in organized labor toward the idea of a "party of our own." Mazzocchi commissioned a survey that revealed that 53 percent of the union leaders, staffers, and members polled agreed, "It's time for labor to build a new political party of working people independent of the two major parties."[8] This was certainly a remarkable finding. Nevertheless, by the early 2000s it was clear that the Labor Party had lost its early momentum. While there were many reasons for its failure, a major problem was that even those union leaders who signed up for the project hesitated to run candidates or endanger existing relations with various Democratic politicians. Its function as a "non-electoral" party was never clear. When George W. Bush and his neo-conservative aides appeared on the scene by 2000, the union leaders flocked to the Democratic banner once again. While there is no question that organized labor must be a central part of any new party, it will have to start at the grassroots among union activists and local unions in urban centers, including smaller ones like Richmond, California, and Lorain County, Ohio, along with other primarily working-class social movement activists and groups.

In electoral terms, the starting point of a new mass political organization means running first at the local and possibly the state levels. National links will be important, but to ensure a democratic structure and practice building from the ground up is essential. In practical terms, campaigns at this level are less costly, more susceptible to grassroots door-to-door campaigning, and more likely to remain close to community and workplace activist groups and to build democratic organization and leadership and candidate accountability. Ballot access is also generally less demanding, and, as argued below, the "spoiler" effect is less of a problem given the high concentration of Democratic office holders and voters in most cities. Below, some examples will be briefly examined.

The other side of this coin is building on the basis of existing labor and social movement struggles in the local area. As argued in chapter 6, we cannot predict when or even if another major working-class upsurge will explode—although there are plenty of reasons to believe it will, due to the enormous pressures on working-class life. But every city in the United States has both its social problems and grassroots efforts to combat them, from the Fight for Fifteen, Black Lives Matter, immigrants' rights organizations, and workers' centers to environmental campaigners, tax reformers, union organizing drives, and embattled unions and their members in America's digital-Dickensian workplaces and lousy jobs. They are not yet mass movements, but they are the material from which bigger, more explosive movements can come. These are the core of any new political organization hoping to gain a working-class base and membership as well as power inside and outside of political office. While the top levels of the union leadership are deeply tied to the Democrats in various ways, local unions can and have been crucial to local-level third-party candidates in most of the cases reviewed below. There are already some embryonic examples of this.

One is the Richmond Progressive Alliance (RPA) in Richmond, California. The account of the RPA here is taken mainly from longtime labor organizer and journalist Steve Early's book, *Refinery Town*. Richmond is "a largely non-white, working-class community of 110,000."[9] For decades Chevron Oil had dominated the city and its politics, at least until Green Party activist Gayle McLaughlin was elected mayor in 2006 with a grassroots campaign that "sent political shockwaves across the Bay Area."[10] Term limits put an end to McLaughlin's role as mayor, but the RPA put together a slate for mayor and city council, with McLaughlin as a council candidate, which won in 2014, increasing the progressive, anti-Chevron majority on the council. But just what is the Richmond Progressive Alliance?

As Early describes it, "The RPA is simultaneously an electoral formation, a membership organization, a coalition of community groups, and a key coordinator of grassroots education and citizen mobilization." Its candidates refuse corporate donations.

"The Alliance relies on membership dues, door-to-door canvassing to expand its grassroots base, and, in election years, small individual donors and modest public matching funds for its city council and mayoral candidates."[11] As it prepared for the elections, it received backing from the Service Employees Local 1021, the California Nurses Association, the National Union of Healthcare Workers, the Amalgamated Transit Union, Communications Workers of America Local 9119, and others.

Chevron for its part put up over $3 million to pay for ads, including vicious negative ads, mostly through a front group called Moving Forward. RPA, however, already had a strong volunteer force from previous fights and campaigns. Plus, RPA "urged canvassers to take time to talk to voters, providing information and having discussions that would go well beyond any script." Furthermore, the unions didn't just give money and endorsements. Service Employees Local 1021 and the California Nurses Association formed a labor-community coalition called Working Families, which "knocked on ten thousand doors and called five thousands absentee voters," according to RPA organizer, socialist, and veteran union activist Mike Parker.[12] Grassroots, door-to-door campaigning and a long history of movement activism defeated Big Oil and Big Money. As Early describes their victory celebration: "When the polls closed there in 2014, labor and community activists, environmental justice campaigners, police reformers, gay rights activists, anti-foreclosure fighters, and defenders of the foreign-born were all partying like they lived in another country. In reality they were just fortunate to reside in a city where more than a decade of local organizing made it possible to defeat candidates funded by one of the richest corporations in the world."[13]

One more thing needs to be said about the RPA. As Early described the membership, "The group united liberal Democrats, socialists, independents, and third-party voters affiliated with the California Greens or Peace and Freedom Party." Liberal Democrats? Hmm? Does this mean that the RPA is not really a case of independent political action? No, this is a fact of life that any effort to build a new political movement or party will confront. A great many people that such a project will and must attract if it is to become a mass organization will be or will have been Democrats, in the sense of registering as one, identifying as one, or even being an office holder. The point is to pull them away from the Democratic Party by providing an alternative, which is what the RPA is doing.

In this case, the county Democratic Party lent a hand to the process. Elections in Richmond are technically nonpartisan, so there is no Democratic ballot line. But candidates can seek a variety of endorsements, including from one or another party. Two of the RPA candidates, being registered Democrats, asked the West Contra Costa Democrats to endorse them in hopes this would bring in more votes or funds. The West Contra Costa Democrats refused. Similarly, the RPA-backed mayoral candidate, Tom Butt, also a registered Democrat and office holder, was turned down by the West Contra Costa Democrats and by the Contra Costa County Democratic Party as a whole.[14] Nevertheless, the problem raised its ugly head when in 2016, the RPA-backed Democratic mayor Butt broke with RPA councillors and candidates running for open seat positions over the issue of rent control that Butt, along with business interests and regular Democrats, opposed.[15]

This is the sort of problem that has plagued efforts at independent political action in the past, from the Populists of the 1890s through the farmer-labor parties of the 1930s. The RPA will survive this in large part because it remains its own independent membership organization with socialists, Greens, and independents in its ranks. Those who think the strategy is to split people from the Democrats might learn from the RPA example that to do that you need an independent movement and organization with a base active on issues beyond election time or political office as an alternative— and that your Democratic allies may not be on the same wavelength.

Despite its problems, this approach is completely different from the "fusion" strategy of the Working Families Party (WFP), which runs official Democratic candidates on its own ballot line. It's a pressure tactic designed, as Dan Cantor, WFP's executive director, puts it, "to yank and pull and prod the Democrats to the left." He uses the analogy of a left "Tea Party."[16] As an effort to move politics leftward it does attract support from unions and union activists. Formed in New York State in 1998, it now operates in six other states and the District of Columbia.[17] In effect, however, the WFP is a semi-autonomous adjunct of the Democratic Party, tying its supporters and activists to the mast of the Democratic Party.

Though one of still few, the RPA is not the only example of successful local independent political action on the left. There is the 2013 election of Kshama Sawant to Seattle's city council as an open socialist with more than ninety thousand votes. Sawant, a member of Socialist Alternative, was an Occupy activist and centered her 2013 campaign around the movement for a city minimum wage of $15, and, as in Richmond, her votes came mostly from low-income people of color. She was reelected in 2015.[18] As of 2014, the Greens could count 131 office holders across the country, almost all in local offices, fifty-three of them in California.[19] The most longstanding and probably best-known example at the state level is the Vermont Progressive Party (VPP), associated with Bernie Sanders. What is most significant about the VPP is that its members not only hold local office but by 2014 had been able to use that base to win seven seats in the Vermont General Assembly and three in the state senate, as well as elect the state's auditor of accounts, who was also endorsed by the Democrats. General Assembly districts in Vermont, however, are very small, with about 4,000 in each.[20]

While many of these third parties receive local union support, independent political action launched specifically by unions is, of course, even more rare, but two examples point to such possibilities. In 2013, the Lorain County AFL-CIO fielded a labor slate in towns across that county and elected two dozen labor candidates, at least three of them as independents in contests against Democrats. They called their slate the Lorain Independent Labor Party. The president of the county labor federation said they did this reluctantly, but "when the leaders of the [Democratic] Party just took us for granted and tried to roll over the rights of working people here, we had to stand up."[21] Explaining the background to labor's political insurgency, Russell Saltamontes writes in *Jacobin*, "In Lorain, decades of workplace and community organizing to improve the standard of living for working-class people finally reached a point of direct confrontation with local elites."[22] It is obvious that this history also underlay the 2014 election victory in Lorain County. We will look in more detail at Lorain County below when discussing the Trump phenomenon.

In 2014, the Chicago Teachers Union (CTU), with its new reform leadership, coming off its successful 2012 nine-day strike, and in cooperation with that city's big SEIU health care local and community groups, formed an independent slate called United Working Families (UWF) to challenge "Mayor 1%" Rahm Emanuel and his followers in the city council in the 2015 elections. Chicago elections are nonpartisan, and while some of the incumbent candidates they endorsed were undoubtedly Democrats, UWF nevertheless ran its own candidates on this independent slate. Only one of their council candidates won. CTU member Susan Sadlowski Garza beat incumbent Democrat John Pope in the South Side working-class Tenth Ward by twenty votes even though Pope spent almost twice as much as Garza.[23] UWF represents both the potential of independent politics and its dilemma in that in the context of nonpartisan elections it is possible to put forth a slate that supports both Democrats and genuine independents. Whether the UWF can evolve into a genuine third force remains to be seen.

Winning state legislative office is more difficult than winning local office. Ballot access, however, is not the major barrier. As Jonathan Martin writes, "Non-major party candidates for state representative in most states requires from zero to several hundred signatures."[24] Despite the fact that US ballot access laws are among the worst of any Western capitalist democracy, state-level third parties are a common feature of US politics. Of the 214 state-level parties with ballot status in 2016, 102 were the state and District of Columbia Democratic and Republican Parties. The remaining 112 were third parties. Most were single-state independent parties, but the Libertarians had thirty-three state parties, the Greens twenty-one, the Constitution Party fifteen, and the Reform and Working Families Party four each.[25] In New York State, with some of the most difficult access laws, a third party or independent candidate for state assembly needs only 1,500 signatures of registered voters, though, of course, it is wise to get many more. For permanent ballot status, a third party needs 50,000 votes in a statewide election. Would-be rebel Democrats may actually face a more difficult time making it onto the ballot. First of all, they need a thousand signatures to get into the primary, not that many fewer than an independent. Additionally, "Candidates endorsed by county Republican or Democratic committees usually get help from hundreds of party volunteers," while unendorsed Democratic primary candidates don't.[26]

Winning office as an independent or third-party candidate, however, is a different matter. The Greens, for example, have run seven hundred candidates for state representative and, as of 2015, had won only five seats.[27] Incumbency, as we saw above, is one problem. While the average cost of a state legislative seat is much less than that for Congress, it has been rising as the states have become a major legislative battlefield for the Right. Furthermore, the size of legislative districts varies considerably. The nation's 5,413 state representative districts each represent an average of almost 60,000 people. State house or assembly districts, however, vary in size from about 3,000 people in New Hampshire to 423,396 in California, with most large states running between 90,000 and 126,000. The Vermont Progressive Party's relative success in that state's general assembly, as we saw, stems in part from the fact that legislative districts there are very small.[28]

On the other hand, redistricting over the years has produced a growing number of "one-party" districts across the country so that in as many as 40 percent of state legislative elections there is only one major party candidate and hence no spoiler effect.[29] Virtually all the representatives in the New York State Assembly from New York City's five counties (boroughs), for example, are Democrats. Only Richmond County (Staten Island) and the one district overlapping Richmond and Kings County (Brooklyn) have one Republican each. Thus, in a great many New York City assembly districts there is little Republican opposition and hence less of the spoiler problem. Nevertheless, it is clear that winning state legislative positions requires a sound local base from which to build.

Building, however, means more than effective grassroots campaigning. As argued above, it means prioritizing the movement side of political action more than is yet typical. The enormous consolidation of business and the rising inequality of income and wealth, along with increased business political spending, has made elections more difficult for radical or even "populist" forces on the left above the local level. Any breakthrough will certainly require an acceleration of the sort of urban-based worker and workplace-based organizing described in chapter 6. Critical to this is the importance of permanent organization that can activate those who do not vote, who as we will see in the discussion in the postscript on the 2016 election and Trump's victory, are many. These non-voters number in the millions, are mostly working class and lower income, are to the left of most voters on key economic issues and not much different on social issues, and have ceased to be the target of political party mobilization efforts.[30] On-the-ground organization based on actual movements and activists can mobilize these left-leaning non-voters by helping them to register and acquire the necessary IDs but more importantly by aiding their unionization and offering a politics that addresses their real concerns and a means to win through ongoing grassroots organization.

Cities, Democrats, and Elections

Chapters 4 through 6 argue that a new terrain of class struggle has arisen based on the major changes in US capitalism in the last thirty years or so: the consolidation of capitalist enterprises, the increased capital intensity on the job, and the intense and vulnerable links provided by the rise of supply chain management and advanced logistics. These interrelated changes in the structure of capital are focused to a large extent on urban centers of so-called service work and the movement of goods, itself now a part of the process of production that serves regional and global manufacturing, and hence on concentrations of the reshaped urban working class of this era. While it will be easier to build a new organization or party in small cities like Richmond, California, or midsize ones like Seattle with nonpartisan electoral systems, the big cities are key to shifting power.

As bastions of the Democratic Party, they are also points of political vulnerability in that most of them are now virtually "one-party" Democratic city-states dependent on a mass working-class voter base that is, by almost any left analysis or recent polls, out of step with most of the mostly middle-class, heavily business-funded "representatives" holding most offices and positions in the party's structure. Cities, as the electoral results of 2016 show, are also less susceptible to large-scale Trump support. Democratic politics vary from city to city, of course. New York, under Mayor Bill de Blasio, is allegedly a bastion of liberalism on the left of that spectrum, while Chicago under Emanuel epitomizes the worst of Democratic neoliberalism. Nevertheless, the overwhelming dominance of the Democrats in most of the larger cities also means there is less of a spoiler effect. Furthermore, this disconnect between the sentiments of the working-class voter base expresses itself in the incredibly low voter turnout that characterizes most municipal and state legislative elections. The turnout in New York mayoral elections, which has been falling for decades, was a mere 24 percent in 2013 when de Blasio was elected.[31] As we will see in the discussion of the 2016 election below, non-voters are actually to the left of those who vote on a number of economic questions—and there are millions of them. A new party that can mobilize previous non-voters has a good chance of winning in the long run. This is a tinderbox awaiting a potential explosion if the disenchanted can be mobilized.

The high concentration of Democratic voters in most big cities means the Republicans are not strong enough to make a third-party challenge a spoiler in most local elections. The New York City Council, for example, has only three Republicans of out fifty-one council members, while the total Republican vote, disproportionately concentrated in those three Republican districts, accounted for only 16 percent of the 2013 council vote. Democrats carried the council elections by over 90 percent of the vote in twenty-one districts, by 80 percent in ten districts, and 70 percent in another five. In six districts the election of the Democrat was uncontested. Thus, only nine out of fifty-one districts saw anything approaching a Republican challenge strong enough to make the third-party candidate a spoiler.[32] Chicago city elections are technically nonpartisan, but looking at ballots cast in that city in the 2016 presidential primaries, the Republicans accounted for only 11 percent of that city's voters.[33] Los Angeles city elections are also nonpartisan, but the only Republican candidate in the 2013 mayoral election, where Democrat fought Democrat, received a mere 16 percent of the vote in the nonpartisan primary.[34] Thus, in these and many other cities, the spoiler effect is not a major factor and becoming the "second" party by no means impossible.

Nor is ballot access at the level of city councils an insurmountable barrier. Ballot access in New York State is generally one of the most restrictive in the country. In New York City Council elections, for example, you need 2,700 signatures from registered voters in a council district with a population of approximately 154,000 to get on the ballot as a third party or independent, though it is wise to get a lot more than that. This takes an effort but is hardly impossible if you have the sort of active membership discussed above. The New York City Council also has term limits, which means open-seat council races are fairly common. There were twenty-one open seats in the 2013 council elections.[35] As we saw, turnout was very low and most won their election with fewer than twenty thousand votes in districts with three or four times that many potential voters.

Discounting even the Democrats' inability to defeat Trump in many heavily working-class areas, there are at least four points of vulnerability for even the most liberal of Democratic city administrations and council members: 1) the fact that their national party has left the cities in a financial mess, making major reforms often unaffordable; 2) the amount of business money Democrats take for their election campaigns; 3) the huge amounts of money given to businesses in the form of tax breaks by Democratic administrations and city councils; and 4) the neglect of grassroots organization in favor of voter targeting by the amassing of demographic, consumer, and personal data and expensive mailings or other *purchased* forms of campaigning discussed earlier.

Viewed in a national context, the cities have become the orphans of the neoliberal era and the Democratic Party. Both Democratic and Republican administrations in Washington, along with congressional majorities of both parties essentially deserted the cities as politicians of both parties fought more and more for the suburban vote and put more emphasis on state politics—and, of course, cut back on spending on concentrations of Black and Latino populations. Most cities, after all, were overwhelmingly Democratic and could be taken for granted, and, in any case, their percentage of the national vote was declining. The neoliberal era saw the change from the 1960s with its urban-oriented antipoverty programs and the Urban Development Action Grants of the 1970s to Reagan's severe cuts in urban programs and the Clinton years, when all the major urban development programs were finally "zeroed out." The exceptions were Community Development Block Grants, which have gone heavily to "downtown"; that is, business development. Building on Reagan's "enterprise zones," another tax break scheme, Clinton gave the cities market-oriented "empowerment zones." Noting this change in Democratic policy, political scientists Judd and Swanstrom point to "the way the past friend of the cities, the Democratic Party, has shied away from urban policy." By 1988 the word "city" had disappeared from the Democratic platform.[36]

More importantly, federal money for the cities dried up under Clinton and later Obama as much as under Reagan or George W. Bush. By 2007, on average only 4 percent of city revenues came from the federal government, and they remained at that level as of 2013, the most recent census figure. Obama's American Recovery and Reinvestment Act sent much to the fiscally strapped states, invested heavily in the sort of transportation and infrastructure projects that support the new logistically linked economy, and allocated some money for school construction, as opposed to teachers' salaries or educational materials, but allotted almost nothing for inner-city neighborhoods and populations.[37] Local Democratic politicians have to contend with the fact that their national party has deserted them and is to a large extent responsible for the fiscal problems and budgetary limits of many cities—surely a source of electoral vulnerability from the left.

The amount of business money that pours into Democratic election campaigns in cities, both directly and, since the *Citizens United* ruling, as "independent" expenditures, is often significant or huge. Since as things stand with no serious Republican or third-party opponent, for Democrats the primaries or the nonpartisan runoffs *are* the election. As a result, they tend to be crowded, expensive, and the target of business money. The general election is frequently more open and less expensive, particularly with a strong grassroots organization.

Looking at the example of New York City, it was in the primaries that real estate's front group Jobs for New York poured its nearly $5 million of "independent" spending into the 2013 council elections, much of it on Democrats in sixteen open-seat contests, for an average of $251,000 per candidate. This is far more than the $150,000 or so in direct spending by the candidates' campaigns, some of which is also business money. Jobs for New York, in turn, gets most of its money from firms "associated with specific development projects"—in other words, developers.[38] Thus, while unions also give large amounts to candidates, the primaries are awash in business money. Even some who don't ask for it get it. This included some $267,000 from Jobs for New York spent in support of Bronx council candidate Ritchie Torres and another $111,000 spent opposing one of his main opponents in the primary, which is ten times what the PACs of the United Federation of Teachers (UFT) and Service Employees International Union (SEIU) Local 32B/J spent on Torres's election. Torres disowned the Jobs for New York campaign in his favor, but the money was spent by Jobs for New York in support for him anyway, and he won.[39] Things were not much different in Chicago's 2015 city council (aldermanic) races where what the Illinois Public Interest Research Group (PIRG) called the "money primary," that is, the fundraising prior to the actual election, determined who would win in the nonpartisan primary election in 93 percent of cases. In that election incumbents outraised and outspent challengers five to one.[40]

Then there is the huge amount of money cities spend on tax breaks for business and the better off. In New York City, for example, these are euphemistically called "tax expenditures." Tax breaks under the city's five largest "expenditures" for real estate, income, and excise taxes for the four fiscal years under de Blasio, 2013 through 2016, increased by 22 percent over those of the previous four years under Bloomberg—from $12.9 billion to $15.7 billion, rising each year.[41] A small amount goes to the elderly or poor for housing, but most goes to big business, developers, gentrifiers, and condo owners. It was these tax breaks that accelerated gentrification in the 1970s and 1980s and pushed big projects such as Trump Place in the 2000s.[42]

These "expenditures" are reviewed and approved by the city council as part of the budget process.[43] Members of the Progressive Caucus have objected to the fact that not all companies or projects receiving such tax breaks pay their employees the minimum wage or live up to their job creation and retention obligations. The Progressive Caucus calls for "thorough evaluation" and "oversight" of projects receiving tax breaks, but, aside from stopping them for "big banks," they do not call for ending or even reining in these vast give-aways.[44] In fact, as a strategy for creating jobs, tax breaks are of limited value. As an article in *Dissent* sympathetic to de Blasio put it, "The effects of such local job creation efforts are modest."[45]

Chicago's Progressive Caucus, with eleven out of fifty council members, simply calls on the Emanuel administration to "reform" a tax diversion system that "directs of hundreds of millions of dollars annually away from the public schools, parks, and other departments into "development projects" rather than calling for its abolition and replacement with a system that spends recovered tax income directly on social needs. Similarly, it only asks that "public-private partnerships," which are another drain on city resources in favor of capital, be "managed with taxpayers as a priority."[46]

Yet these tax breaks and public-private partnerships are aspects of the increasing economic inequality more and more people find unacceptable, both in providing yet more wealth for the wealthy and in limiting what cities can spend directly on housing, education, health care, and so on. All of this tells us that liberal Democrats are vulnerable in their urban lairs. For one thing, liberals who want good things cannot see alternatives beyond the limits imposed by capital. For socialists, the critique of and opposition to such programs as tax abatements and public-private partnerships is transitional in that it points to alternatives that go beyond what capital demands. Furthermore, the redirection of city funds to direct investment in housing, education, and health care would create more services and jobs and challenge the neoliberal assumption that only the market can supply such things efficiently. This sort of fight, of course, will require much more than even radical elected officials. It will require movements and direct actions in the workplaces, streets, public places, and neighborhoods. And, given the limits of municipal resources, it would mean taking the fight to state capitals and Washington, that is, to both the Democrats and Republicans who are participating in the neglect of the cities.

New York is thought of as more "liberal" than most US cities not only for its mayor, de Blasio, but for its city council, which boasts its own Progressive Caucus. Like its congressional namesake it takes left-of-center positions on many issues, but one has to ask just how independent it is. For one thing, its members take business money, including real estate donations. As one city council member commented, "If you look at members of the Progressive Caucus, a lot of them do very well from contributions from the real estate world and other supposed boogeymen of progressive politics." For another, its role has become "more complicated" since the election of de Blasio, according to caucus member Ritchie Torres, and apparently more limited despite having nineteen of the council's fifty-one members, including the speaker of the council. As it is no longer an opposition, Torres says of its function, "I think of it as a support service, not as a litmus test, not a substitute for a party; it's a policy support service."[47] This sounds pretty lame.

Like its congressional counterpart, New York's Progressive Caucus also failed the Sanders litmus test, as only two of its members supported Sanders; one, Torres, did so only the day before the primary—too little, too late. Like the majority of other council members, most caucus members obediently endorsed Clinton or remained safely on the fence. The sole other council member to support Sanders was not a Progressive Caucus member.[48] While who they endorsed in the 2016 presidential primary may not be important to most voters, it well might be to many activists, on whom any new electoral efforts must be based. Similarly, important to some activists is the fact that caucus members, including council speaker Melissa Mark-Viverito, a de Blasio ally, voted for a resolution condemning the Boycott, Divestment and Sanctions (BDS) movement protesting Israel's continued oppression of the Palestinians.[49]

The examples above have focused on large cities, but breakthroughs are even more likely in midsize industrial or formerly industrial urban centers with large working-class populations, like Richmond, California, and Lorain County, Ohio. Because many discussions of third parties focus on national candidates, it is often not recognized how many urban localities across the United States are so thoroughly dominated by Democrats that the spoiler effect is not present, while the failure of the Democrats to support working-class goals is. As John Halle in his discussion of the potential for local union support for independent political action observes:

> Like many other heavily postindustrial areas in the East and Midwest in recent decades, Lorain County largely has been under Democratic control, with the Republican minority having been reduced to rump party (noncompetitive) status. Under these circumstances, with the spoiler factor removed, a labor (or Green) party functions as a de facto second party in races in which it chooses to compete. Here, Democrats' failure to support organized labor becomes a chief campaign issue, rather than being swept under the rug, as would be the case if there commonly were a viable right-wing Republican challenger.[50]

There are scores of such situations that provide an opening for labor-based and -supported independent political action.

The whole point of the Left engaging in electoral politics is or should be to build something new and democratic on a mass scale to gather the active elements of the grassroots labor movement and oppressed communities and groups. This is the antidote to the big spending that has universally infected mainstream politics for decades, leaving the old fashioned door-to-door "ground war" open more often than not. This is particularly true since the main form of "ground war" by today's digital Democrats has increasingly become the "micro-targeting" of groups and individual voters based on data indicating which candidate the person is most likely to back and which the person is most likely to vote for. The massive availability of such personal information and its digital collection and processing by expert firms has surpassed the older focus group and canvassing marketing techniques of voter targeting. Obama used this approach for reelection, but both parties now use it.[51] This is a highly undemocratic approach that encourages low voter turnout among lower-income groups as purchased "expert" business-based forms of campaigning increasingly target high-income groups.[52]

At the same time, where there is working-class dissatisfaction and anger, which is to say almost everywhere, the new Democratic business model is highly vulnerable to grassroots organization and action. As argued in the beginning of this section, a real political alternative must be based on active struggles, movements, and mobilization between as well as during elections if it is to be effective. This can mobilize the troops to beat big spenders, as the Richmond Progressive Alliance did. Even starting at the local level in Democratic-dominated cities and districts requires power from below—workplace organization, active social movements, union organizing drives, strikes, housing struggles, and so on. It is the great contradiction of capitalism that the power of the exploited is to be found above all in the site of that exploitation.

Sources of Power and Exploitation

Marx began his classic analysis of the dynamics of capitalism in *Capital* by examining the social relations of production. It is there that society's class relations and the conflict that characterizes them take form and there that the potential power of the working class originates. Working-class power, however, can only be expressed fully through collective organization. The roots of working-class power, to be sure, lie in its numbers and its position in the production of society's wealth, but these can only be turned into action through organization sometimes produced by the sorts of "spontaneous" upsurges discussed in chapter 6. Spontaneity is mostly the result of organizing we didn't see, initiatives taken by activists who are often leaders without titles. It is important, but grassroots organization is required to transform the explosive moment into sustainable power. These organizations need to be grassroots and democratic to be effective. The starting point here, for the reasons given in the discussion of upsurges, as well as in Marx's exposition of capitalism's social relations in the workplace, is the site of exploitation, "compression," *and* resistance. This is the point of greatest immediate potential power, the greatest racial and gender integration, and also the most likely site of direct democracy through directly elected stewards' organizations and their potential impact on union democracy via rank-and-file movements and beyond.

The workplace, along with prisons and schools, is among history's last remaining universal authoritarian institutions. Absolute monarchies, aristocracies, chattel slavery, fascism, military juntas, and Stalinism have mostly gone. To be sure, many dictatorships remain despite resistance and rebellion, forms of forced labor and human trafficking affect many parts of the world, including the United States, and the return of a slightly modernized fascism is a real danger, whether reflected in the person of a Marine Le Pen or a Donald Trump. But the workplace or "the job" remains the site of authoritarian rule across the entire globe regardless of the nature of the national political regime, state of economic development, or place in the global economy. This is because it is the bedrock of capitalism everywhere, as well as that of the remnants of so-called communist bureaucratic economies, which are themselves becoming penetrated by capitalism. Employee involvement programs in the United States and elsewhere presented no more than a passing fiction of worker participation. Unions modify the tyranny of capital somewhat, and strong workplace organization forms an internal "underground" resistance, while today the source of authority may be electronic or biometric monitoring as well as "close supervision" and bullying. Nevertheless, in essence and practice the workplace is one of the last worldwide bastions of authoritarian rule. Despite all the reorganizations, technological changes, and management innovations, the capital-labor relationship centered in the workplace remains, as Marx wrote long ago, "purely despotic."[53]

Partly for this reason, the workplace and work itself is society's black box. Mostly shunned or superficially treated by the media and most of academia, it is a major site of deteriorating conditions, constant reorganization, digitalized tyranny, increasing stress, and mostly invisible resistance. Due in part to this invisibility and through the understandable disillusionment of many on the left with bureaucratic unions in retreat, recent movement-building discussions have often emphasized community-based organizing, particularly among immigrants and communities of color. Community-based groups such as workers' centers and immigrants' rights groups and social movement organizations of women, African Americans, Latinos, and others, which are important sites of resistance to oppression, are, of course, part of rebuilding an active interracial working-class movement on the ground. A workplace-based movement must reach out to and connect with these communities and movements and take the struggle to the streets and to the political process. After all, a huge proportion of those who reside in such communities are also those who populate the nation's workplaces. Think, for example, of the giant logistics clusters and the contiguous urban neighborhoods that provide their labor force, discussed in chapter 5.

Nevertheless, it is the workplace or the job where the greatest potential collective social power is to be found. It is, more than America's mostly segregated neighborhoods, also society's most interracial site of power despite the persistence of race and gender discrimination and inequality. Yet the workplace has for decades been labor's Achilles' heel as union leaders have abandoned it for the more manageable side of collective bargaining—the ever-retreating "defense" of labor's private welfare state. Union representation on the job has even been dismissed by some leaders as "servicing" in the name of a spurious "organizing model" that bypasses workplace issues. There is, however, a growing realization that it is on the job that the labor movement can begin to be rebuilt from the bottom up, and workplace organization is typically one of the key goals of the rank-and-file union reform movements.

Of course, this rebuilding cannot be confined to workplaces in isolation. The old and new concentrations of workers and the just-in-time networks that connect them must be made live by human interaction and organization. Unions are supposed to do this but often don't or even discourage such horizontal connections. So there is a need to develop grassroots networks of stewards within and between employers and industries, along with action-based alliances in urban areas to organize the unorganized and mobilize mass demonstrations, occupations, and independent political action. Sustainable, dense, overlapping grassroots networks capable of bringing companies, industries, and cities to a halt when needed to disrupt "politics as usual" must be part of the long-term perspective.

We have much to learn in this respect from the Occupy movement, the 2011 Wisconsin uprising, immigrant resistance, and the Black Lives Matter and global justice movements at the recent turn of the century in terms of grassroots mobilization, audacity, and the ability to refocus public attention. Thanks largely to Occupy, by now a great many people know just who the 1 percent are. But one lesson is that movements such as Occupy that are based on a single tactic are not sustainable for long. A rebuilt working-class movement must be able to alter and escalate tactics, to move from demonstration to occupation, mass strike, and independent political action and sometimes to take a step backward and reassess as well. This variety of tactics can be deployed against right-wing initiatives, police violence, work intensification, antilabor legislation, and war, and for single-payer health care, more and better schools and housing, the $15 living wage, the extension of the Medicaid option of the ACA to states where the Right blocked it, and so on. In this way, by focusing on issues that actually matter to people, the activists can begin the uphill fight to break the twin-party clinch of the American Scheme.

All of this is a tall order and will not come about at once or on command. Nevertheless, it flows from the focus on the workplace and the direction of union organizing briefly discussed chapter 6. It should be obvious that socialists have a big role to play in this. Particularly important today are the rank-and-file movements for union democracy, workplace power, and militancy (for a thorough discussion of union democracy see Parker and Gruelle, 2005). They tend to arise from previous struggles in the workplace and union and to project a type of unionism that rejects the bureaucratic culture and "partnership" philosophy of business unionism. In this they are the breeding grounds of tomorrow's "militant minority." Of course, they don't always win, and, even when they do, many eventually fail to make the transformations they initially proposed. But as their numbers increase, they elect the "leaders without titles," develop more contacts with one another, and reach into working-class neighborhoods, the likelihood of achieving their goals and building a mass base increase, and the potential of real change emerges as a *visible* possibility to a growing number of activists.

These movements have been supported and increasingly brought together by the educational and inspirational work of *Labor Notes*, the monthly magazine and the national (even international) network it has created through its national conferences, local "Troublemakers" day schools, and the "how-to" handbooks that have spread throughout much of the labor movement (see appendix G for details). Socialists and other activists can make use of these resources to build workplace and union power as well as local networks. This interaction of rank-and-file movements in the unions and education and network building is an important step in building the "militant minority" that must be at the heart of the big tasks suggested here.

With the exception of the American Postal Workers Union (APWU), Amalgamated Transit Union (ATU), and for a few years in the 1990s the Teamsters, most of these movements that have taken power have done so at the level of the local union—though Teamsters United came very close to winning the union's election in 2016. In the organizing perspective presented above it would be the local unions in a city that would form the backbone of organizing and political efforts. It is also at this level that alliances between unionized workers, those in the process of organizing, and community-based working-class organizations such as workers' centers and immigrants' rights groups could be consummated and still retain a grassroots character.

If this activity is to be politicized, there must be political organization already on the ground. That is the purpose of emphasizing local independent political action and democratic organization. So, once again, the idea of a breakthrough in politics—as in unionization and workplace organization in the nation's cities via a social upsurge—is not a reason to wait but rather to prepare and organize as the few examples of local independent political action offered earlier are at least partially doing. Thus, social movements on the ground and new organizing in the nation's changing workplaces and logistics networks are not something merely "economic" as opposed to "political" but part and parcel of an overall strategy for laying the basis of greater changes to come. Without social upsurge in the cities there can be no electoral breakthrough; without democratic political organization on the ground the next upheaval can be drawn back into that "graveyard of social movements," the Democratic Party.

Independent Political Action and Socialism: Some Speculations

In general, independent political action is transitional in nature—that is, not necessarily explicitly socialist in content or name but built on issues of immediate concern that challenge the neoliberal austerity agenda and the absolute hegemony of capital over so much of our lives. The issues that concern many working-class people are also those that can be acted on at the local and state levels: jobs, schools, housing, health care, taxes, work intensification and stress, living ($15+ per hour) wages, racist police violence, the right to organize unions in both public and private sectors, and so on. These issues address not all but some of the content of the bigger question of inequality, about which a majority of people are concerned. Independent political action is, above all, the means of accumulating an organized mass movement that challenges not only neoliberalism but also the very limits of capital and capitalism. Many of these issues are also those on the minds of middle-class and working-class people who have been attracted to right-wing populist appeals such as Trump's.

What such electoral action cannot do is be the vehicle for the transition to socialism, per se, even if it helps pave the road. "Parliamentary socialism," the idea that a socialist society can be crafted, either gradually or rapidly, though the machinations of legislators operating in a conventional parliamentary context is an old but failed idea. It is ultimately an elitist idea that socialism is something that can be negotiated and legislated from above via "nationalization" to be implemented by the existing bureaucratic state. As Hal Draper put it succinctly in his classic "Two Souls of Socialism," "The great problem of our age is the achievement of *democratic control from below over the vast powers of modern authority*."[54] The modern bourgeois state, no matter how formally democratic, exists to protect private property and control conflict, not to nurture it, whether by means soft (New Deal) or hard (fascism) or the "in between" model of neoliberalism. Its elected branches are only one aspect of this essentially bureaucratic formation. State socialism, Draper also argues, stemming from the theories of Ferdinand Lassalle and later Eduard Bernstein, among many others right up to our own time, is the opposite of what Marx argued for.

Quite aside even from all manner of dubious assumptions about the neutrality, as opposed to relative autonomy, of the capitalist state, there is the problem that socialism in its most democratic form involves the "takeover" and imposition of direct democracy on work and the production of goods and services by the working class itself, not by nationalization from above by a tiny group, even if elected. While leftists might demand nationalization or public ownership of certain industries or services, this can only be a transitional demand, not the sum of socialism itself. The twentieth century is full of examples of this statist approach, from British Labourism in its mild form to Stalinism in its most extreme form, none of which produced socialist democracy. And none of which could resist the undermining influence of capital's global spread or prevent the revenge of capital in the era of neoliberalism. No matter how far down the road this transition from below might be, the emancipation of the working class *remains* the task of the working class itself, to paraphrase Marx. This, in turn, requires the class to become "fit to rule," something it accomplishes mainly through the education provided by prolonged struggle.[55] Independent political action is one aspect of that education through struggle as it gathers forces and pushes things to the limits of capitalism. Only if it develops a mass revolutionary character or tendency can it assist in the creation of socialism from below.

All that seems far away. It is nevertheless interesting that socialism as a concept appears to have lost much of its Cold War stigma and scary image as capitalism loses some of its legitimacy and perhaps its hegemonic place in conventional American ideology. Recent polls indicate that a growing number of voters have a "positive image" of socialism, would vote for a socialist candidate, or even regard themselves as socialists. A 2010 Gallup poll showed while 58 percent of Americans eighteen and older still had a negative view of socialism and still favor good old "free enterprise," a surprising 36 percent had a "positive image" of the "s" word. Among those who identified as Democrats it is 53 percent, while among those who identified as liberals the positive feeling was embraced by 61 percent.[56] A June 2015 Gallup poll showed that 58 percent of adults would vote for a socialist (Bernie?), while a January 2016 Bloomberg Politics/Des Moines Register poll revealed that 43 percent of likely Democratic Iowa caucus voters *identified* as socialists.[57] These latter findings are probably in part attributable to the Bernie Sanders campaign, but certainly the trends produced by capitalism itself well before the presidential primaries played a role. In any case they reveal the unexpected fact that millions of Americans have gone soft on socialism.

There are, of course, at least two problems attached to this new popularity of the once-forbidden "s" word. The first is the matter of what it means to those who give these positive replies when surveyed. After all, the socialist Left itself does not agree on just what this new system should look like. Is it Bernie's vision of a Scandinavian or New Deal–like alternative to neoliberalism or something more robust, involving social ownership and democratic management of production by the working class? Most likely it is more the former, but we won't know until we engage directly over time with this new consciousness of the possible.

One more speculation on the relationship of a socialist future to the seemingly prosaic tasks of workplace organization: strong, democratic workplace (stewards') organization has a prefigurative dimension. If direct democracy in production is a feature of the self-emancipation of the working class, then existing organization that involves aspects of direct democracy has a role to play in the development of socialism from below. And, indeed, this was the case in at least one of the rare revolutionary upsurges of the twentieth century. In the working-class upsurge that followed World War I, workers in many industrial countries or regions developed a new type of organization. The structures of the trade unions of the day, whether craft or industrial, existed outside of and removed from the workplace for the most part, with negotiations conducted by and strikes called (and called off) by full-time officials. In country after country in slightly different ways, industrial workers began to organize on the job through systems of directly elected delegates. In Britain this became the shop stewards' movement, in Germany the Berlin-based revolutionary stewards or delegates, and in Italy the factory councils.[58] In the United States, workplace-based delegate systems also emerged in these years in a number of industries.[59] These were generally understood by revolutionary socialists and syndicalists to be embryonic organs of political power based in the heart of production, similar to the early soviets (workers' councils) in Russia. As Gramsci put it, in the most advanced form "the Factory Council is the model of the proletarian State."[60] For a number of reasons, as we know, these embryonic forms of workers' democracy did not make the transition to socialism.

Granted, it takes a considerable leap of imagination to go from today's average shop steward bogged down in day-to-day grievance "case work" to tomorrow's revolutionary tribune. Nevertheless, as Gramsci argued, it is in the experience of collective democracy in the labor process in the context of a general upheaval that workers can develop what he called in 1919 "communist consciousness."[61] While it is not quite that simple and while workplace organization is not a broad enough social basis for an actual state, it is or can be the initial source of and training ground for the direct democracy at the base that should characterize socialism. From this speculative glimpse into the future, we return now to the analysis that this book has put forward concerning the changes in capitalism and the possibilities of working-class organization.

Pulling the Analysis Together

W e fight now on new terrain. The trends that created barriers, pitfalls, divisions, and minefields for working-class organization and power, while not disappearing, have been altered through capitalism's own inherent dynamics of competition and expansion, which has led to the consolidation, integration, and relocation of capital in ways that are potentially more ad-vantageous for working-class resistance, organization, and power. The older fragmentation has produced its opposite in new forms. To be sure, some of the old problems linger, while new ones arise. Race remains a major fault line within the American working class. Not least of the "new" problems is the soaring wealth of the capitalist class that gives it staying power in a struggle with labor and the near command of conventional American party politics. At the same time, bloated capital has earned the increased enmity of a growing majority of people in the United States and around the world, while much of the working class has been pushed to the edge and simultaneously recon-solidated in capital's embedded but vulnerable technology-driven logistics sinews and concentrations.

There are four major trends and developments that have created the new terrain of class conflict in the United States:

1. The working class itself has changed in its occupational, industrial, and ethno/racial composition. The manufacturing core of the tradi-tional working class has shrunk, due mainly to the enormous increases in productivity, while sectors involved in transportation, warehousing, and other aspects of the "logistics revolution" have grown. The growth of so-called service jobs has been due largely to the increased needs

171

of social reproduction, on the one hand, and capital's requirements for the maintenance of its expanded material infrastructure. While the average workplace in manufacturing has become smaller, those in most other lines of work have increased in size and concentration. Capital intensity and capital-labor ratios have increased in most lines of work. Along with these developments the introduction of lean production methods and their evolution into digital and biometric forms of measuring and monitoring work have accelerated the intensification of labor in most lines of the production of goods and services. As a result, the rate of exploitation has increased over the entire neoliberal period, underlying soaring inequality. More and more jobs are dead-end, low-paid, and low-skilled. Precarity of employment has grown somewhat, but the overall trend is for the economic and working conditions of the working class to have degenerated for all groups, although on average more so for African Americans, Latinos, and women. The result of all this has been the enormous inequality that now characterizes the entire world, with capital's share of both income and wealth soaring. Part of this is both a cause and consequence of the next major piece of this analysis of the current phase of capitalism.

2. Under the pressures of global and domestic competition, capital has seen a period of unprecedented rapid concentration and consolidation through merger movements that accelerated in the mid-1990s. Unlike the mergers of the 1960s and 1970s, which emphasized conglomeration, the consolidation of the past twenty years has been along industrial and product lines. Bigger firms command increased masses of capital, much of it sunk, and employ larger numbers and concentrations of workers producing related products by increasingly similar methods. As a result, capital is often potentially more vulnerable to unionization along industrial lines. In addition, new sources of vulnerability flow from the transformation of streamlined supply chains in the production of goods and services and the way they are moved and distributed.

3. In the last decade or so, these concentrations of capital have been tied together by digitally guided and just-in-time supply chain systems. As with capital in general, supply chains have also become more concentrated, with fewer supply firms along most chains. The key "nodes" in these systems are mostly located on the edges of major

urban metropolitan areas. They depend on large concentrations of labor, much of it low-paid and located in adjacent inner cities. These are "enclosed" urban concentrations of value-adding workers akin to those formerly centered in manufacturing. The timely movement of goods, both domestic and imported, are dependent on these "logistics clusters" and the links between them. Both the clusters and the links have, in many cases, become more geographically and regionally specific. At the same time, most so-called service industries are also dependent on these just-in-time supply chains to provide the equipment and tools necessary to perform the services on which major functions of society—reproduction and maintenance among them—are, in turn, dependent. As a result, the country's larger, more consolidated firms and industries are themselves far more vulnerable to disruption at many points along the just-in-time supply chains.

4. In a number of ways politics have been transformed by the sheer wealth of capital and by its organized efforts to shift the political agenda in favor of its needs and desires—what has become known as neoliberalism. One change is the shift to state-level politics and the rise of the Right in Republican politics. The most obvious and predominant trend, however, has been the enormous increase in the amount of money, lobbying, and influence put into party structures and elections by capital. The high visibility of this and of the policy outcomes that favor capital, such as tax breaks, are a source of vulnerability for the politicians and parties that receive these accelerating funds and deliver on the demands of business and the "1 percent." The increased dependence on big money in elections has reduced the role of human intervention in favor of purchased forms of campaigning. It has also strengthened elite party organization and legislative discipline. At the same time, this concentration of mainstream politics on money and purchased technology and expertise has made electoral politics vulnerable to well-organized mass grassroots human intervention despite the rigged nature of the American Scheme of politics. On the one hand, the increased role of money and direct intervention of capital has made the Democratic Party as an institution less permeable. On the other, the neoliberal politics these have encouraged in this party and the way in which much of this funding is deployed have rendered the Democrats more vulnerable from both the right and, potentially, the left.

The art of working-class advance on this new terrain of class struggle will depend on combining and integrating the unionizing potential of the new configuration of capital with its increased vulnerabilities, on the one hand, and organized, urban-based, mass working-class and social movement activism and grassroots, independent political action, beginning locally and building upward, on the other.

There is no inevitability that organized labor or the working class in general will take advantage of this new landscape. Indeed, the danger of the continuing appeal of a Trump-like figure or politics to sections of the working class remains real. Much depends on the sort of upsurge that cannot be willed or predicted. As argued in chapter 6, the British labor historian Eric Hobsbawm showed that the growth of unions and other social movements cannot be measured by "a mere rising slope." Rather these gains come in "leaps" or "explosions" that sweep into labor's ranks the previously unorganized, including many once conservative or racist workers. While old forms of prejudice and social conservatism do not necessarily disappear automatically, such class "explosions" tend to be transformative in terms of both action and consciousness. The underlying causes of these "leaps" in labor movement growth are not so much economic cycles as "accumulations of inflammable material which only ignite periodically, as it were under compression."[1] "Compression" seems like an apt description of the conditions of the working class in the United States and much of the world today. There are, indeed, massive pressures on more and more working-class people and even middle-class professionals, providing the fuel for a conflagration that awaits a spark or sparks from places no one can foresee.

The task now is not to sit around waiting for an upsurge, much less hoping the Democrats will ride in to the rescue, but to begin building democratic, grassroots organizations, structures, networks, movements, and actions that can hasten and strengthen any social explosion that lies ahead *and* attract those working-class elements currently drawn to right-wing "populism." Many are already doing this; more need to join in. No doubt more research into the contours of capital I have analyzed above will be needed to map strategies and tactics that can take full advantage of the situation that has emerged and is still taking shape. In the final analysis, however, it will be the actions of those on the ground that will open up new possibilities.

Who Put Trump
in the White House?

The media story in the days following the 2016 election was that a huge group of angry white blue-collar workers from Rust Belt communities defected from their traditional Democratic voting patterns and put Donald J. Trump in the White House. While he didn't actually win the popular vote, Trump did carry the majority (58 percent) of white voters. Furthermore, he won the key "battleground" states in the Rust Belt that are the basis of this story. But is this the whole story? Who were these white voters? Was the major shift portrayed in the press actually the decisive shift?

Exit polls taken during the primaries, when the Trump rebellion began, showed that the whole election process was skewed toward the better-off sections of US society and that Trump did better among them than Clinton. While 55 percent of US households fall in the $50,000 or more income bracket, 59 percent of Clinton's votes came from that group and a whopping 68 percent of Trump's. That, of course, could include some better-paid employed industrial workers, though not those who saw their industrial jobs disappear. So, looking at those voters in the general election from the 26 percent of US households earning more than $100,000, who are even less likely to be working class these days, we see that Clinton got 34 percent of her vote and Trump 35 percent of his from these well-to-do voters.[1] In other words, upper-income groups were overrepresented in the voting electorate as a whole, and both

This chapter is based on a two-part article published in *Against the Current* 186 (January–February 2017) and 187 (March–April 2017).

candidates drew a disproportionate part of their vote from the relatively well-to-do, with Trump a bit more reliant on high-income voters. These were the decisive elements in Trump's voter coalition. This in itself doesn't rule out a working-class shift to Trump, but the media's version of this is based on a problematic definition.

In most exit polls and media accounts of this blue-collar rebellion, white "working class" was defined as those white voters without a college degree. There are a number of problems with this definition. One problem is that almost half of those without a college degree don't vote at all. As we will see below, people who don't vote are generally to the left of those who do on economic issues and the role of government. Hence the minority of little more than a fifth of those without degrees that voted for Trump do not represent this demographic very well, and claims about the conservative views of the whole demographic are bogus. Another problem is that while there are just over 135.5 million white men and women who don't have a college degree, there are only about 18.5 million white blue-collar production workers—the prototype of the Trump-voting proletariat.[2] If we double this to account for adult spouses to make it just under 40 million, it still only accounts for a little more than a third of those lacking the allegedly class-defining degree. Of course, there are another 14 million or so white service workers who are working class, but even if we bring them and their spouses in we still account for only about half of the huge 70 percent of white adults in the United States who lack a college degree.

The other side of this definitional problem is that there are also millions of Americans who don't have a college degree and who are not working class. There are, as mentioned above, some 17 million small business owners without that degree. As a 2016 survey by the National Small Business Association tells us, 86 percent of small business owners are white, they are twice as likely to be Republicans as Democrats, almost two-thirds consider themselves conservative (78 percent on economic issues), and 92 percent say they regularly vote in national elections. Plus, they drew an average salary of $112,000 in 2016, compared to $48,320 for the average annual wage.[3] It is doubtful that any significant group of blue-collar workers can match that salary or level of voter turnout even if these entrepreneurs are exaggerating their civic virtue. Add in the spouses and this classically petit bourgeois group alone could more than account for the 29 million votes of those lacking a college degree who voted for Trump.[4]

The problem of equating working class with those lacking a college degree doesn't end there. There are also 1.8 million managers, 8.8 million supervisors, and 1.6 million cops whose jobs don't require a college degree. To this we could add insurance and real estate brokers and agents who require only a license, and so on.[5] Some may have a degree, but it is clear that there are tens of millions of non-working-class white people in the United States who lack such a degree, are more likely to be traditional Republican voters than a majority of white blue-collar workers, and are more likely to vote as those with higher incomes tend to vote. Thus, the proportion of those without a college degree who are petit bourgeois or genuinely middle class and who are more likely to vote and to vote Republican is clearly very large and the equation of the missing degree with working-class status misleading.

To test the extent to which white blue-collar or related workers handed Trump victory, we will look at the swings in union households voting in national elections. This is far from perfect, of course, since only a minority of such workers belong to unions these days, about half are public employees, and nonwhite workers make up a third of the total.[6] Nevertheless, we can safely assume that any swings toward the Republicans came mostly from white union members and their families. It is important to bear in mind as well that the union household vote has declined as a percentage of the total vote in presidential elections, from about 26 to 27 percent in 1980 to 18 percent in 2016, so the impact of the union household vote has diminished, though not disappeared.[7]

Table VIII: Union Household Vote in Presidential Elections, 1976–2016

Year	Democratic	Republican
2016	51%	43% (6% other/no answer)
2012	58%	40%
2008	59%	39%
2004	59%	40%
2000	59%	37% (1% Buchanan, 3% Nader)
1996	60%	30% (9% Perot)
1992	~55%	24% (21% Perot)
1988	57%	43%
1980	48%	45% (7% Anderson)
1976	62%	38%

Sources: Roper Center, "How Groups Voted," 1976–2012, http://ropercenter.cornell.edu/polls/us-elections/how-groups-voted/how-groups-voted/; CNN Politics, election 2016, "Exit Polls, National President," http://edition.cnn.com/election/results/exit-polls/national/president.

Two things are clear from table VIII. First, an average of about 40 percent of union members and their families have been voting Republican in presidential elections for a long time, with the Democrats winning a little under 60 percent of the union household vote for the last four decades. Only in 1948 and 1964 did over 80 percent of union household members vote for the Democratic candidate, Harry Truman and Lyndon B. Johnson, respectively.[8] Nevertheless, in 2016 a relatively small number shifted to Trump by three percentage points, from 40 percent for Romney in 2012 to 43 percent in 2016. This is a shift of just under 800,000 union household voters across the entire country, or 0.6 percent of all those who voted. Even more interesting is that the Democratic union household vote fell by seven points from 2012 to 2016 as union household members defected to a third party, refused to answer the question when surveyed, or didn't vote. While the unspecified "no answer" group lends some credibility to the theory of the "silent Trump voter," this 7 percent drop nonetheless points toward the fact that the Democrats are losing union household voters in national elections not only to Republicans but to third-party candidates and to the massive "party" of nonvoters.

Putting this in historical context, Trump's shift of union household voters is actually less dramatic than the swing from 1976 to 1980 for Reagan and even less so than the fourteen-point desertion of union household voters from Carter in 1980, half of which went to independent John Anderson rather than Reagan in 1980, when the union householders composed 26 percent of all voters.[9] In other words, nationally Trump attracted both a smaller proportion and number of these voters than Reagan. These same voters have swung between Democrats, Republicans, and high-profile third-party candidates such as Anderson, Perot, who got 21 percent of union household voters in 1992, and Nader, who got 3 percent in 2000.[10]

This is not to say that the swing of union household or white working-class voters away from the Democrats to the Republicans doesn't reflect the conservative social views, racism, and in the case of Clinton, sexism of many white working- and middle-class people as well as their anger at their deteriorating situation. Nor is Trump the same as Reagan. Clearly Trump won almost ten million union household votes, compared to almost twelve million for Clinton. We might assume that the broader nonunion white working-class electorate is even more conservative-leaning than union members, but since the level of education turns out to be a dubious measure of working-class status, we have no way of measuring just how many white working-class people actually shifted from the Democrats, either in 2016 or at some point in the past. We only know that the numbers are significant, but that many are not as new to voting Republican as is often thought. This, of course, is not something to take comfort in, but it is an indication of the results of the Democratic Party's choice to target higher-income people who are more likely to vote that began under Bill Clintons and the Democratic Leadership Council's "triangulation" strategy.[11]

Similarly, the relatively high income levels of much of Trump's vote point toward a majority petit bourgeois and middle-class base for Trump, something the *Economist* concluded in its earlier survey of Trump primary voters when it wrote, "The idea that it is the mostly poor, less-educated voters who are drawn to Mr. Trump is a bit of a myth."[12] Nevertheless, it seems clear that a significant number of white working-class people voted for Trump who had voted for Obama in 2008 or 2012. As Mike Davis points out, however, "With the exceptions of Iowa and Ohio, there were no Trump landslides in key states."[13] To get a closer look at how this might have worked across the Rust Belt, where the Democrats lost both the vote and the electoral college, we will look more closely at Ohio and at heavily white, blue-collar counties that moved from Obama in 2012 to Trump in 2016.

In this Rust Belt state, the union household vote was a dramatic 54 percent for Trump. This was a huge change from 2012, when only 37 percent went for Romney and 60 percent for Obama. The Republicans lost Ohio in 2012 but won it in 2016 by 446,841 votes. This would seem to justify the media story. The total two-party vote, however, declined by 253,859 votes between 2012 and 2016, and the union household vote declined by 74,366. Trump's gain of 151,054 union household votes over Romney and 166,867 more than Clinton is obviously significant but less so than the huge drop in the Democratic vote from 2012 to 2016 and not enough to explain Trump's majority. The Ohio Latino vote alone slumped from 10 percent of the total vote to 3 percent in 2016, according to the exit polls. In the actual results Clinton got 433,547 fewer votes than Obama, while Trump got 179,598 more than Romney, not enough to absorb all the missing Democrats.[14] The biggest story here was the drop in Democratic voters.

Thus, the biggest numerical shift was not to Trump, despite the large percentage of union household votes for him, but away from Clinton and the Democrats. The third-party vote increased by two and a half times to 261,318, but not in a way that would have harmed Clinton much, as the Libertarian vote took the lion's share. The Greens at about 45,000 were not a spoiler and couldn't have a made a difference.[15] Clinton's overall loss of votes in Ohio is almost two and a half times larger than Trump's gain. Trump won Ohio because far fewer people voted Democratic than switched to the Republicans. Furthermore, the 2016 Ohio electorate saw an increase in the proportion of higher-income voter. The Ohio electorate saw those earning $50,000 or more go from 59 percent in 2012 to 63 percent in 2016, while those earning $100,000 or more increased from 28 percent to 30 percent. Trump got 57 percent of voters in the $100,000-plus income level, compared to 39 percent for Clinton.[16] This certainly smells like a heavily petit bourgeois, middle-class movement.

The 2016 swing of blue-collar workers to the Republicans in Ohio took place in the Great Lakes counties of the state. The coal counties of southeastern Ohio went Republican some time ago.[17] To examine the Ohio vote more deeply we will look at four of Ohio's Rust Belt counties along Lake Erie, stretching from Cleveland to Toledo, both of which, like most cities, went Democratic in both 2012 and 2016. These four counties, Lorain, Erie, Sandusky, and Ottawa, all went for Obama in 2012 by a total of 124,330 to 98,564. In 2016, this vote was reversed, with Trump getting 113,081 votes to Clinton's 98,789.[18] Again, however, the two-party vote dropped by 11,024. The Democratic loss of 25,541 was larger than the total decline and larger than the shift of 14,517 to Trump, as well as his margin of victory in these four counties. Presumably the story is similar in other blue-collar counties, such as those in northeastern Ohio, home to Youngstown and the legendary GM Lordstown plants. What seems clear about these deindustrialized counties is that disillusioned Democrats and demoralized labor leaders forced to "sell" Clinton, the establishment neoliberal, could not prevent either the shift to Trump or the much larger drop in Democratic voters that gave Trump his majority. A look at Lorain County, the largest of the four will tell us more.

Lorain County's population of just over 300,000 is 80 percent white. It includes the small upper-income Cleveland suburb of Amherst, the small liberal college community of Oberlin, a number of small farming communities and townships, as well as working-class cities Lorain and Elyria. The county's workforce is still 42 percent blue collar. While it still has many employed industrial workers, the local Ford plant has closed, and employment at its biggest steel mill went from 15,000 jobs to fewer than 4,000 by 2014. This is, of course, the county mentioned above where labor elected three independent candidates on the Lorain Independent Labor Party slate in 2014 due to disgust with the local Democrats.[19] In 2012 it chose Obama 78,112 to Romney's 58,092, a majority of over 20,000 votes. In the 2016 primaries, Bernie Sanders got almost as many votes in the Democratic primary (16,587) as Trump did in the Republican primary (16,776).[20]

In 2016 the county went narrowly for Trump 65,346 to Clinton's 64,958, a margin of just 388 votes. Voter turnout was down by 5,900 voters, but the Democratic vote dropped by over 13,000 votes from that in 2012.[21] The fact that Lorain County is 80 percent white means that a lot of white people voted for Clinton, but a significant number just stopped voting. Trump won not only the upper-income Cleveland suburb of Amherst but all the more rural small towns and townships in the county with the sole exception of the tiny college community of Oberlin. Trump's slight majority did not come from the two largest and most "proletarian" towns in the county: Lorain and Elyria, the two places where the Independent Labor candidates won in 2014. The city of Lorain is just over two-thirds white, while Elyria is closer to 78 percent white. Thus, both have substantial white majorities but also a significant African American and/or Latino population.[22]

Table IX: 2012 and 2016 General Election: Ohio, Lorain County, Lorain City, Elyria City

Year	Lorain County	Lorain City	Elyria City
2016			
Clinton	64,958	14,502	10,834
Trump	65,346	7,366	8,351
2012			
Obama	78,112	19,040	14,505
Romney	58,092	6,211	7,412
Increase in Republican Vote 2012 to 2016		+1,155	+939
Decline in Democratic Vote 2012 to 2016		–4,538	-3,671

Sources: Lorain County Board of Elections, 2012, 2016; "General Election, 2012, State Results," *New York Times*, 2012, http://elections.nytimes.com/2012/results/states/ohio.

Both towns went for Obama by large margins: three to one in Lorain and two to one in Elyria in 2012 and for Clinton by smaller two-to-one and five-to-four margins, respectively in 2016. While these two towns still went for Clinton and don't fit the story of a Trump sweep of working-class voters, they still illustrate the problem of the declining Democratic vote. As table IX shows, the turnout in 2016 was down by over 3,000 votes in these two towns, while the drop in the Democratic vote of 8,209 was four times the increase in the Republican vote for Trump of 2,094 votes. In other words, the drop in the Democratic vote surpassed that of the decline in voter turnout and the increase in the Republican vote in these two heavily blue-collar towns. This is consistent with the larger statewide drop in the Democratic vote of 433,547, compared to the drop in the total two-party turnout in Ohio of 253,859.[23]

The picture in Pennsylvania was somewhat different but revealed the same weakness. The Democratic vote in that state also fell but only slightly less than Trump's 68,000-vote margin of victory. His total vote, however, increased by almost 300,000 over Romney's 2012 vote, far greater than the Democratic decline of 62,743. This increase reflected an increased turnout in the two-party vote of over 230,000, virtually all of which went to Trump. Statewide the Democrats declined while the Republicans mobilized thousands of new voters. A look at Erie County, Pennsylvania, a deindustrializing, mostly white, Rust Belt county on the border of Ohio just slightly smaller than Lorain County, gives a picture more like that of Lorain. Here the decline in the Democratic vote from 2012 to 2016 of over 10,000 exceeded Trump's margin of victory of 2,348 by over four times.[24] Erie, which had seen jobs lost at General Electric's huge locomotive plant, was one of only two counties in Pennsylvania that went from blue to red in 2016.[25] Like the Ohio counties, Erie saw the same pattern of a larger drop in Democratic votes than the increase in Trump votes.

One can hardly avoid the conclusion that the Democrats lost the 2016 presidential election in these and other similar Rust Belt counties due to the fact that former Democratic voters in Rust Belt states with relatively large white blue-collar populations failed to turn out for Clinton and other Democrats, even if they did not necessarily vote for Trump or vote at all. While there was a swing among white blue-collar and union household votes to Trump, it was significantly smaller than the overall drop in Democratic voters in these swing blue-collar counties. Below we will see why.

In fact, nationally the Democrats have been losing elections at the national and state level since 2009. In that year, during the 111th Congress the Democrats had 257 members in the House of Representatives. By 2015, in the 114th Congress, that was down to 188 Democrats, the lowest number since the 80th Congress in 1947–49, over which time voter participation rates fell from 48 percent to 42 percent in off-year Congressional elections. In 2016 the Democrats won back just six seats in the House.[26] Between 2009 and 2015 the Democrats lost 203 seats in state senates and 716 in state houses or assemblies. An indication of what was to come in Ohio and Pennsylvania in 2016 could be seen in the loss of twenty-one Democratic seats in the state legislatures of each of these states between 2009 and 2015.[27] Even in the presidential contests, despite Clinton's sizable majority in the 2016 popular vote, the Democrats have received fewer votes in each election since 2008, dropping from 69,498,515 in 2008 to 65,152,112 in 2016, a loss of over four million votes.[28]

In other words, despite, or more likely because of, all the institutional stability, the vast amounts of money raised and deployed, all the digital and "expert" sophistication available to this "party of the people," and the allegedly massive "ground war" force in the battleground states, the Democratic Party as a whole can no longer mobilize enough of those among its traditional core constituencies—Blacks and Latinos, as well as white workers and union members—to win national and even state offices in these key states and possibly elsewhere despite the demographic trends in its favor. While race was certainly a factor in Trump's appeal, the fact is that the Democrats at every level could not get the turnout of African Americans or Latinos they needed to balance out their losses among white voters of all classes.

To be sure, Clinton won a majority of the popular vote nationally, perhaps, as John Nichols gloated in the *Nation,* an "unprecedented" majority that might run as high as two million by the time the official state votes were counted.[29] In fact, her total majority turned out to be 2.9 million.[30] The problem is that 1.5 million of that majority can be accounted for by Clinton's vote tally in New York City alone.[31] The Democratic majority of nearly 4.3 million in California by itself accounts for more than her net 2.9 million majority. The rest of the country continues to see its Democratic vote stagnate or decline. Indeed, between 2012 and 2016, the Democratic vote fell in two-thirds of all states. None of the seventeen states in which it increased were in the Midwest or Great Plains.[32] The reason for its decline is not hard to find.

The Democrats are and have been for decades the party of the (neoliberal) status quo during a period when millions of all races and ethnicities have seen their living standards shrink and future prospects disappear and, as a result, have come to despise the status quo. And, as not only the Clintons' social position but also the many millionaire Democrats in Congress and their business buddies demonstrate for all to see, they are part of the nation's elite. The decline in manufacturing jobs, the shrinking of union representation, the creation of more and more lousy jobs, the withdrawal of aid to the cities, and so on have created not just "angry white men" who voted for Trump but also angry white, Black, Latino, and Asian men and women who, for good and sound reasons, no longer see the Democrats as their defenders. Many in the ranks of this legion have voted with their feet and it wasn't to the polls. According to one estimate, over 100 million eligible voters didn't cast a ballot in the 2016 presidential election.[33] In 2014, the last off-year congressional election, nonvoters numbered almost 128 million adult citizens—a majority of eligible voters.[34]

Strong evidence that the Democrats can no longer motivate or mobilize the majority of voters in much of the country is found in the fact that the millions of nonvoters are on average and in their majority politically to the left of those who do vote on key economic issues that run counter to the neoliberal agenda. As one study put it, "Nonvoters tend to support increasing government services and spending, guaranteeing jobs, and reducing inequality" more than voters and do so by about 17 percentage points. This includes white as well as Black and Latino nonvoters. Furthermore, these nonvoters are as likely to support legal abortion and gay marriage as those who vote. Specifically, they are to the left of voters in that a consistently higher percentage of them think the government should "make union organizing easier," increase funds to the poor and for schools, "guarantee jobs," and "provide health insurance."[35] In short, the Democrats cannot mobilize the forces needed to defeat the Right, including Blacks and Latinos, in part because they cannot implement any policies capable of addressing the plight of the majority that might attract these left-leaning nonvoters. As Mike Davis summarizes the recent history of this desertion of the working class, "Consistently championing global free trade, information elites, and financialization over manufacturing, the Clinton and then Obama White Houses have presided over the death of the industries and industrial unions that were the backbone of New Deal Democrats."[36] It is no wonder that the Democratic vote is shrinking.

While recent voter suppression laws demanding state-issued photo IDs in some seventeen states along with the racial cleansing of voter rolls in many states have undoubtedly limited voting for Blacks, Latinos, and some low-income whites, most left-leaning nonvoters don't vote because they don't see anything compelling to vote for. At the same time, working-class voter participation has remained low because the political parties have reduced the direct door-to-door human contact with lower-income voters in favor of those more likely to turn out on Election Day, who are increasingly targeted by the "experts" and their algorithms.[37] This is not only the case in presidential elections, but in congressional and state- and local-level elections as well. Indeed, the voter participation in off-year congressional elections has fallen even more than that in presidential years. So who put Trump in the White House? The Democrats.

This time, however, the falling Democratic vote meant the victory not of a run-of-the-mill conservative or even a Tea Bagger but of a racist demagogue bent on doing serious damage. And he will. Whether or not, as some on the left speculate, the Republican establishment and/or the ruling class attempt to rein him in, and his first appointments indicate no such thing, he will have the power to harm millions—with or without the cooperation of the Republican Congress or the opposition of a future Democratic Congress. He will certainly revoke the Obama executive order that was to give millions of immigrant "Dreamers" a path to citizenship. Without lifting a pen, he will give the green light to police departments across the country to continue or even accelerate the killing of Black men and the incarceration of many more, and the preservation or upgrading of militarized police forces.

With only what he has already said, the victimization of Muslims or anyone who vaguely looks like they might be a Muslim will escalate—indeed, already did even before he took office. Misogynist language and actions will be acceptable to many. He may not build that wall or attempt to deport eleven million immigrants or even all the two to three million alleged criminals he says are among them, but he will certainly unleash an accelerated reign of terror with increased dawn and workplace raids on immigrant and Latino communities. Without a single piece of legislation he will ratify increased racial and sexual harassment and discrimination. The few small gains from the NLRB are likely to go once he appoints a new member or two. The Supreme Court will most likely get a conservative majority that can overthrow *Roe v. Wade*. And what about foreign policy, war, the future of the Middle East?

There will be resistance. Rather, there already is increased resistance. And this will offer new possibilities for organizing, even in a more hostile atmosphere. At the same time, many, including not a few on the socialist left, will run for cover in the Democratic Party's "Big Tent," arguing that now is not the time to take on the Democrats, that the great task is to elect a Democratic Congress, any Democratic Congress, in 2018 to rein in Trump just as the Republicans blocked Obama after 2010, and so on. It will not even be an argument for reforming the party, just stopping the Trump rampage—although there are already many arguing this party can be pushed to the left by running for office, à la Our Revolution. It will be a tempting and effective argument, particularly if Trump has, indeed, pulled out all the stops or hasn't already appointed someone to the Supreme Court. But such a political direction will only reinforce the Democrats' neoliberalism, digital dependency, and failed strategies.

We had better bear in mind what this approach has *not* done for the past four decades and will not do in the coming years. It will not increase voter turnout for working-class people, especially African American and Latino voters. The rate of voter turnout has fallen for the past few decades, particularly for off-year congressional elections. Both Black and Latino rates of voter participation in off-year elections, long below average, have nose-dived since 2010 and did not recover in 2016 despite the threat of a Trump victory.[38] Nor will the off-the-rack centrist liberalism, much less neoliberalism, of the vast majority of Democratic incumbents and most likely candidates win back those white working-class people or those in union households who have been voting Republican for decades or the recent angry Trump converts. Politics as usual have failed.

They have failed not only in the United States but also across the West, where right-wing "populism" has captured the anger of many working-class as well as petit bourgeois and middle-class people over the impact of neoliberalism, globalization, and capital's periodic crises. The "other" victims of capital's imperial wars and mass economic dispossessions have been made the target of the anger of those who have faced the steamroller of austerity, restructured industries, and "left behind" communities at home. The centrist liberalism and social democracy that participated in both sides of these mass dislocations and deprivations have beaten a hasty retreat where they have not collapsed altogether. There has been a rebellion from the left in Europe, but it has yet to capture or inspire sufficient roots in the working class to defeat the Right. Its overemphasis on electoralism limits this Left's powers of mobilization and grassroots organization. Rather than engaging in political work within the trade unions, the leaders of these new left parties sometimes write them off as simply part of the dying social democracy. None of this is inevitable in Europe or elsewhere.

Don't Moan, Organize!

The growing wealth of the capitalist class and many of their hangers-on has increasingly financed the rightward movement of the Democratic Party and politics in general since the 1970s. The political grasp of capital can be seen to have moved downward from the presidency and Congress to the states where the Republican Right holds sway. Both the grassroots organization that allowed this and the vast amounts of money going to both major parties have transformed party organization and electoral politics in the last four decades. The Republican Right, which has been organizing for decades, has been able to "take over" that party in large part because their ideas, policies, and coded racist and demagogic anti-elitist appeals, at least through the Tea Party, are extensions of those since the days of the Young Americans for Freedom, Barry Goldwater, and Reagan, no matter how unwanted by moderates or sections of capital.[39] As Charlie Post has pointed out, *Citizens United* has also allowed wealthy individuals like the Koch brothers to push things even further than the party elite might wish by funding the Tea Party during its heyday.[40] Trump, his money, and the passions he stirs are the bitter fruit of this progression.

For organized labor, the social movements, and the political Left, including Bernie Sanders and Our Revolution, the effort to move the Democrats in a social democratic direction runs counter to the entire long-standing ideological, policy, funding, and strategic thrust of that party—as well as to the weakened state of social democracy. Thus, the transformation of capital—its consolidation, deep logistical integration, and continuing if uneven accumulation—that creates an opening for organized labor also closes more doors on efforts to move politics to the left through the traditional party channels. *The resolution of this contradiction lies in aggressive labor and grassroots working-class organization and action outside the confines of the Democratic Party.* Given the reality of a Trump presidency, much of this active resistance will be in the streets and workplaces of urban America.

In the United States, where there is no parliamentary opening via proportional representation or serial election rounds, the dimension of social organization is even more central to any perspective that hopes to create a viable political Left based in today's diverse working class. As the analysis in chapters 3 through 6 strongly suggest, organized labor must be at the center of this perspective. Unions and workplace organization are not the only social forces that matter, even within the working class, but they have an immediate source of power most other movements don't in their underutilized ability to halt production—an ability that has been magnified by the "logistics revolution." And they remain the largest organized potential social force for change. Much in the unfolding organization of capitalism in the United States offers opportunities for unions to organize, grow, deepen their urban roots, and expand geographically if they offer the means to fight effectively to the new underpaid, overworked labor force and take advantage of the vulnerabilities inherent in capital's new integrated and largely landlocked terrain. This will certainly require the transformation of most unions through rank-and-file organization that rejects bureaucratic business unionism of the sort we have seen in several national unions and many more local unions in recent years. The influx into organized labor of workers in the nation's growing number and concentrations of low-wage, intensified jobs will add to this dynamic.

On the basis of such a dynamic, political work at the local level can begin to build the base for a genuine transformation in party politics through a new political formation. The center is in retreat everywhere. The fight against the

Right, Trump, and the policies they attempt to implement can be the training ground for an expanded layer of activists and the growth of a militant minority that takes the struggle beyond "politics as usual" and the neoliberalism that has become hated by millions who, nevertheless, see no progressive force or way to resist and overcome it. Capital's new terrain of class war is a treacherous one, but it is also one of new possibilities to build such an alternative. As big a shock as a Trump presidency is certain to be, this is no time to retreat. To echo Joe Hill, "Don't moan, organize!"

ACKNOWLEDGMENTS

Like any work of this sort, this book is the result of knowledge gained not only through research but from countless encounters with friends, colleagues, and activists over many years. It would be impossible to name them all or even to remember all those conversations, exchanges, and joint activities. One group or rather organization that supplied vast amounts of information on the US labor movement over the years comprises those who have worked for or with *Labor Notes*, some of whom appear in appendix G, which presents a brief history of that project, originally written for *Jacobin*. For the rest, I must limit my thanks to the much smaller group who read and commented on one or another chapter: Dan La Botz, Charlie Post, and Jane Slaughter. Finally, let me acknowledge the love, support, and contributions of my long-time partner and cothinker Sheila Cohen.

Thanks, too, to the staff of Haymarket Books for their support and faith that I would produce this book on time.

APPENDIXES

Appendix A: Manufacturing Productivity, Value Added, and Output

A re the various productivity figures cited at various points in chapter 1 an illusion? Martin Neil Baily & Barry P. Bosworth (B&B), among others, argue that the productivity of that period can be attributed almost entirely to the high rates of productivity growth in the computer and electronic products (C&EP) sector. In their table 1, B&B conclude that, excluding computers (C&EP), which did grow much faster than other sectors, there was virtually no increase in value added (VA) (a mere 0.06 percent a year). Since profits come from VA minus labor costs, there could not have been much growth in profits. But there was. This would also seem to eliminate the possibility of much productivity growth. Nevertheless, B&B conclude in their table 3 that productivity gains for the years 1987 to 2011 average 2.3 percent for non-C&EP manufacturing, considerably less than their average for all manufacturing of 3.3 percent in table 3.

B&B's lower estimate was at least partly accomplished by stretching the period under examination that began in 1987 into four years of the Great Recession, when the rates of production and non-C&EP productivity did, indeed, fall—bringing down the long-term average. If we move the goalpost back to include only the twenty-one years of relative growth from 1987 to 2007, before the recession killed it, things look a little different. As the BLS reported, "Between 1987 and 2007, productivity rose in all but one of the 21 aggregate industries." The one was apparel.[1] The table below taken from the same BLS time series as B&B's, but for this twenty-one-year period, shows significant gains in many industries.

Average Annual Productivity Increases, Manufacturing Industries, 1987–2007

Industry	% Change
All Manufacturing	3.6%
Computer and Electronic Products	12.5%
Primary Metals	3.1%
Transportation Equipment	3.2%
Textile Mills	3.7%
Electrical Equipment	3.2%
Household Appliances	4.4%
Industrial Machinery	3.2%
Metal Forgings and Stampings	3.2%
Medical Equipment	3.5%
Basic Chemicals	3.6%
Soap, Cleaning Compounds, and Toiletries	3.5%
Pulp, Paper, and Paperboard	3.1%
Animal Food	3.2%

Sources: BLS, "Major Sector Productivity and Costs: Manufacturing," *Databases, Tables & Calculators by Subject*, 2017, https://data.bls.gov/pdq/SurveyOutputServlet; BLS, "Productivity and Costs by Industry: Manufacturing Industries, 2007, 2009," Table 2, News Release, USDL-09-1502, December 9, 2009.

C&EP as a whole composed about 13 percent of manufacturing ship-ments and value added on average by the end of the 1990s but then fell to 10 percent of VA and 7.8 percent of manufacturing shipments by 2006. As a proportion of the workforce it fell from 11 percent in 1990 to 9 percent in 2007—losing 630,000 jobs. Thus, its impact on overall productivity gains was declining just as manufacturing productivity rose at its fastest for the whole period at 4.7 percent a year from 2000 to 2007.[2]

Over the period 1987–2007, C&EP recorded 12.5 percent average annual productivity increases. This is high but not enough proportionately to erase all other productivity gains. Five non-C&EP aggregate sectors and seven addi-tional individual industries, together employing over a third of the non-C&EP manufacturing workforce, saw annual productivity increases close to or more than 3 percent (just slightly lower than the 1960s). In addition, two aggregate sectors saw increases of 2.5 percent or more, while three aggregate sectors achieved annual gains above 2 percent, which, while low, would be enough to hold down employment gains between the massive job destruction of the reces-sions of the era. Altogether these workers count for over half of the employed non-C&EP manufacturing workforce in 2007.

Looking at trends within this time period, BLS reports productivity gains in many non-C&EP industries. From 1990 to 1999 "output per hour increased in 111 of the 119 industries." Forty-five non-C&EP industries had gains of 3 percent or more, and another thirty had gains of 2 percent or more. In other words, over 40 percent of non-C&EP industries saw gains of 3 percent or more, and fully two-thirds of all industries recorded productivity gains of 2 percent or more. The BLS does not provide a comparable breakdown for the years 2000–2007, but the annual average increase for that period was a very high 4.7 percent, while the average annual gain in C&EP fell from 16 percent in 2003 to 6.2 percent in 2005, 8.7 percent in 2006, and 8 percent by 2007— even as C&EP declined as a percentage of VA and the workforce.[3] Clearly, the idea that C&EP productivity accounted for all or most gains between 1987 and 2007 is not credible. Thus, a majority of manufacturing workers experienced significant increased productivity over this long period. B&B's picture of nearly stagnant non-C&EP manufacturing industries throughout the period is a distortion of reality.

In any case, as far as the impact of productivity on employment levels as shown in this book, those in the C&EP sector who lost jobs due to their out-sized productivity gains, in addition to imports, count as much as any others.

If productivity gains had been negligible in 90 percent of the workforce, lean production, work intensification, new technology, improved JIT logistics, et cetera, would have had little or no impact, something neither enthusiasts nor critics of these innovations argue. In fact, these levels of productivity not only destroyed millions of jobs but also combined with stagnant or falling real wages, were enough to increase the surplus value underlying much of the real income and wealth that moved upward over this period.

BLS productivity figures *understate* the impact on the production workers who actually create the value added. BLS productivity figures are based on total employment, while productivity increases impact the production workforce far more than the nearly 30 percent of non-production employees. From 1979 to 2010 5.7 million production jobs were lost, almost 80 percent of all employment losses in manufacturing.

It is worth noting, as well, that productivity gains also eliminated jobs in some industries that lost production to imports. While the US steel industry, for example, lost production and jobs as imports "captured" increased demand throughout the neoliberal period, domestic steel production nonetheless rose from a little over 60 million tons in 1981 to 70 million tons in 1987 and 110 million tons around 2006 just before the recession—this was the highest level of annual output at least since 1940, with the sole exception of

1973, even with the rise of Chinese imports after 2000.[4] Productivity in US steel and iron mills rose by 5.2 percent a year from 1987 to 2007. This is largely due to the increase in more efficient mini-mills. Clearly this contributed to the loss of some 100,000 jobs even as domestic output rose over this period. Much the same is true for C&EP jobs since, despite imports, output rose over this long period.

In two papers Susan Houseman and various other researchers (2010, 2014) argued that estimates of prices of intermediate inputs (IInp) "overstated . . . real value added growth by 0.2 to 0.5 percentage point(s)." Houseman and coauthors (2014) explain the overestimate in the prices of IInps that go into the BLS price index by a lag in the reporting of price changes as manufacturers switched from high-cost domestic or previously costly imported IInps to even cheaper imports. Thus, even though the cost reduction will eventually be reported, assuming the growth of imports from year to year, the index for any given year will be too low by the increase in unreported price changes. From this they derive an inflation in value added of between 0.2 to 0.5 percentage *points* (not percentage changes) per year. What would the difference in VA rates be? As the table below shows, they would be significant but not all that much. Either adjusted annual rate of VA is still enough to boost productivity and eliminate jobs and/or hold employment levels down during periods of increased output between recessions.

Real Manufacturing Value Added Growth w/wo Houseman et al. Adjustments

Real Value Added	1997–2007	Annual
Unadjusted increase	42.4%	3.9%
Adjusted 0.2 points per year	40.2%	3.7%
Adjusted 0.5 points per year	36.9%	3.4%

Sources: Council of Economic Advisors, *Economic Report of the President* (Washington, DC: US Government Printing Office, 2011), 206, 250; US Census Bureau, *Statistical Abstract of the United States: 2012* (Washington, DC: US Government Printing Office, 2011), 636; Houseman et al., *Offshore Bias in U.S. Manufacturing: Implications for Productivity and Value Added* (Washington, DC: Board of Governors of the Federal Reserve System, 2010), Abstract, n.p.; Houseman et al., *Measuring Manufacturing: How the Computer and Semiconductor Industries Affect the Numbers and Perceptions* (Kalamazoo, MI: W.E. Upjohn Institute for Employment Research, 2014), 43–46.

Furthermore, since productivity is a measure of the change in total output per hour, and VA accounts for about 45 percent of total output, the actual impact of the Houseman adjustments on productivity is much smaller than her and her coauthors' VA figures imply. More like between 0.09 and 0.2 percentage points per year from 1997 to 2007. In other words, not a lot. ·

In addition, since as Houseman and coauthors point out, the destination of imports is not reported by any government agency, there is a lot to be questioned in their method and results. In any case, whatever the effect of these and other biases on past and current government statistics, these adjustments do not substantially alter my argument about the impact of productivity on manufacturing jobs.

Appendix B: Indexes of Real Merchandise Imports and Manufacturing Production Jobs, 1990–2010

(2000 = 100)

Year	Imports (1000s)	Index	Jobs (1000s)	Index
1990	$449,742	36.9	12,738	102.0
1991	$456,215	37.4	12,351	98.9
1992	$504,966	41.4	12,013	96.2
1993	$551,636	45.2	12,060	96.6
1994	$638,716	52.3	12,181	97.5
1995	$753,953	61.8	12,593	100.8
1996	$800,856	65.6	12,517	100.2
1997	$859,268	70.4	12,579	100.7
1998	$848,975	69.6	12,818	102.6
1999	$951,870	78.0	12,605	100.9
2000	$1,220,458	100.0	12,491	100.0
2001	$1,113,615	91.3	12,229	97.9
2002	$1,092,845	89.5	10,993	88.0
2003	$1,209,350	99.1	10,484	83.9
2004	$1,494,689	122.4	10,027	80.3
2005	$1,827,413	149.7	10,045	80.4
2006	$2,174,669	178.2	10,153	81.3
2007	$2,348,354	192.4	10,036	80.4
2008	$3,060.798	250.8	9,914	79.4
2009	$1,871,550	153.3	8,889	71.2
2010	$2,393,875	196.2	8,034	64.3

Sources: US Census Bureau, *Statistical Abstract of the United States, 2004–2005* (Washington, DC: US Government Printing Office, 2004), 819; US Census Bureau, *Statistical Abstract of the United States, 2012* (Washington, DC: US Government Printing Office, 2011), 487, 813; Bureau of Labor Statistics, "Employment, Hours, and Earning from the Current Employment Survey (National) Manufacturing: Production and Nonsupervisory Employees, Thousands," Data, Tables & Calculations by Subject, http://data.bls.gov/pdq/SurveyOutputServlet.

Appendix C: Contingent and Alternative Work, 1995, 2005

Work	1995 (1000s)	2005 (1000s)
Part-Time Economic Reasons, F-T	1,468	1,556
Contingent	(6,034)	(5,705)
Adjusted for Overlap (Table 12)	3,975	3,852
Independent Contractors	8,309	10,342
On-call	2,078	2,454
Temporary Agency	(1,181)	(1,217)
	2,189	2,549
Provided by Contract Firm	652	813
Adjusted Total: Non-brackets	18,671	21,566
Total Employed	123,208	138,952
Precarious as % of Total	15.2%	15.5%

Sources: BLS (1995), *New Data on Contingent and Alternative Employment Examined by BLS,* USDL 95-318, August 17, 1995, Tables 1, 5, 12; *Contingent and Alternative Employment Arrangements, February 2005,* USDL 05-1433, July 27, 2005, Tables 1, 5, 12; US Census Bureau (1996), *Statistical Abstract of the United States* (Washington, DC: US Government Printing Office), 403; US Census Bureau (2005) *Statistical Abstract of the United States* (Washington, DC: US Government Printing Office), 391.

Figures in parentheses are from the BLS 1995 and 2005 reports. "Contingent" is adjusted for overlap with other categories as in table 12. Larger temporary agency figures from the *Statistical Abstracts* 1996 and 2005 are substituted for low counts in the 1995 and 2005 reports. Independent contractors represent those among the "self-employed" who are actually employees, that is, the bogus self-employed. All part-time workers are not included because most are voluntary and/or work in service or retail jobs that have always had shorter hours than the thirty-five that are the official part-time/full-time border. All those self-employed are not included because many are incorporated and actually small business owners or would-be entrepreneurs and are middle class, not working class.

Appendix D: Auto Parts Industry

The statistics in the section on the reorganization of the US auto parts supply industry, including some of the secondary sources, are based primarily on three main, very different data sources. The US Census *County Business Patterns* contains consistent data of the number of establishments, that is, single facilities, not firms, in the auto parts industry, NAICS (North American Industrial Classification System) Code 3363. This definition includes companies whose majority of output is in auto parts but excludes tires as well as electrical and electronic inputs, which obviously have become more important. Nevertheless, this source was used in the McAlinden and Smith (1993) study and by me for figures from 1998 to 2013, to get an idea of the trends in the growth and decline in plants in the industry. These figures are net figures, which conceal plant closings and openings. Figures from the Original Equipment Suppliers Association surveys, cited in the Department of Commerce report (2011), cover a much broader range of companies, many of which may produce only a small portion of their output for the auto industry, such as electronics firms. The dramatic decline in the number of these firms must include not only failed companies but also those who chose to exit the auto parts business and focus more on their "core" production, as well as those Tier 1, 2, or 3 firms forced to merge. Nevertheless, the drop of these companies from 30,000 to 5,000 from 1990 to 2004 speaks strongly of industry consolidation. Finally, there are the figures on plant closings, openings, expansions, downsizing, and locations in Aschoff's study. Her database is drawn from industry publications and press and only covers "events" reported, not overall statistics. This study is most useful for the location information, which generally conforms in its concentrations to US Census *County Business Patterns* data for states.

Appendix E: Real Net Stock of Private Fixed Assets, 1982–2012

($ billions, year-end)

Year	Private	Manuf.	T&W*	Info.	Hosp.
1992	10,540.1	1,189.0	449.9	553.3	210.1
2002	20,722.4	1,699.4	618.5	914.7	345.8
2012	22,287.5	2,050.5	729.2	1,153.4	517.8

Net Stock of Private Fixed Assets adjusted by PPI for capital equipment (1982 = 100).

*Transportation and Warehouse

Production and Nonsupervisory Employees, 1982–2012
(thousands, year-end)

Year	Private	Manuf.	T&W	Info.	Hosp.*
1992	73,478	12,031	2,963	1,889	3,737
2002	88,246	10,523	3,607	2,330	4,206
2012	93,551	8,297	3,880	2,168	4,791

* All Employees

Real Net Stock of Private Assets per Worker, 1982–2012
($, year-end)

Year	Private	Manuf.	T&W	Info.	Hosp.
1992	1,434,457	98,828	151,839.4	292,906	56,222
2002	2,348,254	161,494	171,472.2	392,575	82,216
2012	2,382,390	247,138	187.938.1	532,011	108,078

Real Net Stock of Private Equipment, 1982–2012
($ billions, year-end)

Year	Private	Manuf.	T&W	Info.	Hosp.
1992	1,996.1	556.9	189.1	185.5	45.6
2002	2,882.6	711.1	259.2	272.7	69.9
2012	3,513.5	776.9	289.0	265.6	125.3

Net Stock of Private Equipment adjusted by PPI (1982 = 100).

Sources: BEA, Table 3.1ESI, "Current-Cost Net Stock of Private Fixed Assets by Industry," 2015, www.bea.gov/iTable/print.cfm?; Council of Economic Advisers, *Economic Report of the President 2013* (Washington, DC: US Government Printing Office, 2013), 399; BLS, "Employment, Hours, and Earnings from the Current Employment Survey (National)," Databases, Tables & Calculators by Subject, 2015, http://data.bls.gov/pdq/SurveyOutputServlet.

Appendix F: Strikes and Worker-Hours on Strike, 2002–15*

Year	Strikes	Work-hours
2015	111	39,280,000
2014	108	6,823,000
2013	159	15,317,000
2012	164	11,038,000
2011	149	11,222,000
2010	154	8,877,000
2009	119	19,609,000
2008	183	20,147,000
2007	175	29,734,000
2006	268	25,175,000
2004	273	71,501,000
2003	289	17,078,000
2002	327	17,686,000

* Ending in each year

Source: Federal Mediation and Conciliation Service, *Annual Report*, 2015, 20; 2010, 8; 2006, 7.

A Labor Notes conference in 1981. Pictured: Crystal Lee Sutton, Kim Moody, and Ken Paff. Labor Notes / Flickr

Appendix G: The Rank and File's Paper of Record[1]

The history of *Labor Notes* shows that labor's strength–and socialists' relevance–depend on a militant and independent rank and file.

By most measures 1979 was not an auspicious time to start a radical publication in the United States aimed at labor's rank-and-file activists. Deregulation in transportation was working its way through Congress and soon to pass, threatening national agreements in trucking and airlines. Chrysler went begging to Congress for a financial bailout and soon extracted concessions from the mighty United Auto Workers. These, in turn, opened the floodgates to union givebacks in industry after industry. Federal Reserve chief Paul Volcker jacked up interest rates that soon brought on a double-dip recession that cost two and a half million manufacturing jobs, brought strikes to a screech-

---

1 Kim Moody, "The Rank and File's Paper of Record," *Jacobin*, August 11, 2016, www .jacobinmag.com/2016/08/labor-notes-rank-and-file-reform-unions-concessions-labor.

ing halt, and effectively undermined a decade and a half of labor upsurge even before Reagan fired the striking air traffic controllers in 1981.

The industrial unions that had been the major sites of rank-and-file rebellions, black caucuses, wildcat strikes, and contract rejections during the upsurge lost two million members by the time the recession bottomed out in 1982. The era of labor insurgency and mass social movements was about to give way to that of neoliberalism, union decline, "the end of welfare as we know it," and lean production.

Of course, when *Labor Notes* made its debut in February 1979, we didn't know all of this. "We" were three members of the International Socialists (IS), Jim West, myself, and a little bit later Jane Slaughter, charged with producing and spreading a monthly newsletter (later a magazine) meant to put rank-and-file activists in touch with each other—to present a class view by reporting events and trends across the whole labor movement.

Labor Notes couldn't predict the employers' offensive that began with Chrysler's demand for concessions from autoworkers in fall 1979, but it turned out that our politics prepared us for it. We knew what to say. We also knew, based on over a decade of IS experience in workplace and rank-and-file newsletters, movements, and organizations, that *Labor Notes* could not be seen as, or be anything like, a "front group." It would have to base itself on a broad network of activists whose support and input would be crucial.

IS and its successor Solidarity would continue to support *Labor Notes*, while at the same time respecting its independence. Individual members played important roles both on staff and as union members, but the staff grew beyond those in IS/Solidarity. To grow, *Labor Notes* would have to be, within a broad framework, a center for discussion and debate as well as analysis and news. Socialist ideas, our experience told us, needed a base in an active "class struggle" current within the labor movement to be credible. The task of the *Labor Notes* project was to work with others to create such a current.

How did we do that? Of course, we had a general body of theory that told us about the dynamics of capitalism with its relentless drive for profits and the pressures this put on working-class life. Somewhat more immediate was an understanding of the labor movement and the unions as multilayered social formations with internal contradictions—not only that between "the bureaucracy" and the ranks, but those within the ranks between the activist layer and mostly apathetic members, and the divisions of race and gender. From the start, the magazine addressed these issues by reporting on what women and African American workers were doing in the unions and how rank-and-file workers were still fighting for union democracy and an accountable leadership, as well as fighting the new concessions trend.

We also reported just how the leadership of most unions not only went along with concessions and labor-management cooperation schemes, virtually surrendering the workplace to the employers, but how these became part of the bureaucracy's failed and costly strategy for survival even to this day. Having an analysis or even reporting events and trends, however, is never enough. One of the most important lessons to be drawn from the *Labor Notes* experience is that you have to engage directly in the movement and with the activists—and that radicals can do that when they are willing to relate to people's real concerns and make them aware that others in the movement share those concerns.

Jim West, editor from the start until 2003, describes the basic purpose of the project: "The idea all along was that there were all these grassroots activists and groups in various unions around the country and that our mission was to bring them together—to give them a sense that they were part of a bigger movement." Looking back, Mark Brenner, the current director of the project, argues this worked. "*Labor Notes* succeeded in creating an important space for activists in other unions and various parts of the country to recognize they were having common experiences and to actually build connections with each other."

An important aspect was the focus on rank-and-file activists in the workplace. As Will Johnson, on staff from 2002 to 2007, put it, "*Labor Notes* readers are workplace leaders. What always struck me, both editing articles or in organizing conferences, was the relentless focus on winning power at work." Brenner notes in this regard, "if you want to reengage or connect with members you need to start with where they spend eight, ten, twelve hours a day. I think our emphasis went much farther, arguing that our power as a movement stemmed first and foremost from our power on the job." This, in turn, also meant involvement in the union. Mike Parker, an autoworker for many years and a close associate of *Labor Notes* describes this:

> I think the "focus on the rank-and-file" or "grassroots" is important, but I think the reason that we succeeded where others failed is that we focused on the class struggle. That meant building, involving, mobilizing the rank and file and giving it control, but it also meant that we appreciated organization and the power of the labor movement so we struggled for union reform efforts sometimes led by local (or national) union leaders with mixed or contradictory consciousness.

Brenner adds, "It was crucial that we were one of the only places that was not just blaming the one-sided class war, or trade agreements, or technology, for the decline in union strength. It was critical to our longevity that in any given period we were willing to spell out the ways labor got itself into the mess it was in." And this meant working with and aiding rank-and-file union reform movements, such as the Teamsters for a Democratic Union. Again, Brenner elaborates, "Promoting union reform as a strategy for revitalizing the labor movement is one of our biggest contributions, both theoretically—because it injects politics so squarely into the discussion—but also practically, helping generations of reformers think strategically about how to run for office and win."

Action, education, and organization, not sloganeering, were key both to building rank-and-file power and the success of the magazine. As West put it, "No sectarian language, open to anyone with a rank-and-file perspective, and pretty much focused on trade union issues." Leah Samuel, on staff from 1995 to 2001, agrees. "*Labor Notes* has always emphasized real-world practicality in its approach to helping workers bring about change in their workplaces and unions." Events soon taught us, however, that to bring people together and "give them a sense that they were part of a bigger movement," as West put it, we would need to create a real "center" where activists could learn from one another. The eighteen conferences held between 1981 and 2016 provided such a center.

Former staffer Martha Gruelle puts it this way: "*Labor Notes* is a location—literally, at the conferences, where people can find other unionists who see the world similarly—and in the 'spiritual' sense of knowing these others exist and connecting through the writing, etc. It's hugely important for militant unionists to know they're not alone." The first national conference was in April 1981 at the rundown Book Cadillac Hotel in downtown Detroit. Much to our surprise 576 people registered, while an additional hundred women unionists attended a special Friday evening women's meeting. Crystal Lee Sutton, the real Norma Rae (seen in the photo above) addressed the conference, as did Tony Mazzocchi, then running for president against the old guard of the Oil, Chemical, and Atomic Workers. Mazzocchi called for a new party of labor to oppose the old "twin parties of cancer."

We soon found that it made more sense to let experienced union leaders and activists say some of the more political things—independent politics, for example, and opposition to wars—rather than lectures from the staff, at least in the early years. At the center of the conference, however, were practical workshops on workplace organizing, union democracy, and many other issues and meetings of activists by industry. This would become a growing feature at the heart of all future conferences.

From the start, *Labor Notes* did things that no one else in the labor movement or on the political Left was doing. As Slaughter put it, "*Labor Notes* had great success when we took on subjects that the mainstream labor movement did not know how to tackle, or was facing the wrong way, and offered readers both a political understanding of them and practical help on what to do."

The surrender of the top union leadership in most cases in this period of retreat naturally created a vacuum for intervention on key issues such as concessions on wages, benefits, and working conditions; the introduction of team working and lean production norms that led to work intensification; the lack of democracy that characterized most unions; and the general failure to encourage strong workplace organization. It was a willingness to intervene actively on some of these issues that allowed *Labor Notes* to establish itself as an important educational center.

Confronting Concessions

As 1982 arrived and signs of economic recovery appeared it was clear that the concessions flood was only going to grow. We were convinced that concessions were now a central issue for workers, even nonunion workers.

So Jane Slaughter wrote *Concessions and How to Beat Them* in 1983, analyzing not only the extent and underlying causes of concessions but scores of examples of how workers were resisting and sometimes defeating them. *Concessions* was an instant hit and one of *Labor Notes*'s turning points. Activists across the labor movement used *Concessions* to fight them even when top leaders refused to do so. There were probably more defeats than victories, but the fact that activists saw others fighting encouraged more to resist. In *Concessions*, Slaughter showed that there had been at least two rounds of givebacks and that these waves of retreat saw labor's industry-wide national and pattern agreements shredded, opening the door to a downward spiral of competition. Even as the recession of 1980–82 was turning to recovery, corporate demands for more increased.

The second round had moved from wages to working conditions—an even greater threat. Already in *Concessions* there was an indication of what lay ahead. Slaughter quoted GM chairman Roger Smith's early 1983 declaration: "There's no way we want to put ourselves back in a position to go through the last three years again. All of us are dedicated to keeping our companies lean and mean." Ad hoc concessions would continue right up to today, but new ways to institutionalize them and permanently weaken labor were in the works.

Taking on Circles and Teams

In May 1981, *BusinessWeek* declared the era of "The New Industrial Relations." These were first embodied in "quality of work life" (QWL) programs and later expanded to "total quality management," "employee participation," and more. All put labor-management cooperation—on-the-job class collaboration—at their center.

Mike Parker had been researching these programs since their first public appearance around the late 1970s. In 1985 he produced *Inside the Circle: A Union Guide to QWL*, the first of three handbooks on the topic of labor-management cooperation and lean production. The book gave practical advice on how to resist or undermine this "feel-good" form of union-busting. As Parker noted in the introduction, "There is almost no material available to guide the trade unionist who is trying to come to grips with these new programs from a union point of view." Now there was.

As various forms of employee participation proliferated and morphed into Japanese-inspired lean production, *Labor Notes* kept pace. Parker and Slaughter together produced two additional handbooks, *Choosing Sides: Unions and the Team Concept* in 1988 and *Working Smart: A Union Guide to Participation Programs and Reengineering* in 1994. In these, they coined the term "Management-By-Stress" (MBS), which captured the way in which lean production methods created a new basis for the intensification of work by cutting the workforce while maintaining or increasing output. Teams contributed to this through the process of *kaizen*, or constant improvement in productivity. *Choosing Sides* focused on the auto industry where many of these innovations in work intensification were first or most thoroughly applied. *Working Smart* expanded the analysis to other industries and groups including telecommunications, hospitals, the postal service, home care, women workers, workers of color, and even to Mexico and Sweden. These handbooks sold in the thousands.

From the early to mid-1990s *Labor Notes* created a new place in which workers could learn and exchange ideas about the new management strategies. Jane Slaughter describes this place:

> We also spread the word on labor-management cooperation and lean production through about a dozen "team concept schools" held mostly in Detroit but also Atlanta and the Bay Area. We held one just for the Teamsters

union (under President Ron Carey). These were schools of fifty to eighty people from different unions who came for an intensive three days of learning and figuring out, in teams, how to confront that situation.

Lean production methods continue today in new forms. But, as Slaughter points out, "Labor-management cooperation programs are a dead letter; employers no longer need to pretend to seek employees' involvement."

Aside from simply reverting to bullying and threats of job loss, lean norms became increasingly enforced through electronic and biometric monitoring and measuring technology such as global positioning systems, radio frequency identification, and barcoding.

While lean programs such as total quality management had always been about standardizing jobs and intensifying work, the new types of surveillance further diluted skills and eliminated such creativity as a job might have had.

In addition, the emergence of electronically guided, just-in-time supply chains associated with the "logistics revolution" added external pressures on performance in countless workplaces. These internal and external pressures have spread far beyond traditional blue-collar work into professional occupations such as nursing and teaching.

Often hypnotized by the alleged inevitability of such technology, the leadership of most unions simply ignored the fact that most workplace technology is socially constructed to achieve management goals. *Labor Notes* would attempt to find new ways to deal with and resist evolving management tactics and strategies.

The handbooks and schools helped *Labor Notes* expand from its original base among auto, steel, trucking, and other industrial sectors to telecommunications, health care, transit, the public sector, and other service industries. We also got support from a few smaller unions such as the Oil, Chemical & Atomic Workers (OCAW), United Electrical Workers (UE), and the Farm Labor Organizing Committee (FLOC).

As the working class itself was changing and management was finding new tools of exploitation, we stumbled toward an approach to workplace class conflict that could deal comprehensively with the increasing forms of union avoidance and work intensification. I say "stumbled" because it would be a stretch to say that we put all these factors—new management approaches to lean production, new technology, workplace tactics, union reform movements—together at once. Not everything we tried worked. For example, in 1995 we attempted to raise the shorter workweek as one way to deal with some of the new lean pressures and the increase in precarious work. We produced a pamphlet entitled *Time Out!* making the case for shorter hours. The pamphlet didn't catch on and the project had to be abandoned. We learned a valuable lesson: trying to set the agenda without actual motion among the workplace activists was not going to work.

What we did realize was that even as management tactics were evolving, we were accumulating a vast store of stories about workplace and union resistance and that many of these experiences could be used to fight the boss(es) over a variety of issues.

We held a weekend school on "workplace organizing" in 1989 where dozens of activists told their stories of resistance. We then hired Dan La Botz to pull them together into a new handbook. He produced *A Troublemaker's Handbook: How to Fight Back Where You Work—and Win* in 1991. Jane Slaughter edited a *Troublemaker's Handbook II* in 2005.

Our Troublemakers handbooks used the maxim that people can learn better from a story than from a list of good advice. Like most of our Steward's Corner columns in *Labor Notes*, for each situation or tactic, the books told how a group of workers did something; the reader could then apply the tactics to her or his own situation. This method also had the advantage of using real-life examples, so the author was not just laying down a list of untested ideas— these ideas had worked for someone.

By this time *Labor Notes* really was established as a center of labor education of a type few others could produce. By the nineties, too, the staff had grown significantly. The nineties also saw *Labor Notes* engage directly in international work, largely in cooperation with and through the European-based Transnationals Information Exchange (TIE). Our contribution in the context of the North American Free Trade Agreement (NAFTA) was building cross-border links through meetings in Mexico and tours in all three NAFTA countries of auto and telecommunications workers.

We also worked with the Canadian Auto Workers (CAW), the United Electrical Workers (UE), the Frente Auténtico del Trabajo, and the Centro de Información Laboral y Asesoría Sindical (CILAS) in Mexico City to organize these cross-border events. It was exciting work and the worker-to-worker approach we adopted in the cross-border meetings had an impact on the consciousness of the workers who participated.

The problem here was that most union leaders are tied up in the byzantine protocol of official top-down labor internationalism, making contact between regular workers difficult. It took small, generally underfunded groups like TIE and *Labor Notes*, with help from the small United Electrical Workers, to navigate around the institutional barriers. Yet the resources to continue regular cross-border exchanges and meetings weren't there. *Labor Notes*'s international activity became limited to the biennial *Labor Notes* conferences.

A Plateau

At the same time I say we "stumbled" because from the late 1990s through the early 2000s, *Labor Notes* hit a plateau in terms of subscriptions and conference attendance, which was stuck under one thousand. Part of this was that while we published more good handbooks—notably *Democracy Is Power: Rebuilding Unions from the Bottom Up* by Mike Parker and Martha Gruelle in 1999 on union democracy—we were unable to turn these into the sorts of events we had with the team concept schools.

Any activity in labor or other social movements, however, is also dependent on what is going on around you. The mid-eighties to the mid-nineties saw a number of important high-profile struggles against concessions: P-9 at Hormel, the United Mine Workers at Pittston, the Communications Workers at Verizon, an innovative "inside strategy" at A.E. Staley, the Detroit newspaper strike, and the UPS strike for full-time jobs in 1997, as well as a mini-wave of union reform movements.

Looking back from 1996 in a speech to the National Lawyers Guild, union reform lawyer Paul Levy could report, "There is extensive intra-union activity in a large number of national unions, much more than ever before." In addition to the big victory in the Teamsters with the TDU-backed election of Ron Carey in 1991, Levy noted revolts in a dozen or so major unions. Many of these struggles and movements used *Labor Notes* literature to educate their activists. For example, in the two years leading up to the 1997 Teamster strike at UPS, TDU and the union used *Working Smart* to inform members on the pitfalls of the labor-management/lean production scheme UPS was trying to introduce in hopes of weakening any future union action.

In some places *Labor Notes* staffers and friends helped in defeating UPS's labor-management cooperation program. Staffers and friends were also directly active in the New Directions caucus in the United Auto Workers from the mid-1980s, as well as in the support campaign for the Hormel/P-9 strikers.

The workplace strategy and team concept (lean production) schools in this period attracted hundreds of both mainstream and dissident activists from unions such as the Communications Workers, Oil, Chemical and Atomic Workers, and Grain Millers, among others, contributing indirectly to important anti-concessions and anti-lean struggles in those industries in these years. This active engagement brought both experience and growth. By the late 1990s, however, high-profile strikes became rare and many of the internal rebellions had faded—and with them a good deal of our natural audience.

The debacle that brought Ron Carey down after the 1997 UPS strike had a negative impact on the milieu in which *Labor Notes* operated. Carey's election had been the first big victory of the union reform movement, and the illegal funding scam his hired campaign organizers had run during the 1996 election bolstered the idea that all union leaders were the same. Carey was eventually cleared of any direct involvement in or knowledge of the scam, but the damage was done. It is also possible that the election of John Sweeney as AFL-CIO president on a promise of progressive change deflected some potential *Labor Notes* readers, as did the rise of the Internet. The reform efforts of John Sweeney and the "New Voice" team were largely top-down. As one article in *Labor Notes* put it at the time, "for every problem there was a Washington solution."

The slate's central promise was to ramp up new organizing in order to stop the decline in union membership. While the new AFL-CIO leaders expanded the Organizing Institute to train more organizers, this really meant getting the affiliated unions to put more energy and resources into organizing. The institutional barriers to this proved too great and by 2005 led to a split with the formation of the Change to Win coalition, which itself eventually split. *Labor Notes*, with its emphasis on rank-and-file-based reform, was critical of this bureaucratic approach. While this stance didn't necessarily expand our base at the time, it would pay off as activists in more and more unions began to organize frequently successful grassroots reform movements in the following years.

By the late 1990s the team concept schools and our cross-border work had run their course, and we weren't able to develop the sort of outreach project that struck the chord we had with concessions and team concept. That would await the coming of a new generation of staffers and a change in the situation.

A New Generation

With the opening of the twenty-first century a major transition began as a new generation of younger activists took over the running of *Labor Notes*. Eventually Mark Brenner took over my old job of director after a number of veteran staffers filled in for a while and a series of new editors replaced Jim

West, Martha Gruelle, and Jane Slaughter. These included Chris Kutalik, Mischa Gaus, Jenny Brown, and Alexandra Bradbury, the current editor.

Armed with the publication of *Troublemaker's II* in 2005 this new generation took the Troublemaker's idea to new heights beginning in 2011, with about two dozen local Troublemaker's day schools, prepared with the help of local activists. These schools provided that place in city after city where activists exchanged ideas and helped broaden *Labor Notes*'s reach.

This new activity benefited from a renewed wave of union reform movements among the Teamsters, communications workers, transit workers, postal workers, nurses, and others, reaching a high point with the Chicago Teachers Union's Caucus of Rank and File Educators victory in 2010 and their strike in 2012, along with the Wisconsin uprising of 2011. The period also saw the growing activity of immigrant workers that took off after the Immigrant Workers' Freedom Ride that crossed the country in 2003 and the May 1, 2006, "Day without an Immigrant."

The conferences in 2014 and 2016 reflected the new situation, drawing over two thousand activists to Chicago, where in 2016 it coincided with a one-day Chicago Teachers Union strike—as if to illustrate the viability of the rank-and-file approach.

What Did *Labor Notes* Accomplish?

It hardly needs saying that all the work of the staffers and hundreds of close associates who over the decades helped make *Labor Notes* an institution in the broader labor movement could not stop the decline in union membership, the tidal wave of concessions, the progress and transformation of lean production into its high-tech surveillance, just-in-time regime, or, indeed, the mammoth level of inequality that has taken shape during the lifetime of *Labor Notes*.

That being the case, just what did it accomplish?

Here you have to step back and look beneath the institutional facade of the unions, the big collective bargaining agreements that sometimes make the business page, and the leaders who do occasionally make a public appearance and seek out those who remain mostly invisible to society and even to each other. It is these invisible class warriors whose actions, dedication, and persistence keep the unions afloat and the labor movement alive. These are the people who sit on committees, act as shop stewards, and sometimes hold local union office even when the perks are small—labor's activist layer. Most of these men and women accept much of the ideology of bureaucratic business unionism, waiting and hoping "the union" or someone will do something for them through the sclerotic channels of formal collective bargaining. Many, however, do not and instead take it upon themselves along with others like them to get things done. That is where *Labor Notes* comes in.

The revolutionary syndicalists and Wobblies of old called this layer of workers the "militant minority." But for decades now, this layer has been disorganized and depoliticized. Even during the labor upsurge of the 1960s and 1970s, the various rank-and-file movements, wildcat strikers and union dissidents had precious little contact with one another—isolated and confined largely to their own industry, workplace, or union. Most of the changes, reforms, and civil wars at the top of the labor movement in the last twenty years or so have had little if any impact on this reality. Missing were the radicals who at one time gave overall leadership (or misleadership in some cases) and coherence to this militant minority in the years before and after World War I and during the 1930s and 1940s.

The radicals of the 1970s who entered industry to play this role were too few, too inexperienced, too late, and often too sectarian to carry it off. It was this fragmentation within the 1960s–1970s upsurge that convinced us that something different was needed. The idea of *Labor Notes*, as the earlier quotes from past and present staffers put it, was to bring these activists together, to provide them a place to connect and learn, and the means by which to become visible to one another. The words "Let's Put the Movement Back in the Labor Movement" that first appeared on the masthead in April 1981 were in a sense a call to these activists to take on the task of building a bigger militant minority.

The collapse of the upsurge of the 1970s meant starting on a small scale reaching out to the pockets of resistance that inevitably arose as capital's war on the workers increased. Because old activists dropped out while new ones came in, many reform efforts failed, and the occupational, gender, and racial composition of the workforce changed. This was never a linear process. Nevertheless, it was a process, based on all the activities described above and many more, and of course on the self-activity of thousands of worker activists themselves, that produced the growth of a militant, democratic current—the evidence for which can be seen in the *Labor Notes* conferences and the dozens of local Troublemaker's Schools.

To a greater degree than in the earlier years of *Labor Notes* this emerging current shares a set of operating principles and goals that give it some programmatic and political coherence: union democracy and accountable leadership; rejection of labor-management cooperation; strong workplace and stewards' organizations; direct action and mobilization when needed or possible; racial and gender inclusion and equality; resistance to austerity in society as well as at work; and the realization that the ranks will have to do or win these things themselves. In short: a rejection of the norms of bureaucratic business unionism. *Labor Notes* deserves considerable credit for this political coherence and its spread across the activist layer.

A look at the 2016 conference gives some idea of why *Labor Notes* has played a role in shaping this alternative view of what the labor movement as a whole should stand for. While the workplace and the union remained central to the focus of the conference, of the more than 125 workshops and interest or industry meetings held in Chicago in 2016, nearly fifty dealt with big political, social, and international issues. Yet the political hopes of some of us had been a little more ambitious. Part of the socialist conception of the purpose of *Labor Notes* was that it was a transitional project. That is, to borrow Trotsky's analogy, it was meant to be a "bridge" between the day-to-day struggles and consciousness of the class to a broader class, eventually socialist view of the world. A bridge, of course, has two ends. Theoretically, socialist consciousness and organization would be at the far end of the bridge provided mostly by socialist organization(s).

As the bridge it was not *Labor Notes*'s role to be the socialist educational center, organization, or publication. To attempt that would have limited its audience and the project's effectiveness severely. Rather, the types of ideas the project put forth were transitional ones directed at undermining the conservative consciousness produced by bureaucratic business unionism as well as all the other forces in society that promote acceptance of things as they are. *Labor Notes* accomplished a good deal of this. Indeed, while the emphasis was on building power in the workplace and union, from the start *Labor Notes* took up most of the political, social, and economic issues that affect working-class life. The results of this can be seen at the conferences where there is a working-class political radicalism well beyond what is the norm for the American labor movement. Some of this sentiment was expressed in the nearly universal support for Bernie Sanders that permeated the 2016 conference.

While this political crossing was never seen as the main task, it has nevertheless been less complete than some of us would have wished. Independent political action, for example, is transitional—a bridge—in that it involves a break with the two major parties and their embrace of capitalism and its rules of the game (including the neoliberal framework), without necessarily embracing a fully socialist program. To some extent *Labor Notes* attempted to make this part of its message. Thus, from the start with Tony Mazocchi's labor party speech at the 1981 conference to the coverage of and involvement with such independent political efforts as the Mazzocchi-inspired Labor Party of the mid- to late 1990s and the 2000 Labor for Nader campaign, *Labor Notes* promoted the idea of independent political action. In addition, many of the conferences have featured keynote speakers who put forth the idea of independent politics. Among these in addition to Mazzocchi were Bill Fletcher Jr., who called for a new left party; various Canadian speakers who raised this question; French Marxist Daniel Singer, who argued that the new millennium could be the time of the Left internationally; and, well before he was a household name, independent socialist Bernie Sanders. Yet independent political action is not yet an integral part of the program or set of ideas that characterizes the grassroots labor current or network described above, the potential militant minority.

Could more have been done? It has to be remembered that everything *Labor Notes* did that worked was based on movement activity that was already actually happening. That was a lesson we learned early on. By the end of 2000, once the Labor Party lost its momentum and the Nader campaign came to an end, however, there wasn't really anything to point to and political action seemed a bridge too far.

Should *Labor Notes* have done more educational work on this? Perhaps, but when choices had to be made between educating in practical strategies and actions, on the one hand, and advanced political education or mere propaganda, on the other, for better or worse we almost invariably chose the former. That was the right choice and part of what made the project work as well as it did. Not everyone who worked for *Labor Notes* over the years would agree that the lack of a more political or socialist approach was a problem. Nevertheless for some of us committed to building a more advanced political consciousness in the rank-and-file milieu, the tension between the needs of the here and now and the future remains an unresolved dilemma. There are signs that the times are changing in this regard and more attention to this line of action may be called for.

The contributions of *Labor Notes* and today's changing atmosphere make one of the main lessons of the *Labor Notes*'s experience pressing for the Left today. Socialists from an educated background, as most of us were, can have an impact in the labor movement. The isolation of political radicals from working-class life is largely a self-imposed one. The skills, ideas, and knowledge we have are valued by those trying to fight for change—provided we learn to share them as insiders, not impose them from the sidelines.

The labor movement of today and tomorrow may still be smaller than a generation or two ago, but it is broader in occupations, backgrounds, ethno-racial and gender composition, and increasingly in political openness. If the socialists don't take their place in this evolving movement, its likelihood of revival is diminished as is the hope of building a socialist movement with real social power.

If the *Labor Notes* milieu is not yet quite the militant minority with its strong revolutionary core that Big Bill Haywood, Elizabeth Gurley Flynn, or Eugene Debs would recognize, it is nonetheless a very dense, alive, and contemporary network of worker activists. Held together by the magazine, the handbooks, the conferences, day schools, a website, blog, weekly email updates, archives, and social media, the *Labor Notes* network is a twenty-first-century democratic current within what is still in many ways a mid-twentieth-century bureaucratic labor movement.

Whether this network can evolve into the sort of militant minority that gave political coherence to labor upheavals in the past remains to be seen. But it's clear that without the work of *Labor Notes*, that would not even be a possibility.

BIBLIOGRAPHY

Abraham, Katherine G., and James R. Spletzer. "Are the New Jobs Good Jobs?" In *Labor in the New Economy*, edited by Katherine G. Abraham, James R. Spletzer, and Michael J. Harper, 101–47. Chicago: University of Chicago Press, 2010.

ACLU. *Black, Brown and Targeted: A Report on Boston Police Department Street Encounters from 2007–2010*. Boston: American Civil Liberties Union Foundation of Massachusetts, October 3, 2014.

———. *War Comes Home: The Excessive Militarization of American of Policing*. New York: American Civil Liberties Union, 2014.

ActBlue, "About Us." https://secure.actblue.com/about.

Airlines for America. "U.S. Airline Mergers and Acquisitions." 2015. http://airlines .org?data/u-s-airline-mergers-and-acquisitions.

Allen, Joe. *The Package King: A Rank and File History of United Parcel Service*. Amazon, 2016.

American Hospital Association. *AHA Hospital Statistics*, 2010 edition. Chicago: Health Forum LLC, 2009.

———. *AHA Hospital Statistics*, 2011 edition. Chicago: Health Forum LLC, 2010.

ArcelorMittal. *Driving Solutions: United States Integrated Report: 2015*. Chicago: Arcelor-Mittal, 2015.

———. "Who We Are; Our History." 2016. http://corporate.arcelormittal.com /who-we-are/our-history.

Aschoff, Nicole Marie. *Globalization and Capital Mobility in the Automotive Industry*. Unpublished PhD dissertation, Baltimore: Johns Hopkins University, 2010.

Association of American Railroads. "Railroad Jobs." Association of American Railroads, 2015. www.aar.org/Pages/Careers.

Automotive News. 2013. Supplement, June 17, 2013.

Baily, Martin Neil, and Barry P. Bosworth. "US Manufacturing: Understanding Its Past and Its Potential Future." *Journal of Economic Perspectives* 28, no. 1 (Winter 2014): 3–26.

Ball, Kristie. "Workplace Surveillance: An Overview." *Labor History* 51, no. 1 (February 2010): 87–106.

Ball, Molly. "The Pugnacious, Relentless Progressive Party that Wants to Remake America." *Atlantic*, January 7, 2017. www.theatlantic.com/politics/archive /2016/01/working-families-party/422949.

Ballotpedia. "Ballot Access for Major and Minor Party Candidates." https://

ballotpedia.org/Ballot_access_for_major_and_minor_party_candidates.

———. "Los Angeles, California Mayoral Election, 2013." https://ballotpedia
.org/Los_Angeles,_California_mayoral_election,_2013.

———. "Net Worth of United States Senators and Representatives."
https://ballotpedia.org/Net_worth_of_United_States_Senators_and
_Representatives.

———. "New Democratic Coalition." https://ballotpedia.org/New_Democrat_
Coalition.

———. "New York State Assembly; Current Members." https://ballotpedia.org
/New_York_State_Assembly.

———. "Population Represented by State Legislators." https://ballotpedia.org
/Population_represented_by_state_legislators.

———. "Susan Sadlowski Garza." https://ballotpedia.org/Susan_sadlowski_garza.

Barkan, Ross. "BDS Vote Shows City Council Progressives Are Out of Touch on
Israel." *NY Slant*, September 27, 2016. http://nyslant.com/article/opinion
/bds-vote-shows-city-council-progressives-are-out-of-touch-on-israel.html.

———. "Meet the Only Member of the New York City Council Endorsing Bernie
Sanders." *New York Observer,* January 6, 2016. http://observer.com/2016/01/meet
-the-only-member-of-the-new-york-city-council-endorsing-bernie-sanders/.

Barnett, Jeffery L., Cindy L. Sheckells, Scott Peterson, and Elizabeth M. Tydings.
2012 Census of Governments: Finance—State and Local Government Summary Report.
Washington, DC: US Census Bureau, 2014.

Basso, Pietro. *Modern Times, Ancient Hours: Working Lives in the Twenty-First Century.*
London: Verso, 2003.

Benson, Herman. *Rebels, Reformers, and Racketeers: How Insurgents Transformed the Labor
Movement.* Bloomington, IN: First Books, 2005.

Bernhardt, Annette, Laura Dresser, and Erin Hatton. "The Coffee Pot Wars: Unions
and Firm Restructuring in the Hotel Industry." In *Low-Wage America: How
Employers Are Reshaping Opportunity in the Workplace.* Edited by Eileen Appelbaum,
Annette Bernhardt, and Richard J. Murnane, 33–76. New York: Russell Sage
Foundation, 2003.

Bernstein, Irving. *Turbulent Years: A History of the American Workers, 1933–1941.* Boston:
Houghton Mifflin, 1969.

Binder, Sarah A., Thomas E. Mann, Norman J. Ornstein, and Molly Reynolds.
Mending the Broken Branch: Assessing the 110th Congress, Anticipating the 111th. Washington, DC: Brookings Institution, 2009.

Block, Megan M. "'Stand Up, Fight Back': Why the Attack on Public-Sector Workers Violates the First and Fourteenth Amendments." *University of Pittsburgh Law
Review* 75 (Winter 2013): 189–208.

Blumenthal, Paul. "Crowdpac Helps Small Donors Find a Perfect Match in Politics." *Huffington Post*, October 7, 2014. www.huffingtonpost.com/2014/10/07
/crowdpac_donots_n_5943022.html.

Board of Elections, City of New York. *Annual Report 2012.* New York: Board of Elections, City of New York, 2012.

Board of Election Commissioners of the City of Chicago. "Elections Results: 2016 Primary," 2016. www.chicagolections.com/en/election-results-specifuics-asp.

Bonacich, Edna, and Jake B. Wilson. *Getting the Goods: Ports, Labor, and the Logistics Revolution.* Ithaca, NY: Cornell University Press, 2008.

Bostick, Bruce. "Ohioans Elect Two Dozen City Councilors on Independent Labor Ticket." *Labor Notes,* December 4, 2013. http://labornotes.org/2013/12 /ohioans-elect-two-dozen-city-councilors-independent-labor-ticket.

Bostock, Mike, and Ford Fressenden. "'Stop-and-Frisk' Is All but Gone from New York." *New York Times,* September 19, 2014. www.nytimes.com/interactive /2014/09/19/nyregion.stop-and-frisk-is-all-but-gone-from-new-york.htm.

Botwinick, Howard. *Persistent Inequalities: Wage Disparity under Capitalist Competition.* Princeton, NJ: Princeton University Press, 1993.

Boyle, Kevin. *The UAW and the Heyday of American Liberalism, 1945–1968.* Ithaca, NY: Cornell University Press, 1995.

Bradbury, Alexandra, Mark Brenner, Jenny Brown, Jane Slaughter, and Samantha Winslow. *How to Jump-Start Your Union: Lessons for the Chicago Teachers.* A Labor Notes Book. Detroit: Labor Education and Research Project, 2014.

Brandon, Emily and Kathy Marquardt. "How Did Your 401(k) Really Stack Up in 2008?" *US News & World Report,* February 12, 2009. http://money.usnews.com /money/retirement/articles/2009/02/12/how-did-your-401k-really-stack-up -in-2008.

Braverman, Harry. *Labor and Monopoly Capital: The Degradation of Work in the Twentieth Century.* New York: Monthly Review Press, 1998 (originally 1974).

Brecher, Jeremy, and Tim Costello. "A 'New Labor Movement' in the Shell of the Old?" In *A New Labor Movement for the New Century,* edited by Greg Mantsios, 24–43. New York: Monthly Review Press, 1998.

Bredderman, Will. "Jumaane Williams Endorses Bernie Sanders' Political Revolution." *New York Observer,* April 17, 2016. http://observer.com/2016/04/jumaane -williams-endorses-bernie-sanders-political-revolutionary-moonshot.

Brenner, Johanna. *Women and the Politics of Class.* New York: Monthly Review Press, 2000.

Brenner, Robert. *The Boom and the Bubble: The US in the World Economy.* London: Verso Books, 2002.

Brenner, Aaron, Robert Brenner, and Cal Winslow. *Rebel Rank and File: Labor Militancy and Revolt from Below during the Long 1970s.* London: Verso Books, 2010.

Bronfenbrenner, Kate, and Dorian T. Warren. "Race, Gender, and the Rebirth of Trade Unionism." *New Labor Forum* 16 (Fall 2007): 142–48.

Brooks, G. R. and V. G. Jones. "Hospital Mergers and Market Overlap." *Health Service Research* 31, no. 6 (1997): 701–22.

Broué, Pierre. *The German Revolution, 1917–1923.* Chicago: Haymarket Books, 2006.

Bureau of Economic Analysis (BEA). "BEA Depreciation Estimates," Bureau of Economic Analysis, no date. www.bea.gov/national/FA2004/Tablecandtext.pdf.

———. "Corporate Profits before Taxes by Industry." Table 6.17D. Bureau of Economic Analysis, August 3, 2016. www.bea.gov.

————. Table 3.1ESI. "Current-Cost Net Stock of Private Assets by Industry"; Table 3.1E. "Current-Cost Net Stock of Private Equipment by Industry." Bureau of Economic Analysis, August 31, 2015. https://www.bea.gov/national/faweb /FATableView.asp?SelectedTable=38&FirstYear=1996&LastYear=2001&Freq =Year.

————. Interactive Table for "Gross Output by Industry" and "Intermediate Input by Industry." November 5, 2015. www.bea.gov.

————. *Relation of Private Fixed Investment in Structures (by Type) in the Fixed Assets Accounts to the Corresponding Items in the National Income and Product Accounts.* www .bea.gov/national/FA2004/ST_types.pdf.

Bureau of Justice. "Prisoners in 1994." *Bulletin*, August 1995. https://www.bjs.gov /content/pub/pdf/Pi94.pdf.

————. "Prisoners in 2008." *Bulletin*, December 2009. https://www.bjs.gov/content /pub/pdf/p08.pdf.

————. "Prisoners in 2014." *Bulletin*, September 2015. https://www.bjs.gov/content /pub/pdf/p14.pdf.

Bureau of Labor Statistics (BLS). *Contingent and Alternative Employment Arrangement, February 2005.* USDL 05-1433. Washington, DC: Bureau of Labor Statistics, 2005.

————. *Current Employment Statistics, Establishment Data.* Washington, DC: Bureau of Labor Statistics, 2015. www.bls.gov/web/empsit/ceseebla.htm.

————. "Employed Persons by Class of Worker and Part-Time Status, Seasonally Adjusted." Table A-7. www.bls.gov/web/empsit/cpseea07.htm.

————. "Employee Benefits Survey," Tables 1, 9. www.bls.gov/ncs/ebs/benefits /2015/benefits_health.htm.

————. *Employee Tenure in 2014.* USDL-14-1714. September 18, 2014. Washington, DC: Bureau of Labor Statistics, 2014.

————. *Employee Tenure in 2016.* USDL-16-1867. Washington, DC: Bureau of Labor Statistics, 2016.

————. *Employee Tenure in the Mid-1990s.* USDL 97-25. Washington, DC: Bureau of Labor Statistics, 1997. www.bls.gov/news.release/history/tenure_013097.txt.

————. "Employment, Hours, and Earnings from the Current Employment Statistics Survey (National)." Databases, Tables & Calculators by Subject. http://data.bls.gov/pdq/SurveyOutputServlet.

————. "Employment of Production and Nonsupervisory Employees on Private Nonfarm Payrolls in Industry Sector, Seasonally Adjusted." Table 6a. Current Employment Statistics. www.bls.gov/web/empsit/ceseeb6a.htm.

————. "Employment Projections: Occupations with the Most Growth," Table 1.4. www.bls.gov/emp/ep_table_104.htm.

————. *Employment Projections—2014–24.* USDL-15-2327. Washington, DC: Bureau of Labor Statistics, 2015.

————. *The Employment Situation—November 2015.* USDL-15-2292. Washington, DC: Bureau of Labor Statistics, 2015.

————. *International Comparison of Manufacturing Productivity and Unit Labor Cost*

Trends. USDL-12-2365. Washington, DC: Bureau of Labor Statistics, 2012.
———. "Labor Force Statistics from the Current Population Survey." All Indus-
tries Self-Employed, Unincorporated, Multiple Jobholders. http://data
.bls.gov/pdq/SurveyOutputServlet.
———. "Labor Productivity and Costs." August 9, 2016. https://data.bls.gov
/cgi-bin/print.pl/lpc/prodybar.htm.
———. *Major Work Stoppages in 2015.* USDL-16-0272. Washington, DC: Bureau of
Labor Statistics, 2016.
———. *New Data on Contingent and Alternative Employment Examined by BLS,* USDL
95–318. Washington, DC: Bureau of Labor Statistics, 1995.
———. "Occupational Employment, Job Openings and Worker Characteristics."
Table 1.7. www.bls.gov/emp/ep_table_107.htm.
———. "Occupational Employment Statistics: May 2015 National Occupational
Employment and Wage Estimates United States." www.bls.gov/oes
/current/oes_nat.htm#00-000.
———. "Occupational Employment Statistics, Transportation and Material Mov-
ing Occupations, Chicago-Naperville-Arlington Heights, IL Metropolitan
Division." www.bls.gov/oes_16974.htm.
———. *Productivity and Costs by Industry: Manufacturing, 2005.* USDL-07-0561. Wash-
ington, DC: Bureau of Labor Statistics, 2007.
———. *Productivity and Costs by Industry: Manufacturing Industries, 2006.* USDL-08-
0382. Washington, DC: Bureau of Labor Statistics, 2008.
———. *Productivity and Costs by Industry: Manufacturing Industries, 2007.* USDL-09-
1502. Washington, DC: Bureau of Labor Statistics, 2009.
———. *Union Members in 1995.* USDL 96-41. Washington, DC: Bureau of Labor
Statistics, 1996.
———. *Union Members—2009.* USDL-10-0069. Washington, DC: Bureau of Labor
Statistics, 2010.
———. *Union Members—2010.* USDL-11-0063. Washington, DC: Bureau of Labor
Statistics, 2011.
———. *Union Members—2014.* USDL 15-0072. Washington, DC: Bureau of Labor
Statistics, 2015.
———. *Union Members—2015.* USDL-16-0158. Washington, DC: Bureau of Labor
Statistics, 2016.
Burgess, Keith. "The Political Economy of British Engineering Workers during the
First World War." In *Strikes, Wars, and Revolutions in an International Perspective,* Leo-
pold Haimson and Charles Tilly. Cambridge: Cambridge University Press, 2003.
Burnham, Walter Dean. *Critical Elections and the Mainsprings of American Politics.* New
York: W. W. Norton, 1970.
Burnley, Jr., Willie. "Why There's a Mass Prison Strike Going on Right Now," *attn:,*
October 21, 2016. www.attn.com/stories/12203/massive-prison-strike-occurring
-right-now.
Burris, Val. "The Political Partisanship of American Business: A Study of Corporate
Political Action Committees." *American Sociological Review* 52 (December 1987):

732–44.

Business Source Complete. "REIT Mafia Leads the Charge." EBSCO Host, 2011. http://web.ebschost.com/ehost/detail?vid=3&sid=c"da013d-19de-4e1f-b830.

businessballs.com. "Six Sigma Training, History, Definitions—Six Sigma and Quality Management Glossary." 2011. www.businessballs.com/sixsigma.htm.

Cantor, Dan. "A New Progressive Party." In *Empowering Progressive Third Parties in the United States*, edited by Jonathan H. Martin, 204–7. New York: Routledge, 2016.

Capgemini. *Communications Industry: On the Verge of Massive Consolidation*. London: Capgemini Consulting, Technology, Outsourcing, 2014.

Carter, Zach. "How Hundreds of Law Makers Ended Up Voting to Give Banks $17 Billion," *Huffington Post*, November 6, 2015. http://www.huffingtonpost.com /entry/congress-banks-highway-bill_us_563bc8a6e4b0307f2cacae55.

Center for Constitutional Rights. *Stop and Frisk: The Human Impact, the Stories behind the Numbers, the Effects on Our Communities*. New York: Center for Constitutional Rights, 2012.

Chicago Board of Election Commissioners. *Tabulated Statement of the Returns and Proclamation of the Results of the Canvass of the Election Returns for the March 15, 2016, General Primary Election*. Chicago: Chicago Board of Election Commissioners, 2016.

Chicago City Council Progressive Caucus. "Who We Are." Progressive Caucus Members, 2016. www.chicagoprogressivecaucus.com/who-we-are.

Christopher, Martin. *Logistics and Supply Chain Management*. 4th ed. Harlow, UK: Pearson, 2011.

Circadian. "8-Hour Shifts vs. 12-Hour Shifts: What the Research Says," 2016. www .circadian.com/solutions-services/publications-a-reports/newletters/mana.

Clark, Paul. "Health Care: A Growing Role for Collective Bargaining." In *Collective Bargaining in the Private Sector*, edited by Paul Clark, John T. Delaney, and Ann C. Foster, 91–135. Champaign, IL: Industrial Relations Research Association, 2002.

Clothier, Mark. "Auto-Parts M&A Value Seen Reaching Record $48 Billion This Year." *Bloomberg Business*, August 11, 2015. www.bloomberg.com/news/articles /2015-08-11/auto-parts-m-a-value-seen-reaching-record-48-billion-this-year.

CNN Politics. "Election Center, President, Ohio." 2012. http://edition.cnn.com /election/2012/results/state/OH/president.

———. "National President." http://edition.conn.com/results/exit-polls.

———. "Ohio President." http://edition.cnn.com/election/results//exit-polls/ohio /president.

Collins, Allison. "GE Continues Industrial Push with Metem Deal." *Mergers & Acquisitions*, December 28, 2015. www.themiddlemarket.com/news/ge-continues -industrial-push-with-metem-deal.

Congressional Progressive Caucus. "Caucus Members." https://cpc-grijalva.house.gov/.

Cook Political Report. "2016 National Popular Vote Tracker." December 15, 2016. http://cookpolitical.com/story/10174.

———. "2016 National Popular Vote Tracker." January 2, 2017. http://cookpolitical .com/story/10174.

Cooper, David. "A Majority of Low-Wage Workers Earn So Little That They Must

Rely on Public Assistance to Make Ends Meet." Economic Snapshot: Wages, Income, and Wealth. Economic Policy Institute, February 9, 2016. www.epi.org /publication/a-majority-of-low-wage-workers-earn-so-little-they-must-rely -on-public-assistance-to-make-ends-meet.

Conference Board. *International Comparisons of Manufacturing Productivity and Unit Labor Costs Trends, 2012.* New York: Conference Board, 2013.

Coper, Rudolph. *Failure of a Revolution: Germany in 1918–1919.* Cambridge: Cambridge University Press, 1955.

Council of Economic Advisers. *Economic Report of the President, 2011.* Washington, DC: US Government Printing Office, 2011.

———. *Economic Report of the President, 2013.* Washington, DC: US Government Printing Office, 2013.

Cowen, Deborah. *The Deadly Life of Logistics: Mapping Violence in Global Trade.* Minneapolis: University of Minnesota Press, 2014.

Cranford, Cynthia J., Leah F. Vosko, and Nancy Zukewich. "Precarious Employment in the Canadian Labour Market: A Statistical Portrait." *Just Labour* 3 (Fall 2003): 6–22.

Craypo, Charles. *The Economics of Collective Bargaining: Case Studies in the Private Sector.* Washington, DC: Bureau of National Affairs, 1986.

Crosby, Jeff, and Bill Fletcher Jr. "AFL-CIO Convention Repositions Unions to Speak for All Workers." *Labor Notes,* October 17, 2013.

Cunningham, Doug. "CTU's Karen Lewis: Tentative Deal Is Good for Kids, Teachers and Communities." *Labor Radio,* October 11, 2016.

Cutcher-Gershenfeld, Joel, Dan Brooks, and Martin Mulloy. *The Decline and Resurgence of the U.S. Auto Industry.* Washington, DC: Economic Policy Institute, 2015.

Daily Kos. "Many Progressive Caucus Members Have Endorsed Hillary and Here's the Corrected List." *Daily Kos,* October 1, 2015. www.dailykos.com /story/2015/10/11/1430646/-Many-Progressive-Caucus-members-have -endorsed-Hillary-and-here-s-the-corrected-list.

———. "New York City Council Member Jumaane Williams Endorses Bernie Sanders at Prospect Park Rally." April 18, 2016. www.dailykos.com/story/2016 /4/17/1516643/-BREAKING-NY-City-Council-Member-Jumaane-Williams -Endorses-Bernie-Sanders-at-Prospect-Park-Rally.

Davidson, Roger H., Walter J. Oleszek, Frances E. Lee, and Eric Schickler. *Congress and Its Members.* 15th ed. Los Angeles: CQ Press, 2016.

Davies, Harry, and Danny Yadron. "How Facebook Tracks and Profits from Voters in a $10bn Election." *Guardian,* January 28, 2016. www.theguardian.com/us-news /2016//jan28/facebook-voters-us-election-fed-cruz-targeted-ads-trump.

Davis, Mike. "Not a Revolution—Yet." *Jacobin,* November 16, 2016. www.jacobin-mag.com/2016/11/trump-election-clinton-sanders-whites-turnout.

———. *Prisoners of the American Dream: Politics and Economy in the History of the US Working Class.* London: Verso, 1986.

Democratic Congressional Campaign Committee. "Receipts by Sector." 2014 cycle, 2016 cycle. Open Secrets. www.opensecrets.org/parties/contrib.php

?cycle=2014&cmte=DCCC.

Democratic Party. "Party Organization." www.democrats.org/about/our-party
-organization.

Democratic Senatorial Campaign Committee. "Receipts by Sector." 2014 cycle,
2016 cycle. Open Secrets. www.opensecrets.org/parties/contrib.php?cycle
=2014&cmte=DSCC, www.opensecrets.org/parties/contrib.php?cycle=2016
&cmte=DSCC.

D'Eramo, Marco. *The Pig and the Skyscaper: Chicago: A History of Our Future.* London:
Verso, 2016.

DiMaggio, Dan. "Verizon Strike Shows Corporate Giants Can Be Beat." *Labor Notes,*
June 3, 2016, www.labornotes.org/2016/06/verizon-strikers-show-corporate
-giants-can-be-beat..

———. "Wave of Walkouts at AT&T West." *Labor Notes* 448 (July 2016): 14–16.

Dobbs, Farrell. *Teamster Power.* New York: Pathfinder Press, 1972.

Dollinger, Sol, and Genora Johnson Dollinger. *Not Automatic: Women and the Left in the
Forging of the Auto Workers' Union.* New York: Monthly Review Press, 2000.

Domansky, Elisabeth. "The Rationalization of Class Struggle: Strikes and Strike
Strategy of the German Metalworkers' Union, 1891–1922." In *Strikes, Wars,
and Revolutions in an International Perspective,* edited by Leopold Haimson and
Charles Tilly, 321–55. Cambridge: Cambridge University Press, 2002.

Dovere, Edward-Issac, and Gabriel Debenedetti. "Bernie Sanders' New Group Is
Already in Turmoil." *Politico,* August 23, 2016. www.politico.com.

Draper, Hal. *Karl Marx's Theory of Revolution,* vol. 1, *State and Bureaucracy.* New York:
Monthly Review Press, 1977.

———. *Karl Marx's Theory of Revolution,* vol 2, *The Politics of Social Classes.* New York:
Monthly Review Press, 1978.

———. *Socialism from Below: Essays.* Selected, edited, and introduced by E. Haberkern.
Atlantic Heights, NJ: Humanities Press, 1992.

Draut, Tamara. *Sleeping Giant: How the New Working Class Will Transform America.* New
York: Doubleday, 2016.

Drug Policy Alliance. "A Brief History of the Drug War." Drug Policy Alliance,
2016. www.drugpolicy.org/new-solutions-drug-policy/brief-history-drug-war.

DSPolitical. "Voter Targeted Digital Ads at Fingertips of Thousands of Democratic
Campaigns." 2016. http://dspolitical.com/press-releases/voter-targeted-digi-
tal-ads-now-fingertips-thousands-democratic-campaigns.

Dudzic, Mark, and Katherine Isaac. "Labor Party Time? Not Yet." In *Empowering
Progressive Third Parties in the United States: Defeating Duopoly, Advancing Democracy,*
edited by Jonathan H. Martin, 166–83. New York: Routledge, 2016.

Early, Steve. *The Civil Wars in U.S. Labor: Birth of a New Workers' Movement or Death
Throes of the Old?* Chicago: Haymarket Books, 2011.

———. "House of Labor Needs Repairs, Not Just New Roommates." *Labor Notes,*
September 16, 2013.

———. "In Bay Area Refinery Town: Berniecrats & Clintonites Clash Over Rent
Control." *Counterpunch,* October 21, 2016. http://www.counterpunch

.org/2016/10/21/in-bay-area-refinery-town-berniecrats-clintonites-clash-over
-rent-control/print/.

————. *Refinery Town: Big Oil, Big Money, and the Remaking of an American City.* Boston: Beacon Press, 2017.

Economist. "Industrial Metamorphosis." September 29, 2005. www.economist.com /node/4462685/.

————. "Reshoring Manufacturing: Coming Home." Special Report, January 19, 2013. www.economist.com/node/21569570/.

————. "How America's Police Became So Heavily Armed." *Economist Explains,* May 18, 2015. www.economist.com/blogs/economist-explains/2015/05 /economist-explains-22.

————. "Where Donald Trump's Support Really Comes From." April 20, 2016. www.economist.com/blogs/graphicdetail/2016/04/daily-chart -14?zid=297&ah=3ae0fe266c7447d8a0c7ade5547d62ca.

Edsall, Thomas Byrne. *The New Politics of Inequality.* New York: W. W. Norton, 1984.

Election Projection. "2014 Open Seat Elections." www.electionprojection. com/2014-elections/2014-open-seat-elections.php.

Emmanuel, Adeshina. "Chicago's Black Unemployment Rate Higher than Other Large Metro Areas." *Chicago Reporter,* November 16, 2014. http://chicagoreporter .com/chicagos-black-unemployment-rate-higher-other-large-metro-areas.

Enten, Harry. "How Much Do Democrats Depend on the Union Vote?" *FiveThirty-Eight,* July 1, 2014. http://fivethirtyeight.com/datalab/supreme-court-ruling -wounds-both-democrats-and-unions-neither-fatally.

Epstein, Richard. "Obama's Welcome Silence on the Employee Free Choice Act." *Forbes,* February 10, 2009. https://forbes.com/2009/02/09/card-checks-efca -opinions-columnist_0210_richard_epstein.html.

Erickson, Megan, Katherine Hill, Matt Karp, Connor Kilpatrick, and Bhaskar Sun-kara. "Politics Is the Solution." *Jacobin,* November 9, 2016. www.jacobinmag .com/2016/11/trump-victory-clinton-sanders-democratic-party.

Erie, Steven P. *Rainbow's End: Irish-Americans and the Dilemmas of Urban Machine Politics, 1840–1985.* Los Angeles and Berkeley: University of California Press, 1988.

"Examining Mergers and Acquisitions." Editorial. *Cornell Hospitality Quarterly* 50, no. 2 (May 2009): 138–41.

Farrell, Kevin. "This Is How Dozens of Major Airlines Got Swallowed by the Big 3." *Road Warrior Voices,* November 9, 2015. http://roadwarriorvoices.com/2015 /11/09/this-is-how-dozens-of-major-airlines.

Federal Election Commission. "PAC Financial Activity." 2014. http://classic.fec.gov /disclosure/pacSummary.do.

————. "Presidential Pre-Nomination Campaign Disbursements." June 30, 2016, June 30, 2012, June 30, 2008, June 30, 2000. www.fec.gov.

————. "Party Table 2," "Party Table 3." www.fec.gov.

————. "National Party Committees." 2008–2014, Tables 2 and 3. www.fec.gov.

Federal Mediation & Conciliation Service. *2014 Annual Report.* Washington, DC: Federal Mediation & Conciliation Service, 2014.

Federal Reserve System. "Changes in U.S. Family Finances from 2010 to 2013: Evidence from the Survey of Consumer Finances." *Federal Reserve Bulletin*, 100, no. 4, September 2014.

Feeley, Dianne. "Big Three Contracts: Who Won?" *Against the Current* 180 (January/ February 2016): 4–6.

Feinstein, Mike. "A Green Becomes Mayor: The Election of Gayle McLaughlin in Richmond, California." In *Empowering Progressive Third Parties in the United States*, Jonathan H. Martin, 27–30. New York: Routledge, 2016.

Ferguson, Thomas, and Joel Rogers. *Right Turn: The Decline of the Democrats and the Future of American Politics*. New York: Hill and Wang, 1986.

File, Thom. *Who Votes? Congressional Elections and the American Electorate: 1978–2014*. Washington, DC: US Department of Commerce, 2015.

Fletcher Jr., Bill, and Fernando Gapasin. *Solidarity Divided: The Crisis in Organized Labor and a New Path to Social Justice*. Los Angeles and Berkeley: University of California Press, 2008.

Food & Water Watch. *Consolidation and Buyer Power in the Grocery Industry*. Food & Water Watch, 2010. https://www.foodandwaterwatch.org/insight/consolidation -and-buyer-power-grocery-industry.

Fox, Justin. "Where Are All the Self-Employed Workers?" *Harvard Business Review*, February 7, 2014, 2. https://hbr.org/2014/02/where-are-all-the-self-employed -workers.

Freeman, Joshua B. "De Blasio's New York." *Dissent*, Winter 2015. www.dissentmag-azine.org/article/de-blasio-year-one-new-york-city.

Gabbatt, Adam. "Is Bernie Sanders' Our Revolution Over before It Even Began?" *Guardian*, August 26, 2016. www.theguardian.com/us-news/2016/aug/26/ bernie-sanders-our-revolution-grassroots-jeff-weaver.

Gabriel, Trip. "How Erie Went Red: The Economy Sank, and Trump Rose." *New York Times*, November 12, 2016. www.nytimes.com/2016/11/13/us/politics /pennsylvania-trump-votes.html.

Gallup. "In U.S., Socialist Presidential Candidates Least Appealing." 2010. www .gallup.com/poll/183713.

Gallup News Service. "June Wave 1." Princeton Job # 15-06-006, 2015. http://cns7prod .s3.amazonaws.com/attachments/gallup-historical_trend-june_2015.pdf.

Gaughan, Patrick A. *Mergers, Acquisitions, and Corporate Restructuring*. 6th ed. Hoboken, NJ: John Wiley & Sons, 2015.

Gaus, Mischa. "Technology Push in Hospitals Puts Stress on Workers." *Labor Notes* 364 (November 2009): 1, 13.

Gerstle, Gary. *Liberty and Coercion: The Paradox of American Government from the Found-ing to the Present*. Princeton, NJ: Princeton University Press, 2015.

———. "The Resilient Power of the States across the Long Nineteenth Century." In *The Unsustainable American State*, edited by Lawrence Jacobs and Desmond King, 61–87. Oxford: Oxford University Press, 2009.

Gimenez-Nadal, Jose Ignacio, and Almudena Sevilla-Sanz. "Job Polarization and the Intensification of Work in the United Kingdom and the United States over the

Last Decades: Evidence from Time Diary Data." Paper delivered at the Fourth Society of Labor Educators/European Association of Labour Economists Global Meeting, June 26–28, 2015, Montreal, Quebec, Canada. www.parthen-impact .com/parthen-uploads/78/2015/add_1_258840_lLPu4oUWUf.pdf.

Global Automakers. *Redefining the American Auto Industry: The Growing Impact of International Automakers on the U.S. Economy.* Washington, DC: Global Automakers, 2014.

Golbe, Devra L., and Lawrence J. White. "A Time-Series Analysis of Mergers and Acquisitions in the U.S. Economy." In *Corporate Takeovers: Causes and Consequences,* edited by Alan J. Auerbach, 265–309. Chicago: University of Chicago Press, 1988.

Goldfield, Michael. *The Color of Politics: Race and the Mainsprings of American Politics.* New York, New Press, 1997.

Goldmacher, Shane. "Bernie's Legacy: One of the Most Valuable Donor Lists Ever." *Politico,* June 6, 2016.

Gordon, Suzanne. "Is Sweeney's 'New Voice' A Choice or an Echo." *Labor Notes* 199 (October 1995): 12–13.

Gramsci, Antonio. *Antonio Gramsci: Selections from Political Writings, 1910–1920.* New York: International Publishers, 1977.

Gray, Heather. "The Militarization of U.S. Police Departments." *Counterpunch,* March 10, 2015. www.counterpunch.org/2015/03/10/the-militarization -of-u-s-police-departments.

Green, Donald P., and Michael Schwam-Baird. "Mobilization, Participation, and American Democracy: A Retrospective and Postscript." *Party Politics,* March 2016, 158–64.

Greenbaum, Joan. *Windows on the Workplace: Technology, Jobs, and the Organization of Office Work.* New York: Monthly Review Press, 2004.

Greenberg, Stanley B. *The Two Americas: Our Current Political Deadlock and How to Break It.* New York: Thomas Dunne Books, 2004.

Guardian. "By the Numbers: US Police Kill More in Days than Other Countries Do in Years." June 9, 2015.

Guardian. "The Counted." Database, 2016. www.theguardian.com/us-news/ng -interactive/2015/jun/01/the-counted-police-killings-us-database.

———. "US Elections." November 10, 2016, 6–7.

Gude, Shawn. "The Business Veto." *Jacobin* 20 (Winter 2016). www.jacobinmag .com/issue/up-from-liberalism.

Gunderson, Michelle. "Teachers Compare Notes." *Labor Notes,* April 17, 2015.

Haimson, Leopold. "The Historical Setting in Russia and the West." In *Strikes, Wars, and Revolutions in an International Perspective,* edited by Leopold Haimson and Charles Tilly, 18-32. Cambridge: Cambridge University Press, 2002.

Haimson, Leopold, and Eric Brian. Introduction to part 2. In *Strikes, Wars, and Revolutions in an International Perspective,* edited by Leopold Haimson and Charles Tilly, 35–46. Cambridge: Cambridge University Press, 2002.

Hall, Jonathan V., and Allen B. Krueger. *An Analysis of the Labor Market for Uber's Driver-Partners in the United States.* San Francisco: Uber Technologies, 2015.

Halle, John. "Don't Wait for Labor: The Necessity of Building a Left Third Party at the Grassroots." In *Empowering Progressive Third Parties in the United States: Defeating Duopoly, Advancing Democracy*, edited by Jonathan H. Martin, 184–203. New York: Routledge, 2016.

Hamsher, Jane. "What Happened to the Employee Free Choice Act?" *ShadowProof*, April 13, 2010. https://shaowproof.com/2010/04/13/what-happened-to-the-employee-free-choice-act.

Harrington, Michael. *The Other America: Poverty in the United States*. Baltimore: Penguin Books, 1963.

Harrison, Thomas. "Breaking through by Breaking Free: Why the Left Needs to Declare Its Political Independence." In *Empowering Progressive Third Parties in the United States*, edited by Jonathan H. Martin, 208–39. New York: Routledge, 2016.

Harvey, David. *A Brief History of Neoliberalism*. Oxford: Oxford University Press, 2005.

———. *The Condition of Postmodernism: An Inquiry into the Origins of Cultural Change*. Oxford: Basil Blackwell, 1989.

———. *The Limits to Capital*. Chicago: University of Chicago Press, 1982.

———. *The Ways of the World*. London: Profile Books, 2016.

Hayden, Tom. *The Port Huron Statement: The Visionary Call of the 1960s Revolution*. New York: Thunder's Mouth Press, 2005.

Heideman, Paul. "It's Their Party." *Jacobin* 20 (Winter 2016). www.jacobinmag.com/issue/up-from-liberalism.

Heintz, James. "The Grim State of the States" *New Labor Forum* 18, no. 2 (Spring 2009): 7-15.

Helper, Susan, and Morris M. Kleiner. "When Management Strategies Change: Employe,e Well-Being at an Auto Supplier." In *Low-Wage America: How Employers Are Reshaping Opportunity in the Workplace*, edited by Eileen Appelbaum, Annette Bernhardt, and Richard J. Murnane, 446–78. New York: Russell Sage Foundation, 2003.

Henry, Jim. "Ally, Formerly GMAC, Rebounds to Become Top Auto Finance Story of 2010." *Automotive News*, December 29, 2010. www.autonews.com/article/20101229/FINANCE_AND_INSURANCE/101229913/ally-formerly-gmac-rebounds-to-become-top-auto-finance-story-of-2010.

Henwood, Doug. *Wall Street: How It Works and for Whom*. London: Verso, 1997.

Hernández, Javier C. "Once Again, City Voters Approve Term Limits." *New York Times*, November 3, 2010. www.nytimes.com/2010/11/03limits.html.

Hinton, James. *The First Shop Steward's Movement*. London: George Allen & Unwin, 1973.

Hipple, Steven F. "Self-Employment in the United States." *Monthly Labor Review*, September 2010, 17, 19.

Hirsch, Barry T., and David A. Macpherson. "Union Membership and Coverage Database from the CPS." Unionstats.com, 2010. http://www.unionstats.com.

Hobsbawm, Eric. *Labouring Men: Studies in the History of Labour*. London: Weidenfeld and Nicolson, 1964.

Hoffrogge, Ralf. *Working-Class Politics in the German Revolution: Richard Müller, the Revolutionary Shop Stewards, and the Origins of the Council Movement*. Chicago: Haymarket Books, 2015.

Hogan, Heather. "Scientific Management and the Changing Nature of Work in the St. Petersburg Metalworking Industry, 1900–1914." In *Strikes, Wars, and Revolutions in an International Perspective*, edited by Leopold Haimson and Charles Tilly. Cambridge: Cambridge University Press, 2003.

Houseman, Susan N., Timothy J. Bartik, and Timothy J. Sturgeon. *Measuring Manufacturing: How Computer and Semiconductor Industries Affect the Numbers and Perceptions*. Upjohn Institute Working Paper 14-209. Kalamazoo, MI: W.E. Upjohn Institute for Employment Research, 2014.

Houseman, Susan N., Christopher J. Kurz, Paul Legermann, and Benjamin R. Mandel. *Offshoring Bias in U.S. Manufacturing: Implications for Productivity and Value Added*. Washington, DC: Board of Governors of the Federal Reserve System, 2010.

Human Rights Watch. *Nation Behind Bars*. Human Rights Watch, 2012. www.hrw.org /sites/default/files/related_material/2014_US_Nation_Behind_Bars_0.pdf.

Huws, Ursula. *The Making of a Cybertariat: Virtual Work in a Real World*. New York: Monthly Review Press, 2003.

Ilg, Randy E., and Eleni Theodossiou. "Job Search of the Unemployed by Duration of Unemployment." *Monthly Labor Review*, March 2012, 41–49.

Illinois PIRG. *The Money Primary: Money in the 2015 Chicago Aldermanic Elections*. Illinois PIRG Education Fund, 2015. www.illinoispirgedfund.org/sites/pirg/files /reports/The%20Money%20Primary%20Final%204.1.15_0.pdf.

Indeed. "Small Business Owner Salary." *Indeed*, 2016. www.indeed.com/small -business-owner.htm.

International Labour Organization. *Global Wage Report*. Geneva: International Labour Organization, 2008/9.

———. *Global Wage Report*. Geneva: International Labour Organization, 2011.

———. *Global Wage Report*. Geneva: International Labour Organization, 2013.

———. *Global Wage Report*. Geneva: International Labour Organization, 2014/15.

Institute for Health and Socio-Economic Policy. *Health Information*. Oakland: Institute for Health and Socio-Economic Policy, 2009.

International Organization for Immigration. *World Immigration Report 2010*. Geneva: International Organization for Immigration, 2010.

Irwin, John. "GM Lordstown Plant Faces Strike Threat from UAW Locals." *Automotive News*, January 22, 2016. www.autonews.com/article/20160122//OEM01 /160129940/gm-lordstown-plant-faces-strike-threat-from-uaw-locals.

Jacobson, Gary C. *The Politics of Congressional Elections*. 6th ed. New York: Pearson Longman, 2004.

Jamison, Dave. "It Looks Like Donald Trump Did Really Well with Union Households. That's a Bad Sign for Unions." *Huffington Post*, November 9, 2016. www .huffingtonpost.com/entry/donald-trump-did-really-well-with-union-households _us_582367d0e4b0aac62488cc32.

Jewell, Malcom E., and Sarah M. Morehouse. *Political Parties and Elections in American States*. Washington DC: CQ Press, 2001.

Johnson, Will. "Lean Production." In *Class Action: An Activist Teacher's Handbook*, edited by Shawn Gude and Bhaskar Sunkara, 11–18. New York: Jacobin Foundation, 2014.

Jones, Janelle, John Schmitt and Nicole Woo. *Women, Working Families, and Unions.* Washington, DC: Center for Economic and Policy Research, 2014.

Judd, Dennis R., and Todd Swanstrom. *City Politics: The Political Economy of Urban America.* 9th ed. New York: Routledge, 2015.

Kabaservice, Geoffrey. *Rule and Ruin: The Downfall of Moderation and the Destruction of the Republican Party, from Eisenhower to the Tea Party.* New York: Oxford University Press, 2012.

Kann, Julia. ".Telecom Strikers Win Limits on Outsourcing." *Labor Notes,* February 23, 2015.

Katz, Lewis R. "*Terry v. Ohio* at Thirty-Five: A Revisionist View." *Mississippi Law Journal* 74, no. 2 (2004): 423–86. www.olemiss.edu/depts/ncjrl/pdf /katzMSLJ04.pdf.

Kelly, John. *Rethinking Industrial Relations: Mobilization, Collectivism and Long Waves.* London: Routledge, 1998.

Khalil, Ramy. "How a Socialist Won: Lessons from the Historic Victory of Seattle City Councilmember Kshama Sawant." In *Empowering Progressive Third Parties in the United States,* edited by Jonathan H. Martin, 17–26. New York: Routledge, 2016.

Kivelson, Adrienne. *What Makes New York City Run?* New York: City of New York Education Fund, 2001.

Krebs, Timothy B., and John P. Pelissero. "City Councils." In *Cities, Politics, and Policy: A Comparative Analysis,* edited by John P. Pelissero, 169–95. Washington, DC: CQ Press, 2003.

Kumar, Sameer. "Specialty Hospitals Emulating Focused Factories: A Case Study." *International Journal of Health Care Quality Assurance* 23, no. 1 (2010): 94–109.

La Botz, Dan. "What Happened to the American Working Class?" *New Politics* 12, no. 4 (Winter 2010): 75–87.

———. "The Working Class and Left Politics: Back on the American Radar." *New Politics* 15, no. 1 (Summer 2014): 5–18.

Labor Notes. "Passing the Torch . . . or Lighting a Fire?" *Labor Notes* 366 (September 2009): 1.

Labour Party. "Labour Leadership Election 2016." Labor Party, 2016. www.labour. org.uk/pages/labour-party-leadership-election-2016.

Lafer, Gordon. *The Legislative Attack on American Wages and Labor Standards, 2011–2012.* Washington, DC: Economic Policy Institute, 2013.

Lane, Julia, Philip Moss, Harold Salzman, and Chris Tilly. "Too Many Cooks? Tracking Internal Labor Market Dynamics in Food Services with Case Studies and Qualitative Data." In *Low-Wage America: How Employers Are Reshaping Opportunity in the Workplace,* edited by Eileen Appelbaum, Annette Bernhardt, and Richard J. Murnane, 229–69. New York: Russell Sage Foundation, 2003.

Landy, Joanne. "The Foreign Policies of Sanders, Trump, and Clinton." *New Politics* 16, no. 1 (Summer 2016): 3–13.

LCLAA. *Latino Workers and Unions: A Strategic Partnership for America's Progress.* Washington, DC: Labor Council for Latin American Advancement, 2015.

Leachman, Michael, Nick Albares, Kathleen Masterson, and Marlana Wallace. *Most States Have Cut School Funding, and Some Continue Cutting.* Washington, DC:

Leachman, Michael, and Michael Mazerov. *State Personal Income Tax Cuts: Still a Poor Strategy for Economic Growth.* Washington, DC: Center on Budget and Policy Priorities, 2015.

Le Blanc, Paul. "Radical Labor Subculture: Key to Past and Future Insurgencies." *WorkingUSA* 13 (September 2010): 367–85.

LeRoy, Greg. *The Great American Jobs Scam: Corporate Tax Dodging and the Myth of Job Creation.* San Francisco: Berrett-Koehler Publishers, 2005.

Lichtenstein, Nelson. *The Most Dangerous Man in Detroit: Walter Reuther and the Fate of American Labor.* New York: Basic Books, 1995.

Lipow, Arthur. *Political Parties and Democracy: Explorations in History and Theory.* London: Pluto Press, 1996.

Lorain County Board of Elections. "2012 General Election." 2012. http://media.wix .com/ugd/2568d0_45e5b97f36b54098befa5ee19cb7f8e3.pdf.

———. "2016 Primary Election," "2016 General Election." 2016. http://media.wix .com/ugd/2568d0_45e5b97f36b54098befa5ee19cb7f8e3.pdf.

Luhby, Tami. "How Hillary Clinton Lost." CNN, November 10, 2016. http: //edition.cnn.com/2016/11/09/politics/clinton-votes-african-americans -latinos-women-white-voters.

Ma, Qingzhong, and Peng Liu. "Who's Next? An Analysis of Lodging Industry Acquisitions." *Cornell Hospitality Report* 10, no. 11 (July 2010): 6–11.

Maass, Alan, and Lee Sustar. "Why They Won." *Jacobin,* June 7, 2016. www.jacobinmag .com/2016/06/verizon-strike-contract-deal-cwa-ibew-union-pickets.

MacDonald, James M., Michael E. Ollinger, Kenneth E. Nelson, and Charles R. Handy. *Consolidation in U.S. Meatpacking.* Washington, DC: US Department of Agriculture, 2000.

Mandel, Ernest. *Long Waves of Capitalist Development: A Marxist Interpretation.* Rev. ed. London: Verso, 1995.

Mangan, John, Chandra Lalwani, Tim Butcher, and Roya Javadpour. *Global Logistics and Supply Chain Management.* Chichester UK: John Wiley & Sons, 2012.

Mapping Police Violence. "National Trends." 2016. http://mappingpoliceviolence .org/nationaltrends.

Marable, Manning. *Black American Politics: From the Washington Marches to Jesse Jackson.* London: Verso, 1985.

Marcin, Tim. "Latest Popular Vote Election Results: Clinton Leads Trump by 2.5 Million as Recount Effort Continues." *International Business Times,* December 1, 2016. www.ibtimes.com/latest-2016-popular-vote-election-results-clinton -leads-trump-25-million-recount-2453280?utm_source=internal&utm _campaign=incontent&utm_medium=related2.

Martin, Jonathan H., editor. *Empowering Progressive Third Parties in the United States: Defeating Duopoly, Advancing Democracy.* New York: Routledge, 2016.

Martin Associates. *The Economic Impacts of the Port of Chicago.* Lancaster, PA: Martin

Associates, 2011.

Marx, Karl. *Wage-Labour and Capital.* New York: International Publishers, 1933.

————. *Grundrisse: Introduction to the Critique of Political Economy.* Harmondsworth, UK: Penguin Books, 1973.

————. *Capital,* volume 2. Harmondsworth, UK: Penguin Books, 1978.

————. *Capital,* volume 1. London: Penguin Books, 1990.

————. *Capital,* volume 3. London: Penguin Books, 1981.

McAlinden, Sean P., and Brett Smith. "The Changing Structure of the U.S. Automotive Parts Industry." Washington, DC: US Department of Commerce, 1993.

McAndrew, Mike. "Could You Run for New York State Legislature?" Syracuse.com, 2016. www.syracuse.com/politics/index.ssf/2016/06.will_ny_lawmakers_run_unopposed__for_re-election.html.

McCabe, Bret. "Does the Militarization of American Police Help Them Serve and Protect?" *Johns Hopkins Magazine,* Spring 2015. https://hub.jhu.edu/magazine/2015/spring/aclu-militarization-of-police/.

McElwee, Sean. "Why Non-Voters Matter." *Atlantic,* September 15, 2015. www.theatlantic.com/politics/archive/2015/09/why-non-voters-matter/405.

————. "Why the Voting Gap Matters." *Demos,* October 23, 2014. www.demos.org/publication/why-voting-gap-matters.

McKay, Sonia, Steve Jefferys, Anna Paraksevopoulou, and Janoj Keles. *Study on Precarious Work and Social Rights.* London: London Metropolitan University, 2012.

McNally, David. *Global Slump: The Economic and Politics of Crisis and Resistance.* Oakland: PM Press, 2011.

McNally, David, and Susan Ferguson. "Precarious Migrants: Gender, Race and the Social Reproduction of a Global Working Class." In *Socialist Register 2015,* edited by Leo Panitch and Greg Albo, 1–23. London: Merlin Press, 2014.

Merle, Renae. "U.S. Regulators Strike at Two Big Consolidation Deals." *Washington Post,* December 7, 2015. www.washingtonpost.com/business/economy/us-regulators-strike-at-two-big-consolidation-deals.

Metzgar, Jack. *Striking Steel: Solidarity Remembered.* Philadelphia: Temple University Press, 2000.

Milkman, Ruth, and Stephanie Luce. *The State of the Unions 2015: A Profile of Organized Labor in New York City, New York State, and the United States.* New York: Joseph S. Murphy Institute for Worker Education and Labor Studies, 2015.

Mirus Capital Advisors. "Foodservice Consolidation Wave Washes over Food and Beverage Manufacturers." Mirus Capital Advisors, 2014. http://merger.com/foodservice-consolidation-wave-crashes-food-beverage-manufacturers.

Mishel, Lawrence. *Despite Freelancers Union/Upwork Claim, Freelancing Is Not Becoming America's Main Source of Income.* Briefing Paper #415. Washington, DC: Economic Policy Institute, 2015.

Mishel, Lawrence, Jared Bernstein, and Heidi Shierholz. *The State of Working America, 2008/2009.* Ithaca, NY: Cornell University Press, 2009.

Mishel, Lawrence, Josh Bivens, Elsie Gould, and Heidi Shierholz. *The State of Work-*

ing America. 12th ed. Ithaca, NY: Cornell University Press, 2012.

Montgomery, David. *The Fall of the House of Labor: The Workplace, the State, and American Labor Activism, 1865–1925.* Cambridge: Cambridge University Press, 1989.

———. "Strikes of Machinists in the United States, 1870–1922." In *Strikes, Wars, and Revolutions in an International Perspective,* edited by Leopold Haimson and Charles Tilly, 269–88. Cambridge: Cambridge University Press, 2002.

Moody, Kim. "Competition and Conflict: Union Growth in the US Hospital Industry." *Economic & Industrial Democracy* 35, no. 1 (February 2014): 5–25.

———. "Contextualizing Organized Labour in Expansion and Crisis: The Case of the US." *Historical Materialism* 20, no. 1 (2012): 3–30.

———. "The Direction of Union Mergers in the United States: The Rise of Conglomerate Unionism." *British Journal of Industrial Relations* 47, no. 4 (December 2009): 676–700.

———. *From Welfare State to Real Estate: Regime Change in New York City, 1974 to the Present.* New York: New Press, 2007.

———. *An Injury to All: The Decline of American Unionism.* New York: Verso, 1988.

———. *Political Directions for Labor.* Detroit: Labor Education & Research Project, 1979.

———. "Rapid Change in Auto Industry Throws Uncertainty over '99 Contract Talks." *Labor Notes* 245 (August 1999): 8–9.

———. "Understanding the Rank-and-File Rebellion in the Long 1970s." In *Rebel Rank and File: Labor Militancy and Revolt from below During the Long 1970s,* edited by Aaron Brenner, Robert Brenner, and Cal Winslow, 105–46. London: Verso, 2010.

———. "Union Organizing in the US: New Tactics, Old Barriers." In *The Future of Union Organizing: Building for Tomorrow,* edited by Gregor Gall, 10–27. Houndsmill, UK: Palgrave Macmillan, 2009.

———. *US Labor in Trouble and Transition: The Failure of Reform from Above, the Promise of Revival from Below.* London: Verso, 2007.

Moody, Kim, and Simone Sagovac. *Time Out! The Case for a Shorter Work Week.* Detroit: Labor Notes, 1995.

Moody, Kim, and Jim Woodward. *Battle Line: The Coal Strike of '78.* Detroit: Sun Press, 1978.

Morath, Eric. "Gig Economy Attracts Many Workers, Few Full-Time Jobs." *Wall Street Journal,* February 18, 2016. http://blogs.wsj.com/economics/2016/02/18 /gig-economy.

Morrissey, Monique. *The State of American Retirement: How 401(k)s Have Failed Most American Workers.* Washington, DC: Economic Policy Institute, 2016.

Motorola. *From Cost Center to Growth Center: Warehousing 2018.* Oakdale, MN: Motorola Supply Chain Services, 2013.

Mutzabaugh, Ben. "Era of Airline Merger Mania Comes to a Close with Last US Airways Flight." *USA Today,* October 16, 2015. www.usatoday.com/story/travel /flights/todayinthesky.

Narro, Victor. "AFL-CIO Convention: A Historic Opening in the Labor Movement." *AFL-CIO Now,* October 18, 2013. www.aflcio.org/About/Exec-Council

/Conventions/2013/AFL-CIO-Now-2013/(post)/99661.

National Conference of State Legislatures (NCSL). "2009 State and Legislative Partisan Composition." National Conference of State Legislatures, 2009. www.ncsl.org/documents/statevote/legiscontrol_2009.pdf.

———. "2015 State and Legislative Partisan Composition." National Conference of State Legislatures, 2015. www.ncsl.org/documents/statevote/legiscontrol_2015.pdf.

———. "State Partisan Composition." National Conference of State Legislatures, 2016. www.ncsl.org/research/about-state-legislatures/partisan-composition.aspx.

———. "Voter Identification Requirements/Voter ID Laws." National Conference of State Legislatures, 2016. www.ncsl.org/research/elections-and-campaigns/voter-id.aspex.

National Institute on Money in State Politics. "2014 Candidate Elections Overview." 2015. www.followthemoney.org/research/institute-reports/2014-candidate-elections-overview.

———. "2013 and 2014: Money and Incumbency in Legislative Races." 2016. www.followthemoney.org/research/institute-reports/2013-and-2014-money-and-incumbency-in-state-legislative-races.

National Provisioner. "The U.S. Meatpacking Industry: Investment Invasion." September 23, 2015. www.provisioneronline.com/articles/102363.

National Small Business Association. *NSBA 2016 Politics of Small Business Survey.* Washington, DC: National Small Business Association, 2016.

"NEWSwatch." *Labor Notes* 439 (October 2015): 5.

New York City Campaign Finance Board. *2013 Post-Election Report.* New York: New York City Campaign Finance Board, 2014.

New York City Department of Finance. *Annual Report on Tax Expenditures,* Fiscal Years 2009–2016. New York: Tax Policy Division, 2009–2016.

New York State Board of Elections. *State of New York 2014 Election Law.* Albany: New York State Board of Elections, 2014.

New York Times. "City Council." November 5, 2013. www.nytimes.com/projects/elections/2013/general/city-council/results.html.

———. "Debbie Wasserman Schultz Wins Congressional Primary in Florida, According to A.P." August 31, 2016. www.nytimes.com/elections/results/florida-congressional-23-primary-wasserman-schultz-canova.

———. "Election 2012: Pennsylvania." 2012. http://elections.nytimes.com/2012/results/states/pennsylvania.

———. "Election 2016: Exit Polls." 2016. www.nytimes.com/interactive/2016/11/08/us/politics/election-exit-polls.html.

———. "Election 2016: New York Results." 2016. www.nytimes.com/elections/results/new-york.

———. "Election 2016: Ohio Results." November 15, 2016. www.nytimes.com/elections/results/ohio.

———. "Election 2016: Pennsylvania Results." 2016. www.nytimes.com/elections/results/pennsylvania.

———. "President, 100% Reporting." 2012. http://elections.nytimes.com

/2-12/results/states/ohio.

New York Times/CBS News Poll. "Americans' Views on Income Inequality and Workers' Rights." *New York Times,* June 2, 2015. www.nytimes.com/interactive /2015/06/03/business/income-inequality-workers-rights-international -trade-poll.html.

Nicholas, Peter. "Hillary Clinton Backs Debbie Wasserman Schultz during Florida Campaign Stop." *Wall Street Journal,* August 9, 2016. http://blogs.wsj.com /washwire/2016/08/09/hillary-clinton-backs-wasserman-schultz-during -florida-campaign-stop.

Nichols, John. "Hillary Clinton's Popular-Vote Victory Is Unprecedented—and Still Growing." *Nation,* November 17, 2016. www.thenation.com/article/hillary -clintons-popular-vote-victory-is-unprecedented-and-still-growing.

Noble, David. *Forces of Production: A Social History of Industrial Automation.* New York: Oxford University Press, 1986.

OccupyForum. "Don't Give Money to Democratic Party Front Group ActBlue." Forum post, 2011. http://occupywallst.org/forum/dont-give-money-to -democratic-party-front-group-ac.

Office of Management and Budget. *The President's Budget for Fiscal Year 2017.* Washington, DC: The White House, 2016.

Ogburn, Stephanie Paige. "Cattlemen Struggle against Giant Meatpackers and Economic Squeezes." *High Country News,* March 21, 2011. www.hcn.org/issues/43.5 /cattlemen-struggle-against-giant-meatpackers-and-economic-squeezes.

Ollinger, Michael, Sang V. Nguyen, Donald P. Blayney, Bill Chambers, and Ken Nelson. *Effects of Food Industry Mergers and Acquisitions on Employment and Wages.* Washington, DC: United States Department of Agriculture, 2005.

O'Mahony, Mary, and Bart van Ark. *EU Productivity and Competitiveness: An Industry Perspective.* Luxembourg: Office for Official Publications of the European Communities, 2003.

OpenSecrets. "ActBlue." 2016. www.opensecrets.org/usearch/?q=ActBlue&cx =0106779074629555562473%3Anlldkv0jvam&cof=FORID%3A11.

———. "Democratic Congressional Campaign Committee Receipts by Sector." 2014. www.opensecrets.org/parties/contrib.php?cycle=2014&cmte=DCCC.

———. "Democratic Congressional Campaign Committee Receipts by Sector." 2016. www.opensecrets.org/parties/contrib.php?cycle=2016&cmte=DCCC.

———. "Democratic Legislative Campaign Committee." 2016. www.opensecrets .org/527s/527cmtedetail_contribs.php?ein=521870839&cycle=2016.

———. "Democratic National Committee." 2016. www.opensecrets.org/parties /contrib.php?cycle=2016&cmte=DNC.

———. "Democratic Senatorial Campaign Committee Receipts by Sector." 2014. www.opensecrets.org/parties/indus.php?cmte=DSCC&cycle=2014.

———. "Democratic Senatorial Campaign Committee Receipts by Sector." 2016. www.opensecrets.org/parties/indus.php?cmte=DSCC&cycle=2016.

———. "Lobbying Database." 2016. https://www.opensecrets.org/lobby/.

———. "Massachusetts Senate Race." 2012. www.opensecrets.org/races/summary

.php?id=MAS1&cycle=2012.
———. "PAC Contributions to Federal Candidates." 2010. www.opensecrets.org
/pacs/sector.php?cycle=2010&txt=P01.
———. "PAC Contributions to Federal Candidates." 2016. www.opensecrets.org
/pacs/alphalist.php.
———. "Presidential Pre-Nomination Campaign Disbursements." 2016.
https://www.opensecrets.org/pres16.
———. "Who's Up and Who's Down?" 2016. www.opensecrets.org/lobby/top
.php?showYear=2016&indexType=i.
Ostlind, Emilene. "The Big Four Meatpackers." *High Country News*, March 21, 2011.
www.hcn.org/issues/43.5.
Our Revolution. "Candidates," 2016. https://ourrevolution.com/candidates.
———. "Election 2016 Our Revolution Live Tracker." 2016. https://ourrevolution.
com/election-2016.
Parker, Mike, and Martha Gruelle. *Democracy Is Power: Rebuilding Unions from the
Bottom Up.* Detroit: Labor Notes, 2005.
Parker, Mike, and Jane Slaughter. *Working Smart: A Union Guide to Participation Pro-
grams and Reengineering.* Detroit: Labor Notes, 1994.
Parmes, Amie, and Kevin Cirilli. "The $5 Billion Presidential Campaign" *The Hill*,
January 21, 2015.
Parramore, Lynn Stuart. "How 401(k)s Rewarded the Rich and Turned the Rest of
Us into Big Losers." BillMoyers.com, 2013. http://billmoyers.com/2013/09/25
/how-401ks-rewarded-the-rich-and-turned-the-rest-of-us-into-big-losers.
Pauli, Keven P., and Tammy Y. Arthur. "Computer Monitoring: The Hidden War
of Control." *International Journal of Management & Information Systems* 15, no. 1
(2011): 49–58.
Pautler, Paul A. *Evidence on Mergers and Acquisitions.* Working Paper 243. Washington
DC: Federal Trade Comission, 2001. www.ftc.gov/reports/evidence-mergers
-acquisitions.
Pazmino, Gloria. "After Public Anguish, Bronx Councilman Endorses Sanders on
Eve of Primary." *Politico*, April 18, 2016. www.politico.com/states/new-york
/city-hall/story/2016/04/after-public-anguish-bronx-councilman-endorses
-sanders-on-eve-of-primary-033574.
Perlstein, Rick. "It Goes Way, Way Back." *New Republic*, June 14, 2016. https:
//newrepublic.com/article/133776/split.
Perry, L., and P. Wilson. *Trends in Work Stoppages: A Global Perspective.* Working Paper
No. 47. Geneva: International Labour Office, 2004.
Petitjean, Clément. "What Happened to the French Left?" In *Europe in Revolt*, edited
by Catarina Príncipe and Bhaskar Sunkara, 87–106. Chicago: Haymarket
Books, 2016.
Pew Research Center. "The Party of the Nonvoters," October 11, 2014. www
.people-press.org/2014/10/31/the-party-of-nonvoters-2.
Piketty, Thomas. *Capital in the Twenty-First Century.* Cambridge, MA: Harvard Uni-
versity Press, 2014.

Piore, Michael. "Unions: A Reorientation to Survive." In *Labor Economics and Industrial Relations: Markets and Institutions,* edited by Clark Kerr and Paul D. Staudohar, 512–41. Cambridge MA: Harvard University Press, 1994.

Politics & Policy. "Campaigns and Voter Information: Elections in a Digital Age." 2016. http://politicsandpolicy.org/article/campaigns-and-voter-information -elections-digital-era.

Polyani, Karl. *The Great Transformation: The Political and Economic Origins of Our Time.* Boston: Beacon Press, 2001.

Post, Charlie. "The Future of the Republican Party." *Jacobin,* December 23, 2014. www.jacobinmag.com/2014/12/republican-party-tea-party/.

Preis, Art. *Labor's Giant Step: Twenty Years of the CIO.* New York: Pioneer Press, 1964.

PriceWaterhouseCooper. *Assembling Value: Second-Quarter 2015 Global Industrial Manufacturing Industry Mergers and Acquisitions Analysis.* London: PriceWaterhouseCoooper, 2015.

———. *Automotive M&A Insights: Mid-Year 2014.* London: PriceWaterhouseCooper, 2014.

Projects Five Thirty-Eight. "The Endorsement Primary." 2016. http://projects .fivethirtyeight.com/2016-endorsement-primary.

———. "How Much Do Democrats Depend on the Union Vote?" 2014. http:// fivethirtyeight.com/datalab/supreme-court-ruling-wounds-both-democrats -and-unions-neither-fatally.

Progressive Caucus. "Making the City Stronger." *Huffington Post,* June 1, 2012. www.huffingtonpost.com.new-york-city-council-progessive-caucus /new-york-city-economic-development-corporation_b_156057.html.

———. "13 Bold Progressive Ideas for NYC in 2013." http://13boldideas.org /wp-content/uploads/2013/03/13boldideas_depth.pdf.

Railway Technology. "The World's 10 Longest Railway Networks." February 20, 2014. www.railway-technology.com/features/featurethe-worlds-longest -railway-networks-4180878/.

Reshoring Initiative. *Reshoring Initiative Data Report: Reshoring and FDI Boost US Manufacturing in 2014.* Kildeer, IL: Reshoring Initiative, 2015.

Rice, Josie Duffy. "The Biggest Prison Strike in American History Is Happening Now." *Daily Kos,* October 4, 2016. www.dailykos.com/2016/10/04/1577788/-The -biggest-national-prison-strike-in-American-history-is-happening-now.

Richards, Gwynne. *Warehouse Management: A Complete Guide to Improving Efficiency and Minimizing Costs in the Modern Warehouse.* London: Kogan Page, 2014.

Rivera, Liliana, Yossi Sheffi, and Roy Welsch. "Logistics Agglomeration in the US." *Transportation Research Part A* 59 (2014): 222–38. http://sheffi.mit.edu/sites /default/files/Logistics%20Agglomeration%20in%20the%20US.pdf.

Roberts, Dan, Ben Jacobs, and Alan Yuhas. "Debbie Wasserman Schultz to Resign as DNC Chair as Email Scandal Rocks Democrats." *Guardian,* July 25, 2016. www.theguardian.com/us-news/2016/jul/24/debbie-wasserman-schultz -resigns-dnc-chair-emails-sanders.

Roberts, Sam. "New York: Voter Turnout Appears to Be Record Low." *New York*

Times, November 6, 2013. www.nytimes.com/news/election-2013/2013/11/06
/new-york-turnout-appears-headed-for-record-low.

Robin, Corey. "The Big-Donor Math." *Jacobin,* June 2016. www.jacobinmag.com
/2016/06/money-politics-donors-trump-clinton-business-campaign-finance.

Roebuck, Jeremy. "Civil Rights Group: Stop-and-Frisk Still Targets Minorities."
Philadelphia Inquirer, February 25, 2015. www.philly.com/philly/news/20150225
_Civil_rights_group__Phila__police_still_target_minorities.html.

Roper Center. "How Groups Voted." Cornell University, 1976–2012. http://
ropercenter.cornell.edu/polls/us-elections/how-groups-voted/how-groups
-voted.

Rosenfeld, Steven. "Why the New Sanders Group Our Revolution Is Leaving Many
Bernie Backers Scratching Their Heads." *Alternet,* August 31, 2016. www.alter-
net.org/election-2016/why-new-sanders-group-our-revolution-leaving
-many-bernie-backers-scratching-their.

Rustin, Bayard. "From Protest to Politics." *Commentary* 39 (February 1965): 25–31.

Saad, Lydia. "Americans' Support for Labor Unions Continues to Recover."
Gallup, August 17, 2015. www.gallup.com/poll/184622/americans-support-la-
bor-unions-continues-recover.aspx.

Saez, Emmanuel, and Gabriel Zucman. "Wealth Inequality in the United States
since 1913: Evidence from Capitalized Income Tax Data." 2015. http://gabri-
el-zucman.eu/files/SaezZucman2015.pdf.

Sainato, Michael. "Wasserman Schultz's Primary Challenger Petitions Joe Biden to
Rescind Endorsement." *Observer,* August 4, 2016. http://observer.com/2016/08/
wasserman-schultzs-primary-challenger-petitions-joe-biden-to-rescind-en-
dorsement.

St. Louis Federal Reserve Board. "Industrial Capacity: Total Index." 2015.
https://research.stlouisfed.org/fred2/series/CAPB50001S/downloaddata.

Saltamontes, Russell. "A Union County." *Jacobin,* October 6, 2014. www.jacobinmag
.org/2014/a-union-county.

Savage, Mike, et al. "A New Model of Social Class? Findings from the BBC's Great
British Survey Experiment." *Sociology* 47 no. 2 (2013): 219–50.

Schmitt, John. *Unions and Upward Mobility for Immigrant Workers.* Washington, DC:
Center for Economic and Policy Research, 2010.

Schmitt, John, and Ben Zipperer. *The Decline of African-American Representation in
Unions and Manufacturing, 1979–2007.* Washington, DC: Center for Economic
and Policy Research, 2008.

Schuknecht, Catherine. "City Council Candidates Get Boost from Bernie Sanders."
Richmond Confidential, September 8, 2016. http://richmondconfidential
.org/2016/09/08/city-council-candidates-get-boost-from-bernie-sanders.

Schwartz, Robert. "Dues Checkoff Survives Contract Expiration, Labor Board
Rules." *Labor Notes* 439 (October 2015): 11.

Schulman, Jason. "Bernie Sanders and the Dilemma of the Democratic Party." *New
Politics* 15, no. 4 (2016): 7–12.

Shafer, Byron E. "The Partisan Legacy: Are There Any New Democrats? (And by the Way, Was There a Republican Revolution?)" In *The Clinton Legacy*, edited by Colin Campbell and Bert A. Rockman, 1–32. New York: Chatham House Publishers, 2000.

Shah, Neil. "Americans' Net Worth Reaches High of $84.9 Trillion." *Wall Street Journal*, June 11, 2015. www.wsj.com/articles/americans-net-worth-hits-high -of-84.9-trillion-1434038401.

Shaikh, Anwar. *Capitalism: Competition, Conflict, Crises*. New York: Oxford University Press, 2016.

———. "The First Great Depression of the 21st Century." In *Socialist Register 2011: The Crisis This Time*, edited by Leo Panitch, Greg Albo, and Vivek Chibber, 44–63. London: Merlin Press, 2010.

Shaikh, Anwar, and E. Ahmet Tonak. *Measuring the Wealth of Nations: The Political Economy of National Accounts*. Cambridge: Cambridge University Press, 1994.

Shank, Virginia. "Fifty Years Later, GM Lordstown Still Going Strong." *Salem News*, April 25, 2016. www.salemnews.net/news/local-news/2016/04/fifty-years-lat-er-gm-lordstown-still-going-strong.

Sheffi, Yossi. *Logistics Clusters: Delivering Value and Driving Growth*. Cambridge, MA: MIT Press, 2012.

———. "Logistics-Intensive Clusters: Global Competitiveness and Regional Growth." In *Handbook of Global Logistics*, edited by James Bookbinder, 463–500. New York: Springer Science+Business Media, 2013.

Silver, Beverly J. *Forces of Labor: Workers' Movements and Globalization since 1870*. Cambridge: Cambridge University Press, 2003.

Silver, Nate. "The Mythology of Trump's 'Working Class' Support." *FiveThirty-Eight*, May 3, 2016. http://fivethirtyeight.com/features/the-mythology-of -trumps-working-class-support/.

Skocpol, Theda. *Boomerang: Health Care Reform and the Turn against Government*. New York: W. W. Norton, 1997.

———. *Protecting Soldiers and Mothers: The Political Origins of Social Policy in the United States*. Cambridge, MA: Harvard University Press, 1992.

Slaughter, Jane. "Three Recent Wins Prove Old-Fashioned Union Power Isn't Dead Yet." *Labor Notes* 448 (July 2016), 8–9.

Small Business Administration. *Demographic Characteristics of Business Owners and Employees, 2013*. Washington, DC: US Small Business Administration Office of Advocacy, 2015.

Smith, Ben. "The End of the DLC Era." *Politico*, February 7, 2011. www.politico .com/story/2011/02/the-end-of-the-dlc-era-049041.

Smith, Kevin B., and Alan Greenblatt. *Governing States and Localities*. 5th ed. Los Angeles: CQ Press, 2016.

Social Enterprise Conference. "Erin Hill: ActBlue, Executive Director." 2014. https://thesocialenterpriseconferen2014.sched.org/speaker/erin_hill.1s3ffr3m.

Socialist Party–Social Democratic Federation. *A Way Forward: Political Realignment in America*. New York: Socialist Party-Social Democratic Federation, 1960.

SourceWatch. "Bundling." November 3, 2010. www.sourcewatch.org/index.php/

Bundling.

Spriano, Paolo. *The Occupation of the Factories: Italy 1920.* London: Pluto Press, 1975.

Sreenivasan, Hari. "The Digital Campaign." *Frontline*, PBS, 2012. www.pbs.org/wgbh/frontline/film/digital-campaign/transcript.

Standing, Guy. *The Precariat: The New Dangerous Class.* London: Bloomsbury Academic, 2011.

Stobart, Luke. "Can Podemos Reclaim Its Earlier Momentum?" In *Europe in Revolt*, edited by Catarina Príncipe and Bhaskar Sunkara, 175–90. Chicago: Haymarket Books, 2016.

Story, Louise. "As Companies Seek Tax Deals, Governments Pay High Price." *New York Times*, December 1, 2012. www.nytimes.com/2012/12/02/us/how-local-taxpayers-bankroll-corporations.htm.

Sugimoto, Takashi. "E-commerce Giant Driving Massive US Retail Consolidation." *Nikkei Asian Review*, February 9, 2015. http://asia.nikkei.com/Business/Trends/E-commerce-giant-driving-massive-US-retail-consolidation.

Sullivan, Sean. "What Is a 501(c)(4), Anyway?" *Washington Post*, May 13, 2013. www.washingtonpost.com/news/the-fix/wp/2013/05/13/what-is-a-501c4-anyway/?utm_term=.d41a34f77936.

Sunkara, Bhaskar. "Bernie for President?" *Jacobin*, May 1, 2015. www.jacobinmag.com/2015/05/bernie-sanders-president-vermont-socialist/.

Sweet, Lynn. "Sweet Exclusive: Who's on Sanders' Illinois Delegate Slate?" *Chicago Sun-Times*, January 5, 2016. http://chicago.suntimes.com/politics/sweet-exclusive-whos-on-sanders-illinois-delegate-slate.

Sysco. *Annual Report.* Houston: Sysco, 2015.

Taylor, Jessica. "Taking Aim at Money in Politics, Feingold Announces Comeback Bid." NPR, May 14, 2015. www.npr.org/sections/itsallpolitics/2015/05/14/406700612/taking-aim-at-money-in-politics-feingold-announces-comeback-bid.

TD Bank. "Introducing TD Auto Finance." 2011. www.tdbank.com/chryslerfinancial.

Teamsters United. "Fred Zuckerman Statement on the IBT Election." November 17, 2016. www.teamstersunited.org/statement_from_fred_zuckerman_on_the_ibt_election.

Thomas-Breitfeld, Sean, Linda Burnham, Steven Pitts, Marc Bayard, and Algernon Austin. *#BlackWorkersMatter.* New York: Discount Foundation and Oakland, CA: Neighborhood Funders Group, 2014.

Thomson Reuters. *Mergers & Acquisitions Review.* Thomson Reuters Financial Advisors, New York. Full Year 2010, 2; Full Year 2012, 2; Full Year 2014, 2.

Tim Canova for Congress. "Debbie Wasserman Schultz Fails to Receive AFL-CIO Endorsement." 2016. https://timcanova.com/news/debbie-wasserman-schultz-fails-receive-afl-cio-endorsement.

Trangle, Sarina. "Now a Dominant Force, the Progressive Caucus Finds Its Vision Complicated." *City & State*, September 25, 2015. http://cityandstateny.com/articles/poliotics/new-york-city/now-a-dominant-force-the-progressive-caucus-finds-its-vision-comlicated.html#.V_ZwxugrKM8.

Transport Topics. Top 100 for Hire Carriers. Arlington, VA: Transport Topics Publishing Group, 2014.

Tsai, Tyjen, and Paola Scommegna. "U.S. Has World's Highest Incarceration Rate." Population Reference Bureau, 2012. www.prb.org/Publications/Articles/2012/us-incarceration.aspex.

Tucker, Will. "Personal Wealth: A Nation of Extremes, and a Congress Too: A Yearly Report from the Center for Responsive Politics." OpenSecrets, 2015. https://www.opensecrets.org/news/2015/11/personal-wealth-a-nation-of-extremes-and-a-congress-too/.

UNCTC. *World Investment Report 1991*. New York: United Nations Centre on Transnational Corporations, 1991.

———. *World Investment Report 2006*. New York: United Nations Centre on Transnational Corporations, 2006.

UNCTAD. *World Investment Report 2013*. Geneva: United Nations Conference on Trade and Development, 2013.

———. *World Investment Report 2014*. Geneva: United Nations Conference on Trade and Development, 2014.

UNIDO. *Industrial Development Report 2013*. Vienna: United Nations Industrial Development Organization, 2013.

United States Elections Project. "2016 November General Election Turnout Rates." 2016. www.electproject.org/2016g.

UN Secretary-General. *International Migration and Development: Report of the Secretary-General*. New York: United Nations General Assembly, 2014.

US Census Bureau. *County Business Patterns* (NAICS), 2015. www.census.gov/econ/cbp/.

———. "HINC-06. Income Distribution to $250,000 or More for Households." www.census.gov/data/tables/time-series/demo/income-poverty/cps-hinc/hinc-06.2015.html.

———. *A Look at the 1940 Census*. https://www.census.gov/newsroom/cspan/1940census/CSPAN_1940slides.pdf.

———. "Quick Facts, Chicago, Illinois." 2016. www.census.gov/quickfacts/table/PST045217/1714000.

———. "Quick Facts, Elyria City, Ohio," 2016. www.census.gov/quickfacts/table/PST045215/3925256.

———. "Quick Facts, Lorain City, Ohio," 2016. www.census.gov/quickfacts/table/PST045215/3944856.

———. "Quick Facts, Lorain County, Ohio," 2016. www.census.gov/quickfacts/table/PST045215/39093.

———. "State and Local Government Finances by Level of Government and by State: 2013." 2015. http://factfinder.census.gov/faces/tableservices/jsf/pages/productview.xhtml?src=bkmk.

———. *Statistical Abstract of the United States*. Washington, DC: US Government Printing Office. (Assorted years between 1983 and 2012.)

———. "Table 1, Educational Attainment of the Population 18 Years and Over, by Age, Sex, Race, and Hispanic Origin: 2014." Current Population Strategy, 2014, www.census.gov/hhes/socdemo/education/data/cps/2014/tables.html.

USDA ERS. *Retail Trends.* US Department of Agriculture, Economic Research Service, 2015. www.ers.usda.gov/food-market-prices.

US Department of Commerce. *US Automotive Parts Industry Annual Assessment.* Washington, DC: US Department of Commerce, 2009.

———. *On the Road: US Automotive Parts Industry Annual Assessment.* Washington, DC: US Department of Commerce, 2011.

US Department of Labor. "LM-2, OLMS, Public Disclosure Home." 2016. https://olms.dol-esa.gov/query/getOrgQryResult.do.

US Electoral College. "2012 Presidential Election." 2012. www.archives.gov/federal -register/electoral-college/2012/results/state/OH/president.

US Government Spending. "State & Local Spending by Function." 2016. www.usgovernmentspending.com/statelocal_spending_2016USm.

US House of Representatives. "Party Divisions of the House of Representatives." 2016. http://history.house.gov/Institution/Party-Divisions/Party-Divisions/.

US Steel. "History of US Steel." 2016. www.ussteel.com/uss/portal/home/aboutus /history.

———. *2007 Annual Report and Form 10-K.* Pittsburgh: United States Steel Corporation, 2007.

———. *2014 Annual Report and Form 10-K.* Pittsburgh: United States Steel Corporation, 2014.

Vandaele, K. *Sustaining or Abandoning Social Peace? Strike Developments and Trends in Europe since the 1990s.* Brussels: European Trade Union Institute, 2011.

Van den Heuvel, Frank P., Liliana Rivera, Karel H. van Donselaar, Ad de Jong, Yossi Sheffi, Peter W. De Langen, and Jan C. Fransoo. *Relationship between Freight Accessibility and Logistics Employment in US Counties.* Beta Working Paper series 401. Eindhoven: Beta Research School for Occupations, Management and Logistics, 2013.

VanDerhel, Jack. *The Impact of the Recent Financial Crisis on 401(k) Account Balances.* Issue Brief. Washington, DC: Employee Benefit Research Institute, 2009.

Vlisela, James, Jr. "Michael Madigan is the King of Illinois." *Chicago Magazine,* November 20, 2013. www.chicagomag.com/Chicago-Magazine/December-2013 /michael-madigan.

Warehouse Workers for Justice. *Bad Jobs in Goods Movement: Warehouse Work in Will County, Illinois.* Chicago: Warehouse Workers for Justice, 2010.

———. "Chicago Is One of the Most Important Transportation and Distribution Hubs in the World." 2016. www.warehouseworker.org/industry.html.

Washington Post. Police Shootings database, 2015, 2016. www.washingtonpost.com /graphics/national/police-shootings/.

Watkins, Susan. "Oppositions." *New Left Review* 98 (March–April, 2016): 5–30.

Weir, Stan. *Singlejack Solidarity.* Edited by George Lipsitz. Minneapolis: University of Minnesota Press, 2004.

Wells Capital Management. "Where Wall Street Meets Main Street . . . Corner of Capital and Labor." *Economic & Market Perspective Update.* August 20, 2013.

www.wellscap.com/pdf/emp/20130820.pdf.

Wikipedia. "Endorsements for the Democratic Party Presidential Primaries, 2016." 2016. https://en.wikipedia.org/wiki/Endorsements_for_the_Democratic _Party_presidential_primaries,_2016.

Willens, Max. "Election 2016 Ads: Xaxis Will Target Voters Using Their Digital and Real-Life Data." *ibtimes*, November 9, 2015. www.ibtimes.com /election-2016-political-ads-xaxis-will-target-voters-using-their-digital-real -life-2176196.

Winslow, Samantha. "Safety Is Life or Death, Say Refinery Strikers," *Labor Notes*, February 26, 2015. www.labornotes.org/2015/02/safety-life-or-death-say -refinery-strikers.

————. "Small Victory for Independent Politics in Chicago, as Rahm Prevails." *Labor Notes*, April 9, 2015. http://labornotes.org/blogs/2015/04/small-victory -independent-politics-chicago-rahm-prevails.

Woo, Nicole, Cherrie Bucknor, and John Schmitt. *Asian American and Pacific Islander Workers' Union Membership*. Washington, DC: Center for Economic and Policy Research, 2015.

Wood, Steve. "Revisiting the US Food Retail Consolidation Wave: Regulation, Market Power and Spatial Outcomes." *Journal of Economic Geography* 13, no. 2 (March 2013): 299–326.

Yuskavage, Robert E., Erich H. Strassner, and Gabriel W. Medeiros. *Domestic Outsourcing and Imported Output in the U.S. Economy: Insights from Integrated Economic Accounts*. Washington, DC: Bureau of Economic Analysis, 2008.

Zweig, Michael, *The Working-Class Majority: America's Best-Kept Secret*. Ithaca, NY: Cornell University Press, 2000.

NOTES

Introduction

1. Anwar Shaikh, "The First Great Depression of the 21st Century," in *Socialist Register 2011: The Crisis This* Time, ed. Leo Panitch, Greg Albo, and Vivek Chibber (London: Merlin Press, 2010), 45–50; David McNally, *Global Slump: The Economic and Politics of Crisis and Resistance* (Oakland: PM Press, 2011), 33–45; International Labour Organization, *Global Wage Report* (Geneva: International Labour Organization, 2014/15), 8.

2. International Labour Organization (ILO), *Global Wage Report* (Geneva: International Labour Organization, 2011), 68; ILO, *Global Wage Report* (Geneva: International Labour Organization, 2014), 97; ILO, *Global Wage Report* (Geneva: International Labour Organization, 2008/9), 9–10; ILO, *Global Wage Report* (Geneva: International Labour Organization, 2013), 41–45.

3. International Labour Organization, *Global Wage Report* 2011, 68; ILO, *Global Wage Report* 2014, 97; UNCTC, *World Investment Report 1991* (New York: United Nations Centre on Transnational Corporations, 1991), 5; UNCTAD, *World Investment Report 2013* (Geneva: United Nations Conference on Trade and Development, 2013), 24; UNIDO, *Industrial Development Report 2013* (Vienna: United Nations Industrial Development Organization, 2013), 171.

4. UN Secretary-General, "International Migration and Development: Report of the Secretary-General" (New York: United Nations General Assembly, July 30, 2014), 2–3; International Organization for Immigration, *World Immigration Report 2010* (Geneva: International Organization for Immigration, 2010), 149, 153, 165, 185, 221.

5. Dan La Botz, "What Happened to the American Working Class?" *New Politics* 12, no. 4 (Winter 2010): 75–87.

6. David Harvey, *A Brief History of Neoliberalism* (Oxford: Oxford University Press 2005), 19–36.

Chapter One: The Roots of Change

1. Guy Standing, *The Precariat: The New Dangerous Class* (London: Bloomsbury Academic, 2011), 7–8.

2. See, for example, Mike Savage et al., "A New Model of Social Class? Findings from the BBC's Great British Survey Experiment," *Sociology* 47, no. 2 (2013): 219–50.

3. Tamara Draut, *Sleeping Giant: How the New Working Class Will Transform America* (New York: Doubleday, 2016).

4. Karl Marx, *Capital*, vol. 1 (London: Penguin Books, 1990), 724.

5. UNIDO, *Industrial Development Report 2013*, 171.

6. Bureau of Labor Statistics, Table 3.1ESI, "Current-Cost Net Stock of Private Assets by Industry,"; US Census Bureau, *Statistical Abstract of the United States, 1983* (Washington, DC: US Government Printing Office, 1982–83), 396–97.

7. UNCTAD, *World Investment Report 2013*, 130–31.

8. Nicole Marie Aschoff, "Globalization and Capital Mobility in the Automotive Industry," PhD dissertation (Baltimore, MD: Johns Hopkins University, 2010).

9. Susan N. Houseman, Christopher J. Kurz, Paul Legermann, and Benjamin R. Mandel, *Offshoring Bias in U.S. Manufacturing: Implications for Productivity and Value Added* (Washington, DC: Board of Governors of the Federal Reserve System, 2010), 7; Robert E. Yuskavage, Erich H. Strassner, and Gabriel W. Medeiros, *Domestic Outsourcing and Imported Output in the U.S. Economy: Insights from Integrated Economic Accounts* (Washington, DC: Bureau of Economic Analysis, 2008), 41–43; Bureau of Economic Analysis (BEA), Table 3.1ESI, "Current-Cost Net Stock of Private Assets by Industry" and Table 3.1E, "Current-Cost Net Stock of Private Equipment by Industry," August 31, 2015; UNCTAD, *World Investment Report 2013*, 130–31.

10. BEA, Table 3.1ESI and Table 3.1E; Yuskavage, Strassner, and Medeiros, *Domestic Outsourcing and Imported Output*, 44, 45.

11. *Economist*, "Reshoring Manufacturing: Coming Home," Special Report, January 19, 2013, www.economist.com/node/21569570; Reshoring Initiative, *Reshoring Initiative Data Report: Reshoring and FDI Boost US Manufacturing in 2014* (Kildeer, IL: Reshoring Initiative, 2015).

12. Council of Economic Advisers, *Economic Report of the President, 2011* (Washington, DC: US Government Printing Office), 206, 250.

13. US Census Bureau, *Statistical Abstract of the United States, 2011* (Washington, DC: US Government Printing Office, 2011), 408, 647; Arcelor/Mittal, *Driving Solutions: United States Integrated Report: 2015* (Chicago: ArcelorMittal, 2015), 21, 25.

14. *Economist*, "Industrial Metamorphosis," September 29, 2005, www.economist.com/node/4462685.

15. Council of Economic Advisers, *Economic Report of the President, 2011*, 250–52; St. Louis Federal Reserve, "Industrial Capacity: Total Index," 2015, https://research.stlouisfed.org/fred2/series/CAPB50001S/downloaddata.

16. Kim Moody, *US Labor in Trouble and Transition: The Failure of Reform from Above, the Promise of Revival from Below* (London: Verso, 2007), 31–32.

17. Yuskavage, Strasser and Medeiros, *Domestic Outsourcing and Imported Output*, 5.

18. BEA, Table 3.1ESI and Table 3.1E; Council of Economic Advisers, *Economic Report of the President, 2011*, 250.

19. Marx, *Capital*, vol. 1, 773–74.

20. Mike Davis, *Prisoners of the American Dream: Politics and Economy in the History of the US Working Class* (London: Verso, 1986), 117–27.

21. See Aaron Brenner, Robert Brenner, and Cal Winslow, *Rebel Rank and File: Labor Mil-*

itancy and Revolt from Below during the Long 1970s (London: Verso Books, 2010).

22. Robert Brenner, *The Boom and the Bubble: The US in the World* Economy (London: Verso, 2002), 24; Anwar Shaikh and E. Ahmet Tonak, *Measuring the Wealth of Nations: The Political Economy of National Accounts* (Cambridge: Cambridge University Press, 1994), 126–27.

23. McNally, *Global Slump*, 33–37; Harvey, *Brief History of Neoliberalism*, 23–25.

24. Moody, "Contextualizing Organized Labour in Expansion and Crisis: The Case of the US," *Historical Materialism* 20, no. 1 (2012): 5–7.

25. Moody, "Contextualizing Organized Labour," 3–30.

26. Mike Parker and Jane Slaughter, *Working Smart: A Union Guide to Participation Programs and Reengineering* (Detroit: Labor Notes, 1994); Pietro Basso, *Modern Times, Ancient Hours: Working Lives in the Twenty-First Century* (London: Verso, 2003), 60–64.

27. Joel Cutcher-Gershenfeld, Dan Brooks, and Martin Mulloy, *The Decline and Resurgence of the U.S. Auto Industry* (Washington, DC: Economic Policy Institute, 2015), 22.

28. businessballs.com, "Six Sigma Training, History, Definitions—Six Sigma and Quality Management Glossary," 2011, www.businessballs.com/sixsigma.htm.

29. Susan Helper and Morris M. Kleiner, "When Management Strategies Change: Employee Well-Being at an Auto Supplier," in *Low-Wage America: How Employers Are Reshaping Opportunity in the Workplace*, ed. Eileen Appelbaum, Annette Bernhardt, and Richard J. Murnane (New York: Russell Sage Foundation, 2003), 447–48.

30. Parker and Slaughter, *Working Smart*, 24–38.

31. Basso, *Modern Times, Ancient Hours*, 63–64; Marx, *Capital*, vol. 1, 534.

32. *Barking Dog*, NUMMI plant, California, November 1997, n. p.

33. Jose Ignacio Gimenez-Nadal and Almudena Sevilla-Sanz, "Job Polarization and the Intensification of Work in the United Kingdom and the United States over the Last Decades: Evidence from Time Diary Data," paper delivered at the Fourth Society of Labor Educators/European Association of Labour Economists Global Meeting, June 26–28, 2015, Montreal, Quebec, Canada, www.parthen-impact.com/parthen-uploads/78/2015/add_1_258840_lLPu4oUWUf.pdf, 3–11.

34. Dianne Feeley, "Big Three Contracts: Who Won?," *Against the Current* 180 (January/February 2016): 5.

35. Kim Moody and Simone Sagovac, *Time Out! The Case for a Shorter Work Week* (Detroit: Labor Notes, 1995), 15–16; Virginia Shank, "Fifty Years Later, GM Lordstown Still Going Strong," *Salem News*, April 25, 2016, www.salemnews.net/news/local-news/2016/04/fifty-years-later-gm-lordstown-still-going-strong; John Irwin, "GM Lordstown Plant Faces Strike Threat from UAW Locals," *Automotive News*, January 22, 2016, www.autonews.com/article/20160122//OEM01/160129940/gm-lordstown-plant-faces-strike-threat-from-uaw-locals.

36. Circadian.com, "8-Hour Shifts vs. 12-Hour Shifts: What the Research Says," 2016, www.circadian.com/solutions-services/publications-a-reports/newletters/mana.

37. Shaik, *Capitalism: Competition, Conflict, Crises* (New York: Oxford University Press, 2016), 134.

38. Shaikh, *Capitalism: Competition, Conflict, Crises*, 138–38.

39. Shaikh, *Capitalism: Competition, Conflict, Crises*, 134–64.

40. Kristie Ball, "Workplace Surveillance: An Overview," *Labor History* 51, no. 1 (February

2010): 87–106; Keven P. Pauli and Tammy Y. Arthur, "Computer Monitoring: The Hidden War of Control," *International Journal of Management & Information Systems* 15, no. 1 (2011): 49–58; John Mangan, Chandra Lalwani, Tim Butcher, and Roya Javadpour, *Global Logistics and Supply Chain Management* (Chichester, UK: John Wiley & Sons, 2012), 237–40.

41. Marx, *Capital*, vol. 1, 536.

42. Harry Braverman, *Labor and Monopoly Capital: The Degradation of Work in the Twentieth Century* (New York: Monthly Review Press, 1998), 127–62; David Noble, *Forces of Production: A Social History of Industrial Automation* (New York: Oxford University Press, 1986), 144–92.

43. US Census Bureau, *Statistical Abstract of the United States, 1991* (Washington, DC: US Government Printing Office, 1991), 411–12.

44. US Census Bureau, *Statistical Abstract of the United States, 2011* (Washington, DC: US Government Printing Office, 2011), 416.

45. Mary O'Mahony and Bart van Ark, *EU Productivity and Competitiveness: An Industry Perspective* (Luxembourg: Office for Official Publications of the European Communities, 2003), 29; Conference Board, *International Comparisons of Manufacturing Productivity and Unit Labor Costs Trends, 2012* (New York: Conference Board, 2013), 7; Bureau of Labor Statistics (BLS), "Labor Productivity and Costs," August 9, 2016, https://data .bls.gov/cgi-bin/print.pl/lpc/prodybar.htm.

46. BLS, *International Comparison of Manufacturing Productivity and Unit Labor Cost Trends*, USDL-12-2365 (Washington, DC: Bureau of Labor Statistics, 2012), 5.

47. US Census Bureau, *Statistical Abstract of the United States, 2011*, 406.

48. US Census Bureau, *Statistical Abstract of the United States, 2011*, 416–17.

49. Janelle Jones, John Schmitt, and Nicole Woo, *Women, Working Families, and Unions* (Washington, DC: Center for Economic and Policy Research, 2014), 3.

50. Marx, *Capital*, vol. 1, 578.

51. US Census Bureau, *Statistical Abstract of the United States, 2001*, 96; US Census Bureau, *Statistical Abstract of the United States, 2011*, 105.

52. US Census Bureau, *Statistical Abstract of the United States, 2011*, 410.

53. US Census Bureau, *Statistical Abstract of the United States, 2011*, 398, 408–11.

54. Marx, *Capital*, vol. 1, 301, 450, 874; Shaikh and Tonak, *Measuring the Wealth of Nations*, 206–8.

55. Ursula Huws, *The Making of a Cybertariat: Virtual Work in a Real World* (New York: Monthly Review Press, 2003), 126–51; Shaikh and Tonak, *Measuring the Wealth of Nations*, 22–23.

56. Shaikh and Tonak, *Measuring the Wealth of Nations*, 20–32.

57. Joan Greenbaum, *Windows on the Workplace: Technology, Jobs, and the Organization of Office Work* (New York: Monthly Review Press, 2004), 81.

58. Sameer Kumar, "Specialty Hospitals Emulating Focused Factories: A Case Study," *International Journal of Health Care Quality Assurance* 23, no. 1 (2010): 95.

59. Will Johnson, "Lean Production," in *Class Action: An Activist Teacher's Handbook*, ed. Shawn Gude and Bhaskar Sunkara (New York: Jacobin Foundation, 2014), 11–18.

60. *Economist*, "Industrial Metamorphosis."

Chapter Two: Precarious Work

1. Sonia McKay, Steve Jefferys, Anna Paraksevopoulou, and Janoj Keles, *Study on Precarious Work and Social Rights* (London: London Metropolitan University, 2012), 17–18.
2. Marx, *Capital*, vol. 1, 782.
3. Marx, *Capital*, vol. 1, 785.
4. US Census Bureau, *Statistical Abstract of the United States, 2011*, 390.
5. Bureau of Labor Statistics, *New Data on Contingent and Alternative Employment Examined by BLS*, USDL 95-318 (Washington, DC: Bureau of Labor Statistics, 1995), Tables 1, 5, 12; BLS, *Contingent and Alternative Employment Arrangement, February 2005*, USDL 05-1433 (Washington, DC: Bureau of Labor Statistics, 2005), Tables 1, 5, 12; US Census Bureau, *Statistical Abstract of the United States, 2011*, 410; US Census Bureau, *Statistical Abstract of the United States, 2006*, 386; US Census Bureau, *Statistical Abstract of the United States, 1996*, 401, 403; see appendix C for calculations.
6. US Census Bureau, *Statistical Abstract of the United States, 1985*, US Census Bureau, *Statistical Abstract of the United States, 1996*, 421; US Census Bureau, *Statistical Abstract of the United States, 2011*, 410; BLS, "Labor Force Statistics from the Current Population Survey."
7. McKay et al., *Study on Precarious Work*, 7, 16; Cynthia J. Cranford, Leah F. Vosko, and Nancy Zukewich, "Precarious Employment in the Canadian Labour Market: A Statistical Portrait," *Just Labour* 3 (Fall 2003): 10.
8. Lawrence Mishel, Jared Bernstein, and Heidi Shierholz, *The State of Working America, 2008/2009* (Ithaca, NY: Cornell University Press, 2009), 257, 259.
9. BLS, *Employee Tenure in the Mid-1990s*, USDL 97-25 (Washington, DC: Bureau of Labor Statistics), 1997, Table 1, www.bls.gov/news.release/history/tenure_013097.txt; BLS, *Employee Tenure in 2014*, USDL-14-1714 (Washington, DC: Bureau of Labor Statistics, 2014), Table 1.
10. Justin Fox, "Where Are All the Self-Employed Workers?," *Harvard Business Review*, (February 7, 2014): 2, https://hbr.org/2014/02/where-are-all-the-self-employed-workers.
11. Eric Morath, "Gig Economy Attracts Many Workers, Few Full-Time Jobs," *Wall Street Journal*, February 18, 2016, http://blogs.wsj.com/economics/2016/02/18/gig-economy.
12. US Census Bureau, *Statistical Abstract of the United States, 2010*, 390; US Census Bureau, *Statistical Abstract of the United States, 2009*, 381; US Census Bureau, *Statistical Abstract of the United States, 2008*, 385; US Census Bureau, *Statistical Abstract of the United States, 2006*, 398; US Census Bureau, *Statistical Abstract of the United States, 2004/05*, 382; US Census Bureau, *Statistical Abstract of the United States, 2003*, 396; US Census Bureau, *Statistical Abstract of the United States, 2002*, 378; US Census Bureau, *Statistical Abstract of the United States, 2001*, 377; US Census Bureau, *Statistical Abstract of the United States, 2000*, 413; US Census Bureau, *Statistical Abstract of the United States, 1999*, 421; US Census Bureau, *Statistical Abstract of the United States, 1998*, 414; US Census Bureau, *Statistical Abstract of the United States, 1997*, 407; US Census Bureau, *Statistical Abstract of the United States, 1996*, 403; BLS, "Labor Force Statistics from the Current Population Survey," All Industries Self-Employed, Unincorporated, Multiple Jobholders, 2016, http://data.bls.gov/pdq/SurveyOutputServlet.

13. Fox, "Where Are All the Self-Employed," 8; US Census Bureau, *Statistical Abstract of the United States, 1982–83*, 384.

14. Mishel, *Despite Freelancers*, 2015.

15. Steven F. Hipple, "Self-Employment in the United States." *Monthly Labor Review* (September 2010): 17, 19; BLS, "Labor Force Statistics.

16. Jonathan V. Hall and Alen B. Krueger, *An Analysis of the Labor Market for Uber's Driver-Partners in the United States* (Uber Technologies, 2015).

17. US Census Bureau, *Statistical Abstract of the United States, 2009*, 392; US Census Bureau, *Statistical Abstract of the United States, 2011*, 405; Randy E. Ilg and Eleni Theodossiou, "Job Search of the Unemployed by Duration of Unemployment," *Monthly Labor Review*, March 2012: 43.

18. Shaikh, *Capitalism: Competition, Conflict*, 663–65.

19. Harry Braverman, *Labor and Monopoly Capital*.

20. Council of Economic Advisers, *Economic Report of the President, 2013* (Washington, DC: US Government Printing Office, 2013), 380.

21. David Cooper, "A Majority of Low-Wage Workers Earn So Little That They Must Rely on Public Assistance to Make Ends Meet," Economic Snapshot: Wages, Income, and Wealth, Economic Policy Institute, February 9, 2016, www.epi.org/publication /a-majority-of-low-wage-workers-earn-so-little-they-must-rely-on-public-assistance -to-make-ends-meet.

22. Mishel, Bivens, Gould, and Shierholz, *State of Working America*, 102; Shaikh, *Capitalism: Competition, Conflict*, 755.

23. Mishel, Bivens, Gould, and Shierholz, *State of Working America*, 175–204.

24. Council of Economic Advisers, *Economic Report of the President, 2013*, 435.

25. Jack VanDerhel, *The Impact of the Recent Financial Crisis on 401(k) Account Balances*, Issue Brief (Washington, DC: Employee Benefit Research Institute, 2009), 3–4; Emily Brandon and Kathy Marquardt, "How Did Your 401(k) Really Stack Up in 2008?," *US News & World Report*, February 12, 2009, http://money.usnews.com/money/retirement /articles/2009/02/12/how-did-your-401k-really-stack-up-in-2008.

26. Monique Morrissey, *The State of American Retirement: How 401(k)s Have Failed Most American Workers* (Washington, DC: Economic Policy Institute, 2016), 1–34; Lynn Stuart Parramore, "How 401(k)s Rewarded the Rich and Turned the Rest of Us into Big Losers," 2013, http://billmoyers.com/2013/09/25/how-401ks-rewarded-the-rich -and-turned-the-rest-of-us-into-big-losers.

27. BLS, "Employee Benefits Survey, Table 1, 2015, www.bls.gov/ncs/ebs/benefits/2015 /benefits_health.htm; Morrissey, *State of American Retirement*, 16.

28. Katherine G. Abraham and James R. Spletzer. "Are the New Jobs Good Jobs?," in *Labor in the New Economy*, ed. Katherine G. Abraham, James R. Spletzer, and Michael J. Harper (Chicago: University of Chicago Press, 2010). 101–43.

29. BLS, *Employment Projections—2014–24*, USDL-15-2327 (Washington, DC: Bureau of Labor Statistics, 2015), Table 4; BLS "Employment Projections: Occupations with the Most Growth," www.bls.gov/emp/ep_table_104.htm, Table 1.4; US Census, *Statistical Abstract of the United States, 2011*, 398.

30. Thomas Piketty, *Capital in the Twenty-First Century* (Cambridge, MA: Harvard Uni-

versity Press, 2014), 294–96.

31. Shaikh, *Capitalism: Competition, Conflict*, 130.

32. Shaikh, *Capitalism: Competition, Conflict*, 52–54, 729–36, 755 (emphasis in original).

Chapter Three: Growing Diversity in the Midst of Change

1. David McNally and Susan Ferguson, "Precarious Migrants: Gender, Race and the Social Reproduction of a Global Working Class," in *Socialist Register 2015*, ed. Leo Panitch and Greg Albo (London: Merlin Press, 2014), 9–11; McNally, *Global Slump*, 113–45.

2. US Census Bureau, *A Look at the 1940 Census* (Washington DC: US Census Bureau, 2012), 11.

3. US Census Bureau, *Statistical Abstract of the United States, 1982/83*, 21, 388–90; US Census Bureau, *Statistical Abstract of the United States, 2012*, 14, 393–96.

4. Kate Bronfenbrenner and Dorian T. Warren, "Race, Gender, and the Rebirth of Trade Unionism," *New Labor Forum* 16, nos. 3–4 (Fall 2007): 142–47.

5. BLS, *Union Members—2014*, USDL 15-0072 (Washington, DC: Bureau of Labor Statistics, 2015), Table 1; BLS *Union Members in 1995*, USDL 96-41 (Washington, DC: Bureau of Labor Statistics, 1996), Table 1; John Schmitt, *Unions and Upward Mobility for Immigrant Workers* (Washington, DC: Center for Economic and Policy Research, 2010), 1.

6. Ruth Milkman and Stephanie Luce, *The State of the Unions 2015: A Profile of Organized Labor in New York City, New York State, and the United States* (New York: Joseph S. Murphy Institute for Worker Education and Labor Studies, 2015), 4, 18; LCLAA, *Latino Workers and Unions: A Strategic Partnership for America's Progress* (Washington, DC: Labor Council for Latin American Advancement, 2015), 10.

7. Nicole Woo, Cherrie Bucknor, and John Schmitt, *Asian American and Pacific Islander Workers' Union Membership* (Washington, DC: Center for Economic and Policy Research, 2015), 1.

8. John Schmitt and Ben Zipperer, *The Decline of African-American Representation in Unions and Manufacturing, 1979–2007* (Washington, DC: Center for Economic and Policy Research, 2008), 1–3; Sean Thomas-Breitfeld, Linda Burnham, Steven Pitts, Marc Bayard, and Algernon Austin, *#BlackWorkersMatter* (New York: Discount Foundation; Oakland: Neighborhood Funders Group), 7–14.

9. US Census Bureau, *Statistical Abstract of the United States*, 2011, 421.

10. Mishel, Bivens, Gould, and Shierholz, *State of Working America*, 192–93.

11. Hal Draper, *Karl Marx's Theory of Revolution: The Politics of Social Classes*, vol. 2 (New York: Monthly Review Press, 1978), 35–38.

12. BLS, "Employment, Hours, and Earnings from the Current Employment Statistics Survey (National)," Databases, Tables & Calculators by Subject, 2015, http://data .bls.gov/pdq/SurveyOutputServlet.

13. Michael Zweig, *The Working-Class Majority: America's Best-Kept Secret* (Ithaca, NY: Cornell University Press, 2000), 28–34.

Chapter Four: Competition, Concentration, and Centralization of Capital

1. Patrick A. Gaughan, *Mergers, Acquisitions, and Corporate Restructuring*, 6th ed. (Hobo-ken, NJ: John Wiley & Sons, 2015), 41–74; Devra L. Golbe and Lawrence J. White, "A Time-Series Analysis of Mergers and Acquisitions in the U.S. Economy," in *Corporate Takeovers: Causes and Consequences*, ed. Alan J. Auerbach (Chicago: University of Chicago Press, 1988), 269–75.

2. Gaughan, *Mergers, Acquisitions, and Corporate Restructuring*, 42.

3. For more on gross profit rate minus interest rate, see Marx, *Capital*, vol. 3, 493–514; Shaikh, "First Great Depression," 52; Gaughan, *Mergers, Acquisitions, and Corporate Restructuring*, 49–74; Paul A. Paulter, *Evidence on Mergers and Acquisitions*, Working Paper 243 (Washington, DC: Federal Trade Commission, 2001), www.ftc.gov/reports /evidence-mergers-acquisitions, 58.

4. Marx, *Capital*, vol. 1, 775–78.

5. Marx, *Capital*, vol. 1, 776–77.

6. Golbe and White, "A Time-Series Analysis," 272–73; Doug Henwood, *Wall Street: How It Works and for Whom* (London: Verso, 1997), 277–82; Gaughan, *Mergers, Acquisitions, and Corporate Restructuring*, 22, 41–74, 350.

7. UNCTAD, *World Investment Report 2014* (Geneva: United Nations Conference on Trade and Development, 2014), 213; UNCTAD, *World Investment Report 2006* (New York and Geneva: United Nations Conference on Trade and Development, 2006), 9.

8. Marx, *Capital*, vol. 1, 777.

9. UNCTC, *World Investment Report 1991*, 5; UNCTAD, *World Investment Report 2013*, 24; Gaughan, *Mergers, Acquisitions, and Corporate Restructuring*, 49–74.

10. Golbe and White, "A Time-Series Analysis," 270–71; US Census Bureau, *Statistical Abstract of the United States, 1990* (Washington, DC: US Government Printing Office, 1990), 534; US Census Bureau, *Statistical Abstract of the United States, 2001*, 492–93; US Census Bureau, *Statistical Abstract of the United States, 2006*, 520; Thomson Reuters, *Mergers & Acquisitions Review*, Full Year 2010, 2012, 2014, 2; Renae Merle, "U.S. Regulators Strike at Two Big Consolidation Deals," *Washington Post*, December 7, 2015, www.washingtonpost.com/business/economy/us-regulators-strike-at-two -big-consolidation-deals/2015/12/07/607007a8-9d32-11e5-8728-1af6af208198 _story.html.

11. PriceWaterhouseCooper, *Assembling Value: Second-Quarter 2015 Global Industrial Manufacturing Industry Mergers and Acquisitions Analysis* (London: PriceWaterhouseCooper LLP, 2015); Gaughan, *Mergers, Acquisitions, and Corporate Restructuring*, 62–74; Henwood, *Wall Street*, 279.

12. Gaughan, *Mergers, Acquisitions, and Corporate Restructuring*, 394.

13. Allison Collins, "GE Continues Industrial Push with Metem Deal," *Mergers & Acquisitions*, December 28, 2015, www.themiddlemarket.com/news/ge-continues -industrial-push-with-metem-deal.

14. Jim Henry, "Ally, Formerly GMAC, Rebounds to Become Top Auto Finance Story of 2010," *Automotive News*, December 29, 2010, www.autonews.com/article/20101229

/FINANCE_AND_INSURANCE/101229913/ally-formerly-gmac-rebounds-to
-become-top-auto-finance-story-of-2010.

15.. TD Bank, "Introducing TD Auto Finance," 2011, www.tdbank.com/chryslerfinancial.

16. US Steel, *2007 Annual Report and Form 10-K* (Pittsburgh: United States Steel Corporation, 2007), 4; US Steel, "History of US Steel," 2016, www.ussteel.com/uss/portal
/home/aboutus/history.

17. Howard Botwinick, *Persistent Inequalities: Wage Disparity under Capitalist Competition* (Princeton, NJ: Princeton University Press, 1993), 209.

18. Charles Craypo, *The Economics of Collective Bargaining: Case Studies in the Private Sector* (Washington, DC: Bureau of National Affairs, 1986), 200.

19. Michael Ollinger, Sang V. Nguyen, Donald P. Blayney, Bill Chambers, and Ken Nelson, *Effects of Food Industry Mergers and Acquisitions on Employment and Wages* (Washington, DC: United States Department of Agriculture, 2005), 5–7; US Census Bureau, *Statistical Abstract of the United States, 2001*, 394.

20. Golbe and White, "A Time-Series Analysis," 272–73; Gaughan, *Mergers, Acquisitions, and Corporate Restructuring*, 48–49.

21. Global Automakers, *Redefining the American Auto Industry: The Growing Impact of International Automakers on the U.S. Economy* (Washington, DC: Global Automakers, 2014), 3, 7.

22. Sean P. McAlinden and Brett Smith, *The Changing Structure of the U.S. Automotive Parts Industry* (Washington, DC: US Department of Commerce, 1993), 30; US Census Bureau, *County Business Patterns* (NAICS), 2015, www.census.gov/programs-surveys
/cbp.html.

23. McAlinden and Smith, *Automotive Parts Industry*, 4; Aschoff, *Globalization and Capital Mobility*, 49–70; US Census Bureau, *County Business Patterns*; see appendix D for the different measures of the auto parts industry used here.

24. US Department of Commerce, *On the Road: U.S. Automotive Parts Industry Annual Assessment* (Washington, DC: US Department of Commerce, 2011), 4–7; Kim Moody, "Rapid Change in Auto Industry Throws Uncertainty over '99 Contract Talks," *Labor Notes* 245 (August 1999): 8–9; *Automotive News*, Supplement, June 17, 2013, 11–12.

25. US Department of Commerce, "On the Road," 4–7, 15, 33; *Automotive News*, Supplement, 3; Mark Clothier, "Auto-Parts M&A Value Seen Reaching Record $48 Billion This Year," *Bloomberg Business*, August 11, 2015, www.bloomberg.com/news/articles
/2015-08-11/auto-parts-m-a-value-seen-reaching-record-48-billion-this-year.

26. US Department of Commerce, "On the Road," 4–7, 15, 33; PriceWaterhouseCooper, *Automotive M&A Insights: Mid-Year 2014* (London: PriceWaterhouseCooper LLP, 2014); US Department of Commerce, *US Automotive Parts Industry Annual Assessment* (Washington, DC: US Department of Commerce, 2009), 17; Aschoff, *Globalization and Capital Mobility*, 49, 57; US Census Bureau, *Statistical Abstract of the United States, 2001*, 393; US Census Bureau, *Statistical Abstract of the United States, 2012*, 408; BLS, "Employment of Production and Nonsupervisory Employees."

27. Helper and Kleiner, "When Management Strategies Change," 447–49.

28. Ollinger, *Effects of Food Industry Mergers*, 5–6.

29. US Census Bureau, *Statistical Abstract of the United States, 2001*, 394.

30. James M. MacDonald, Michael E. Ollinger, Kenneth E. Nelson, and Charles R.

Handy, *Consolidation in U.S. Meatpacking* (Washington, DC: US Department of Agriculture, 2000), 8–15.

31. Stephanie Paige Ogburn, "Cattlemen Struggle against Giant Meatpackers and Economic Squeezes," *High Country News*, March 21, 2011, www.hcn.org/issues/43.5/cattlemen -struggle-against-giant-meatpackers-and-economic-squeezes; *National Provisioner*, "The U.S. Meatpacking Industry: Investment Invasion," *National Provisioner*, September 23, 2015, www.provisioneronline.com/articles/102363.

32. BLS, "Employment of Production and Nonsupervisory Employees."

33. US Steel, *Annual Report*, 2007, 4; US Steel, "History of US Steel."

34. Arcelor/Mittal, *Driving Solutions*, 7, 26; Arcelor/Mittal, "Who We Are; Our History," 2016, http://corporate.arcelormittal.com/who-we-are/our-history; US Steel, *Annual Report 2014*, 9.

35. Association of American Railroads, "Railroad Jobs," 2015, www.aar.org/Pages/Careers.

36. Transport Topics, "Top 100 for Hire Carriers," Transport Topics Publishing Group, 2014; US Census Bureau, *Statistical Abstract of the United States, 2012*, 409.

37. Kevin Farrell, "This Is How Dozens of Major Airlines Got Swallowed by the Big 3," *Road Warrior Voices*, November 9, 2015, http://roadwarriorvoices.com/2015/11/09 /this-is-how-dozens-of-major-airlines; US Census Bureau, *Statistical Abstract of the United States, 2012*, 409; Ben Mutzabaugh, "Era of Airline Merger Mania Comes to a Close with Last US Airways Flight," *USA Today*, October 16, 2015, www.usatoday .com/story/travel/flights/todayinthesky.

38. Capgemini, *Communications Industry: On the Verge of Massive Consolidation* (London: Capgemini Consulting, Technology, Outsourcing, 2014), 4.

39. American Hospital Association, *AHA Hospital Statistics*, 2011 ed. (Chicago: Health Forum, 2010), 4; American Hospital Association, 2011, 12; Brooks and Jones, "Hospital Mergers," 701–2; Clark, "Health Care," 94.

40. Annette Bernhardt, Laura Dresser, and Erin Hatton, "The Coffee Pot Wars: Unions and Firm Restructuring in the Hotel Industry," in *Low-Wage America: How Employers Are Reshaping Opportunity in the* Workplace, ed. Eileen Appelbaum, Annette Bernhardt, and Richard J. Murnane, 33–76 (New York: Russell Sage Foundation, 2003), 38.

41. Qingzhong Ma and Peng Liu, "Who's Next? An Analysis of Lodging Industry Acquisitions," *Cornell Hospitality Report* 10, no. 11 (July 2010): 6–11; From the Editor, "Examining Mergers and Acquisitions", *Cornell Hospitality Quarterly*, May 2009, 140; Business Source Complete, "REIT Mafia Leads the Charge," EBSCO Host, 2011, http://web.ebschost.com/ehost/detail?vid=3&sid=c"da013d-19de-4e1f-b830.

42. Takashi Sugimoto, "E-commerce Giant Driving Massive US Retail Consolidation," *Nikkei Asian Review*, February 9, 2015, http://asia.nikkei.con/Business/Trends; Gwynne Richards, *Warehouse Management: A Complete Guide to Improving Efficiency and Minimizing Costs in the Modern Warehouse* (London: Kogan Page, 2014), 22; US Census Bureau, *Statistical Abstract of the United States, 2001*, 653; US Census Bureau, *Statistical Abstract of the United States, 2012*, 409, 662.

43. Food & Water Watch, *Consolidation and Buyer Power in the Grocery Industry*, 2010, www .foodandwaterwatch.org/insight/consolidation-and-buyer-power-grocery-industry; Steve Wood, "Revisiting the US Food Retail Consolidation Wave: Regulation, Mar-

ket Power and Spatial Outcomes," *Journal of Economic Geography* 13, no. 2 (March 2013): 299–326.

44. USDA ERS, *Retail Trends*, US Department of Agriculture, Economic Research Service, 2015, www.ers.usda.gov/food-market-prices; Food & Water Watch, *Consolidation and Buyer Power.*

45. Julia Lane, Philip Moss, Harold Salzman, and Chris Tilly, "Too Many Cooks? Tracking Internal Labor Market Dynamics in Food Services with Case Studies and Qualitative Data," in *Low-Wage America: How Employers Are Reshaping Opportunity in the Workplace*, ed. Eileen Appelbaum, Annette Bernhardt, and Richard J. Murnane, 229–69 (New York: Russell Sage Foundation, 2003), 237.

46. Sysco, *Annual Report* (Houston: Sysco, 2015), 53; Mirus Capital Advisors, "Foodservice Consolidation Wave Washes over Food and Beverage Manufacturers," 2014, http://merger.com/foodservice-consolidation-wave-crashes-food-beverage-manufacturers.

47. Botwinick, *Persistent Inequalities*, 150–56.

48. Council of Economic Advisers, *Economic Report of the President 2013*, 399; BLS, "Employment, Hours, and Earnings"; BLS, Table 6a, "Employment of Production and Nonsupervisory Employees on Private Nonfarm Payrolls in Industry Sector, Seasonally Adjusted," Current Employment Statistics, 2015, www.bls.gov/web/empsit /ceseeb6a.htm; BLS, "Employment, Hours, and Earnings," Appendix E.

49. Jeffery L. Barnett, Cindy L. Sheckells, Scott Peterson, and Elizabeth M. Tydings, *2012 Census of Governments: Finance—State and Local Government Summary Report* (Washington, DC: US Census Bureau, 2014), 8, 12; US Census Bureau *Statistical Abstract of the United States, 2012*, 275–76; Warehouse Workers for Justice, "Chicago Is One of the Most Important Transportation and Distribution Hubs in the World," 2016, www .warehouseworker.org/industry.html.

50. St. Louis Federal Reserve, "Industrial Capacity"; Wells Capital Management, "Where Wall Street Meets Main Street . . . Corner of Capital and Labor," *Economic & Market Perspective Update*, August 20, 2013, 1–4.

51. US Census Bureau, *Statistical Abstract of the United States, 2012*, 644.

52. Shaikh, *Capitalism: Competition, Conflict*, 751.

53. US Census Bureau, *Statistical Abstract of the United States, 1990*, 528; US Census Bureau, *Statistical Abstract of the United States, 2001*, 484; US Census Bureau, *Statistical Abstract of the United States, 2012*, 501.

54. Marx, *Capital*, vol. 1, 799.

55. Shaikh, "First Great Depression," 52; Shaikh, *Capitalism: Competition, Conflict*, 734–36.

56. Lawrence Mishel, Josh Bivens, Elsie Gould, and Heidi Shierholz, *The State of Working America*, 12th ed. (Ithaca, NY: Cornell University Press, 2012), 235–41; ILO, *Global Wage Report*, 8–10.

57. "Americans' Views on Income Inequality and Workers' Rights," *New York Times*/ CBS News Poll, June 2, 2015, www.nytimes.com/interactive/2015/06/03/business /income-inequality-workers-rights-international-trade-poll.html.

58. Botwinick, *Persistent Inequalities*, 129–36; Karl Marx, *Wage-Labour and Capital* (New York: International Publishers, 1933), 43.

Chapter Five: Logistics

1. Marx, *Capital*, vol. 1, 505–6.

2. Yossi Sheffi, *Logistics Clusters: Delivering Value and Driving Growth* (Cambridge, MA: MIT Press, 2012), 77, 238, 265–67; Yossi Sheffi, "Logistics-Intensive Clusters: Global Competitiveness and Regional Growth," in *Handbook of Global Logistics*, ed. James Bookbinder, 463–500 (New York: Springer Science+Business Media, 2013), 472; Frank P. Van den Heuvel, Liliana Rivera, Karel H. van Donselaar, Ad de Jong, Yossi Sheffi, Peter W. De Langen, and Jan C. Fransoo, *Relationship between Freight Accessibility and Logistics Employment in US Counties*, Beta Working Paper series 401 (Eindhoven: Beta Research School for Occupations, Management and Logistics, 2013), 21; Warehouse Workers for Justice, "Chicago Is One."

3. Quoted in Deborah Cowen, *The Deadly Life of Logistics: Mapping Violence in Global Trade* (Minneapolis: University of Minnesota Press, 2014), 183.

4. Marx, *Capital*, vol. 3, 163.

5. Sheffi, *Logistics Clusters*, 147.

6. Harvey, *The Ways of the World* (London: Profile Books, 2016), 134–42.

7. US Census Bureau, *Statistical Abstract of the United States, 2012*, 31, 383.

8. Liliana Rivera, Yossi Sheffi, and Roy Welsch, "Logistics Agglomerations in the US," *Transportation Research Part A* 59 (2014): 223.

9. Martin Associates, *The Economic Impacts of the Port of Chicago*, 11.

10. Warehouse Workers for Justice, *Bad Jobs in Goods Movement: Warehouse Work in Will County, Illinois* (Chicago: Warehouse Workers for Justice, 2010), 9; Sheffi, *Logistics Clusters*, 150, 178; BLS, "Occupational Employment Statistics, Transportation and Material Moving Occupations, Chicago-Naperville-Arlington Heights, IL Metropolitan Division," www.bls.gov/oes_16974.htm.

11. Warehouse Workers for Justice, *Bad Jobs in Goods Movement*, 10–17.

12. Van den Heuvel et al., *Freight Accessibility and Logistics*, 9.

13. US Census Bureau, "Quick Facts, Chicago, Illinois"; Adeshina Emmanuel, "Chicago's Black Unemployment Rate Higher than Other Large Metro Areas," *Chicago Reporter*, November 16, 2014, http://chicagoreporter.com/chicagos-black-unemployment-rate-higher-other-large-metro-areas.

14. Van den Heuvel et al., *Freight Accessibility and Logistics*, 21.

15. Association of American Railroads, "Railroad Jobs."

16. Karl Marx, *Grundrisse: Introduction to the Critique of Political Economy* (Harmondsworth UK: Penguin Books, 1973), 533–34.

17. Marx, *Capital*, vol. 2, 226–27.

18. Richards, *Warehouse Management*, 6, 10; Motorola, *From Cost Center to Growth Center: Warehousing 2018* (Oakdale, MN: Motorola Supply Chain Services, 2013), 8; Sheffi, *Logistics Clusters*, 121–46; Edna Bonicich and Jake B. Wilson, *Getting the Goods: Ports, Labor, and the Logistics Revolution* (Ithaca, NY: Cornell University Press, 2008), 126.

19. BEA, *Relation of Private Fixed Investment in Structures (by Type) in the Fixed Assets Accounts to the Corresponding Items in the National Income and Product Accounts*, 2015, www.bea.gov/national/FA2004/ST_types.pdf.

20. Draper, *Marx's Theory of Revolution*, 35–38.
21. Martin Christopher. *Logistics and Supply Chain Management*, 4th ed. (Harlow UK: Pearson, 2011), 28.
22. Marx, *Grundrisse*, 538.
23. Marx, *Grundrisse*, 524.
24. Sheffi, *Logistics Clusters*, 159.
25. Bonacich and Wilson, *Getting the Goods*, 130.
26. Sheffi, *Logistics Clusters*, 171.
27. US Department of Commerce, *On the Road*, 7.
28. Christopher, *Logistics and Supply*, 193.
29. Marx, *Capital*, vol. 3, 310–11.
30. BEA, Interactive Tables; BEA, "BEA Depreciation Estimates," no date, www.bea. gov/national/FA2004/Tablecandtext.pdf, 8–13.
31. David Harvey, *The Limits to Capital* (Chicago: University of Chicago Press, 1982), 386.
32. US Census Bureau, *Statistical Abstract of the United States, 2012*, 675; "The World's 10 Longest Railway Networks," Railway Technology, February 20, 2014, www.railway -technology.com/features/featurethe-worlds-longest-railway-networks-4180878/.
33. Moody, *U.S. Labor in Trouble*, 44.
34. Harvey, *Limits to Capital*, 442.
35. Harvey, *The Condition of Postmodernism: An Inquiry into the Origins of Cultural Change* (Oxford: Basil Blackwell, 1989), 147.

Chapter Six: The Coming Upsurge?

1. Eric Hobsbawm, *Labouring Men: Studies in the History of Labour* (London: Weidenfeld and Nicolson, 1964), 126–39.
2. John Kelly, *Rethinking Industrial Relations: Mobilization, Collectivism and Long Waves* (London: Routledge, 1998), 91; Beverly J. Silver, *Forces of Labor: Workers' Movements and Globalization since 1870* (Cambridge: Cambridge University Press, 2003), 127; Ernest Mandel, *Long Waves of Capitalist Development: A Marxist Interpretation*, rev. ed. (London: Verso, 1995), 39.
3. Mandel, *Long Waves*, 37–38.
4. Kelly, *Rethinking Industrial Relations*, 1.
5. Mandel, *Long Waves*, 119; Kelly, *Rethinking Industrial Relations*, 98.
6. Haimson, "The Historical Setting," 28–29.
7. Montgomery, "Strikes of Machinists in the United States, 1870–1922," in *Strikes, Wars, and Revolutions in an International Perspective*, ed. Leopold Haimson and Charles Tilly (Cambridge: Cambridge University Press, 2002), 278–82; Elisabeth Domansky, "The Rationalization of Class Struggle: Strikes and Strike Strategy of the German Metalworkers' Union, 1891–1922," in *Strikes, Wars, and Revolutions in an International Perspective*, ed. Leopold Haimson and Charles Tilly (Cambridge: Cambridge University Press, 2002), 328; Heather Hogan, "Scientific Management and the Changing Nature of Work in the St. Petersburg Metalworking Industry, 1900–1914," in *Strikes,*

Wars, and Revolutions in an International Perspective, ed. Leopold Haimson and Charles Tilly (Cambridge: Cambridge University Press, 2003), 357–65; Keith Burgess, "The Political Economy of British Engineering Workers during the First World War," in *Strikes, Wars, and Revolutions in an International Perspective*, Leopold Haimson and Charles Tilly (Cambridge: Cambridge University Press, 2002), 295–310.

8. James Hinton, *The First Shop Steward's Movement* (London: George Allen & Unwin, 1973); Pierre Broué, *The German Revolution, 1917–1923* (Chicago: Haymarket Books, 2006), 67–68; Ralf Hoffrogge, *Working-Class Politics in the German Revolution: Richard Müller, the Revolutionary Shop Stewards, and the Origins of the Council Movement* (Chicago: Haymarket Books, 2015); Paolo Spriano, *The Occupation of the Factories: Italy 1920* (London: Pluto Press, 1975).

9. David Montgomery, *The Fall of the House of Labor: The Workplace, the State, and American Labor Activism, 1865–1925* (Cambridge: Cambridge University Press, 1989), 425–38.

10. Hoffrogge, *Working-Class Politics*, 15–20.

11. Leopold Haimson and Eric Brian, introduction to part 2, *Strikes, Wars, and Revolutions in an International* Perspective, ed. Leopold Haimson and Charles Tilly (Cambridge: Cambridge University Press, 2002), 38.

12. Hobsbawm, *Labouring Men*, 139.

13. Davis, *Prisoners of the American Dream*, 119–24; Stan Weir, *Singlejack Solidarity*, ed. George Lipsitz (Minneapolis: University of Minnesota Press, 2004), 305.

14. Kelly, *Rethinking Industrial Relations*, 1.

15. Montgomery, *Fall of the House of Labor*, 2.

16. Irving Bernstein, *Turbulent Years: A History of the American Workers, 1933–1941* (Boston: Houghton Mifflin Company, 1969), 217–317; Dobbs, *Teamster Power*; Art Preis, *Labor's Giant Step: Twenty Years of the CIO* (New York: Pioneer Press, 1964), 19–33.

17. Sol Dollinger and Genora Johnson Dollinger, *Not Automatic: Women and the Left in the Forging of the Auto Workers' Union* (New York: Monthly Review Press, 2000), 123–60.

18. Paul Le Blanc, "Radical Labor Subculture: Key to Past and Future Insurgencies," *WorkingUSA* 13 (September 2010): 374.

19. Kim Moody, "Understanding the Rank-and-File Rebellion in the Long 1970s," in *Rebel Rank and File: Labor Militancy and Revolt from Below during the Long 1970s*, ed. Aaron Brenner, Robert Brenner, and Cal Winslow (London: Verso, 2010), 144.

20. BLS, *Major Work Stoppages in 2015*, USDL-16-0272 (Washington, DC: Bureau of Labor Statistics, 2016), Table 3; *2014 Annual Report* (Washington, DC: Federal Mediation & Conciliation Service, 2014), 20.

21. Moody, "The Direction of Union Mergers in the United States: The Rise of Conglomerate Unionism," *British Journal of Industrial Relations* 47, no. 4 (December 2009): 676–700.

22. Piore, "Unions," 512–41.

23. Jeremy Brecher and Tim Costello. "A 'New Labor Movement' in the Shell of the Old?" in *A New Labor Movement for the New Century*, ed. Greg Mantsios (New York: Monthly Review Press, 1998), 40.

24. Suzanne Gordon, "Is Sweeney's 'New Voice' A Choice or an Echo," *Labor Notes* 199 (October 1995), 12–13.

25. Kim Moody, "Union Organizing in the US: New Tactics, Old Barriers," in *The Future of Union Organizing: Building for Tomorrow*, ed. Gregor Gall (Houndsmill, UK: Palgrave Macmillan, 2009), 13–19; Kim Moody, "Competition and Conflict: Union Growth in the US Hospital Industry," *Economic & Industrial Democracy* 35, no. 1 (February 2014): 5–25.

26. Herman Benson. *Rebels, Reformers, and Racketeers: How Insurgents Transformed the Labor Movement* (Bloomington, IN: First Books, 2005), 211.

27. US Department of Labor, "LM-2, OLMS, Public Disclosure Home," 2016, https://olms.dol-esa.gov/query/getOrgQryResult.do.

28. *Labor Notes*, "Passing the Torch . . . or Lighting a Fire?," *Labor Notes* 366 (September 2009): 1.

29. Steve Early, *The Civil Wars in U.S. Labor: Birth of a New Workers' Movement or Death Throes of the Old?* (Chicago: Haymarket Books, 2011), 281–82.

30. Jeff Crosby and Bill Fletcher Jr., "AFL-CIO Convention Repositions Unions to Speak for All Workers," *Labor Notes*, October 17, 2013; Steve Early, "House of Labor Needs Repairs, Not Just New Roommates," *Labor Notes*, September 16, 2013; Harry Enten, "How Much Do Democrats Depend on the Union Vote?," *FiveThirtyEight*, http://fivethirtyeight.com/datalab/supreme-court-ruling-wounds-both-democrats-and-unions-neither-fatally; Victor Narro, "AFL-CIO Convention: A Historic Opening in the Labor Movement," *AFL-CIO Now*, October 18, 2013, www.aflcio.org/About/Exec-Council/Conventions/2013/AFL-CIO-Now-2013/(post)/99661.

31. L. Perry and P. Wilson, *Trends in Work Stoppages: A Global Perspective*, Working Paper No. 47 (Geneva: International Labour Office, 2004), 37.

32. K. Vandaele, *Sustaining or Abandoning Social Peace? Strike Developments and Trends in Europe since the 1990s* (Brussels: European Trade Union Institute, 2011), 26–29.

33. Moody, "Competition and Conflict," 230.

34. Samantha Winslow, "Safety Is Life or Death, Say Refinery Strikers," *Labor Notes*, February 26, 2015.

35. Kann, Julia, "Telecom Strikers Win Limits on Outsourcing," *Labor Notes*, February 23, 2015.

36. BLS, *Major Work Stoppages in 2015*, 5.

37. Dan DiMaggio, "Verizon Strike Shows Corporate Giants Can Be Beat," *Labor Notes*, June 3, 2016; Alan Maass and Lee Sustar, "Why They Won," *Jacobin*, June 7, 2016, www.jacobinmag.com/2016/06/verizon-strike-contract-deal-cwa-ibew-union-pickets.

38. Dan DiMaggio, "Wave of Walkouts at AT&T West," *Labor Notes* 448 (July 2016): 14, 16.

39. Jane Slaughter, "Three Recent Wins Prove Old-Fashioned Union Power Isn't Dead Yet," *Labor Notes* 448 (July 2016): 8–9.

40. For details, see Alexandra Bradbury, Mark Brenner, Jenny Brown, Jane Slaughter, and Samantha Winslow, *How to Jump-Start Your Union: Lessons for the Chicago Teachers* (Detroit: Labor Education and Research Project, 2014).

41. Doug Cunningham, "CTU's Karen Lewis: Tentative Deal Is Good for Kids, Teachers and Communities," *Labor Radio*, October 11, 2016.

42. Dobbs, *Teamster Power*, 145–55.

43. Barry T. Hirsch and David A. Macpherson, "Union Membership and Coverage

Database from the CPS," 2010, www.unionstats.com; Milkman and Luce, *State of the Unions 2015*, 1.

44. Robert Schwartz, "Dues Checkoff Survives Contract Expiration, Labor Board Rules," *Labor Notes* 439 (October 2015): 11.

45. "NEWSwatch," *Labor Notes* 439 (October 2015): 5.

46. Lydia Saad, "Americans' Support for Labor Unions Continues to Recover," Gallup, August 17, 2015, www.gallup.com/poll/184622/americans-support-labor-unions -continues-recover.aspx.

47. Bill Fletcher and Fernando Gapasin, *Solidarity Divided: The Crisis in Organized Labor and a New Path to Social Justice* (Los Angeles and Berkeley: University of California Press, 2008), 259.

48. Michelle Gunderson, "Teachers Compare Notes, *Labor Notes*, April 17, 2015.

49. Teamsters United, "Fred Zuckerman Statement on the IBT Election," November 17, 2016, www.teamstersunited.org/statement_from_fred_zuckerman_on_the_ibt _election.

50. Joe Allen, *The Package King: A Rank and File History of United Parcel Service* (Amazon, 2016), 108–37.

Chapter Seven: Capital and the Return of the States

1. Stanley B. Greenberg, *The Two Americas: Our Current Political Deadlock and How to Break It* (New York: Thomas Dunne Books, 2004), 132–35; Roper Center, "How Groups Voted," 1996, 2000.

2. Tami Luhby, "How Hillary Clinton Lost," CNN, November 10, 2016, http://edition .cnn.com/2016/11/09/politics/clinton-votes-african-americans-latinos-women -white-voters.

3. Megan Erickson, Katherine Hill, Matt Karp, Connor Kilpatrick, and Bhaskar Sun-kara, "Politics Is the Solution," *Jacobin*, November 9, 2016, www.jacobinmag.com /2016/11/trump-victory-clinton-sanders-democratic-party.

4. CNN Politics, "Election Center, President, Ohio," 2012. http://edition.cnn.com /election/2012/results/state/OH/president; CNN Politics, "Ohio President," 2016, http://edition.cnn.com/election/results//exit-polls/ohio/president; *New York Times*, "Election 2016: Exit Polls," 2016, www.nytimes.com/interactive/2016/11/08/us /politics/election-exit-polls.html; Jamison, 2016; *Guardian*, "U.S. Elections," No-vember 10, 2016.

5. *New York Times*, "Election 2016: Exit Polls"; Small Business Administration, *Demo-graphic Characteristics of Business Owners and Employees, 2013* (Washington, DC: US Small Business Administration Office of Advocacy, 2016), 1; National Small Business Association, *NSBA 2016 Politics of Small Business Survey* (Washington, DC: National Small Business Association, 2016), 5–6.

6. US Census Bureau, "On the Road," 267.

7. Draper, *Karl Marx's Theory*, vol. 1, 320.

8. Draper, *Karl Marx's* Theory, vol. 1, 311–26.

9. Theda Skocpol, *Protecting Soldiers and Mothers: The Political Origins of Social Policy in the United States* (Cambridge, MA: Harvard University Press, 1992), 102–51.

10. Gary Gerstle, "The Resilient Power of the States across the Long Nineteenth Century," in *The Unsustainable American State*, ed. Lawrence Jacobs and Desmond King (Oxford: Oxford University Press, 2009), 61–87.

11. Moody, *An Injury to All*, 127–46.

12. Gary Gerstle, *Liberty and Coercion: The Paradox of American Government from the Founding to the Present* (Princeton, NJ: Princeton University Press, 2015), 318–19, 327–29, 332–34.

13. Kevin B. Smith and Alan Greenblatt, *Governing States and Localities*, 5th ed. (Los Angeles: CQ Press, 2016), 209, 223–28.

14. Smith and Greenblatt, *Governing States and Localities*, 182.

15. Greg LeRoy, *The Great American Jobs Scam: Corporate Tax Dodging and the Myth of Job Creation* (San Francisco: Berrett-Koehler Publishers, 2005), 2.

16. Louise Story, "As Companies Seek Tax Deals, Governments Pay High Price," *New York Times*, December 1, 2012, www.nytimes.com/2012/12/02/us/how-local-taxpayers-bankroll-corporations.htm.

17. LeRoy, *Great American Jobs Scam* 5, 23.

18. Barnett, *2012 Census of Governments*, 2; Heintz, "The Grim State of the States," 10–13; Michael Leachman and Michael Mazerov, *State Personal Income Tax Cuts: Still a Poor Strategy for Economic Growth* (Washington, DC: Center on Budget and Policy Priorities, 2015), 1–6; LeRoy, *Great American Jobs Scam*, 172.

19. Gordon Lafer, *The Legislative Attack on American Wages and Labor Standards, 2011–2012* (Washington, DC: Economic Policy Institute, 2013), 14.

20. Lafer, *Legislative Attack on American Wages*, 1–10; Megan M. Block, "'Stand Up, Fight Back': Why the Attack on Public-Sector Workers Violates the First and Fourteenth Amendments," *University of Pittsburgh Law Review* 75 (Winter 2013): 189–94.

21. Thomas Harrison, "Breaking through by Breaking Free: Why the Left Needs to Declare Its Political Independence," in *Empowering Progressive Third Parties in the United States*, ed. Jonathan H. Martin (New York: Routledge, 2016), 231.

22. US Census Bureau, *Statistical Abstract of the United States, 2012*, 395, 411; BLS, *The Employment Situation—November 2015*, USDL-15-2292, Table B1 (Washington, DC: Bureau of Labor Statistics, 2015).

23. Michael Leachman, Nick Albares, Kathleen Masterson, and Marlana Wallace, *Most States Have Cut School Funding, and Some Continue Cutting* (Washington, DC: Center on Budget and Policy Priorities, 2015), 2; US Census Bureau, *Statistical Abstract of the United States, 2012*, 394.

24. BLS, *Union Members—2010*, Table 3; BLS.

25. Lafer, *Legislative Attack on American Wages*, 18–19.

26. Gerstle, *Liberty and Coercion*, 311–43; National Conference of State Legislatures, "State Partisan Composition," National Conference of State Legislatures, September 26, 2016, www.ncsl.org/research/about-state-legislatures/partisan-composition.aspx.

27. Arthur Lipow, *Political Parties and Democracy: Explorations in History and Theory* (London: Pluto Press, 1996), 81.

28. Drug Policy Alliance, "A Brief History of the Drug War," 2016, www.drugpolicy .org/new-solutions-drug-policy/brief-history-drug-war.

29. Smith and Greenblatt, *Governing States and Localities*, 448–49; Bureau of Justice, "Prisoners in 2014," *Bulletin*, September 2015, 1, 29; Bureau of Justice, "Prisoners in 2008," *Bulletin*, December 2009, 1, 2; Bureau of Justice, "Prisoners in 1994" *Bulletin*, August 1995, 1, 8, 9; Tyjen Tsai and Paola Scommegna, "U.S. Has World's Highest Incarceration Rate," Population Reference Bureau, 2012, www.prb.org/Publications /Articles/2012/us-incarceration.aspex.

30. Human Rights Watch, *Nation Behind Bars: A Human Rights Solution*, 2012, www.hrw .org/sites/default/files/related_material/2014_US_Nation_Behind_Bars_0.pdf, 5.

31. Smith and Greenblatt, *Governing States and Localities*, 454.

32. Human Rights Watch, *Nation Behind Bars*, 5; Bureau of Justice Statistics, "Prisoners in 2014," 2; Smith and Greenblatt, *Governing States and Localities*, 450.

33. Smith and Greenblatt, *Governing States and Localities*, 451.

34. Rice, Josie Duffy, "The Biggest Prison Strike in American History Is Happening Now," *Daily Kos*, October 4, 2016, www.dailykos.com/2016/10/04/1577788/-The-biggest -national-prison-strike-in-American-history-is-happening-now; Willie Burnley Jr., "Why There's a Mass Prison Strike Going on Right Now," *attn:*, October 21, 2016. www .attn.com/stories/12203/massive-prison-strike-occurring-right-now.

35. Katz, "*Terry v. Ohio*," 423–86.

36. Jeremy Roebuck, "Civil Rights Group: Stop-and-Frisk Still Targets Minorities," *Philadelphia Inquirer*, February 25, 2015, www.philly.com/philly/news/20150225_Civil _rights_group__Phila__police_still_target_minorities.html.

37. ACLU, *Black, Brown and Targeted: A Report on Boston Police Department Street Encounters from 2007–2010* (Boston: American Civil Liberties Union Foundation of Massachusetts, October 3, 2014), 1.

38. Center for Constitutional Rights, *Stop and Frisk: The Human Impact, the Stories behind the Numbers, the Effects on Our Communities* (New York: Center for Constitutional Rights, 2012), 3; Moody, *From Welfare State to Real Estate: Regime Change in New York City, 1974 to the Present* (New York: New Press), 2007b, 157.

39. Mike Bostock and Ford Fressenden, "'Stop-and-Frisk' Is All but Gone from New York," *New York Times*, September 19, 2014, www.nytimes.com/interactive/2014/09 /19/nyregion.stop-and-frisk-is-all-but-gone-from-new-york.htm.

40. Mapping Police Violence, "National Trends," 2016, http://mappingpoliceviolence.org /nationaltrends/; *Guardian*, "By the numbers", June 9, 2015. *Guardian*, "The Counted," database, 2016, www.theguardian.com/us-news/ng-interactive/2015/jun/01/the-counted -police-killings-us-database; *Washington Post*, Police Shootings database, 2015, 2016, www.washingtonpost.com/graphics/national/police-shootings/.

41. *Guardian*, "By the Numbers"; *Washington Post*, Police Shootings database, 2015, 2016.

42. Mapping Police Violence, "National Trends."

43. Heather Gray, "The Militarization of U.S. Police Departments," *Counterpunch*, March 10, 2015, www.counterpunch.org/2015/03/10/the-militarization-of-u-s-police-departments; ACLU, *War Comes Home: The Excessive Militarization of American of Policing* (New York: American Civil Liberties Union, 2014).

44. ACLU, *War Comes Home*, 16, 24, 25; Bret McCabe, "Does the Militarization of American Police Help Them Serve and Protect?" *Johns Hopkins Magazine*, Spring 2015, 230.
45. ACLU, *War Comes Home*, 2.
46. *Economist*, "How America's Police Became So Heavily Armed," *Economist Explains*, May 18, 2015, www.economist.com/blogs/economist-explains/2015/05/economist -explains-22.
47. ACLU, *War Comes Home*, 2, 35, 37.
48. US Government Spending, "State & Local Spending by Function," 2016, www .usgovernmentspending.com/statelocal_spending_2016; Office of Management and Budget, *The President's Budget for Fiscal Year 2017* (Washington, DC: The White House, 2016), 115.
49. Gerstle, *Liberty and Coercion*, 262–70.
50. Susan Watkins, "Oppositions," *New Left Review* 98 (March–April, 2016): 21.
51. Gerstle, *Liberty and Coercion*, 331.
52. Byron E. Shafer, "The Partisan Legacy: Are There Any New Democrats? (And by the Way, Was There a Republican Revolution?)" in *The Clinton Legacy*, ed. Colin Campbell and Bert A. Rockman (New York: Chatham House Publishers, 2000), 4.
53. Joanne Landy, "The Foreign Policies of Sanders, Trump, and Clinton," *New Politics* 16, no. 1 (Summer 2016): 10.

Chapter Eight: Prisoners of the American Scheme

1. Rustin, Bayard, "From Protest to Politics," *Commentary* 39 (February 1965): n.p.
2. Polanyi, *The Great Transformation*.
3. Thomas Ferguson and Joel Rogers, *Right Turn: The Decline of the Democrats and the Future of American Politics* (New York: Hill and Wang, 1986), 46–51.
4. Gerstle, *Liberty and Coercion*, 245–47.
5. Gude, "The Business Veto," *Jacobin* 20 (Winter 2016), www.jacobinmag.com/issue/up -from-liberalism.
6. Ferguson and Rogers, *Right Turn*, 55–56.
7. Socialist Party–Social Democratic Federation, 1960; Tom Hayden, *The Port Huron Statement: The Visionary Call of the 1960s Revolution* (New York: Thunder's Mouth Press, 2005), 135–36.
8. Harrington, *The Other America*, 183–85.
9. Steven P. Erie, *Rainbow's End: Irish-Americans and the Dilemmas of Urban Machine Politics, 1840–1985* (Los Angeles and Berkeley: University of California Press, 1988), 140–90.
10. Dennis R. Judd and Todd Swanstrom, *City Politics: The Political Economy of Urban Amer- ica*, 9th ed. (New York: Routledge, 2015), 68.
11. Walter Dean Burnham, *Critical Elections and the Mainsprings of American Politics* (New York: W. W. Norton, 1970), 120.
12. Roger H. Davidson, Walter J. Oleszek, Frances E. Lee, and Eric Schickler, *Congress and Its Members*, 15th ed. (Los Angeles: CQ Press, 2016), 87–88, 257–59.
13. Burnham, *Critical Elections*, x.

14. Ferguson and Rogers, *Right Turn*, 37.
15. Greenberg, *Two Americas*, 42.
16. Lichtenstein, *The Most Dangerous Man in Detroit*, 442.
17. Kevin Boyle, *The UAW and the Heyday of American Liberalism, 1945–1968* (Ithaca, NY: Cornell University Press, 1995), 260.
18. Boyle, *UAW and the Heyday*, 260.
19. Weir, *Singlejack Solidarity*, 294–323.
20. Brenner, Brenner, and Winslow, *Rebel Rank and File*.
21. Davis, *Prisoners of the American Dream*, 256–300.
22. Johanna Brenner, *Women and the Politics of Class* (New York: Monthly Review Press, 2000), 247.
23. Kim Moody, *Political Directions for Labor* (Detroit: Labor Education & Research Project, 1979), 19–26.
24. Moody, *Political Directions for Labor*, 19–26; Ferguson and Rogers, *Right Turn*, 78–113, 138–39; Paul Heideman, "It's Their Party," *Jacobin* 20 (Winter 2016), www.jacobinmag .com/issue/up-from-liberalism.
25. Kim Moody and Jim Woodward, *Battle Line: The Coal Strike of '78* (Detroit: Sun Press, 1978), 63–68.
26. Moody, *An Injury to All*, 127–39.
27. Heideman, "It's Their Party."
28. Shaikh, *Capitalism: Competition, Conflict*, 65–66.
29. Thomas Byrne Edsall, *The New Politics of Inequality* (New York: W. W. Norton, 1984), 128.
30. Val Burris, "The Political Partisanship of American Business: A Study of Corporate Political Action Committees," *American Sociological Review* 52 (December 1987): 732; Moody, *An Injury to All*, 127–35.
31. Ferguson and Rogers, *Right Turn*, 143–57.
32. Marable, *Black American Politics*, 254, 380–81.
33. Goldfield, *The Color of Politics*, 357–58.
34. Ben Smith, "The End of the DLC Era," Politico, February 7, 2011, www.politico .com/story/2011/02/the-end-of-the-dlc-era-049041.
35. Davis, *Prisoners of the American Dream*, 292.
36. Harrison, *Breaking through by Breaking Free*, 229.
37. Shafer, "The Partisan Legacy," 12.
38. Sean McElewee, "Why Non-Voters Matter," *Atlantic*, September 15, 2015, www .theatlantic.com/politics/archive/2015/09/why-non-voters-matter/405.
39. Skocpol, *Protecting Soldiers and Mothers*.

Chapter Nine: The Democratic Party Cul-de-sac

1. See Jason Schulman, "Bernie Sanders and the Dilemma of the Democratic Party," *New Politics* 15, no. 4 (2016), for a recent version of this argument.
2. Epstein, "Obama's Welcome Silence."
3. Jane Hamsher, "What Happened to the Employee Free Choice Act?" *ShadowProof*, April

13, 2010, https://shaowproof.com/2010/04/13/what-happened-to-the-employee-free -choice-act.

4. Lipow, *Political Parties and Democracy*, 20–21.

5. Watkins, "Oppositions," 15–17; Labour Party, "Labour Leadership Election 2016," 2016, www.labour.org.uk/pages/labour-party-leadership-election-2016.

6. Marco d'Eramo, *The Pig and the Skyscaper: Chicago: A History of Our Future* (London: Verso, 2016), 374–75.

7. Lipow, *Political Parties and Democracy*, 16, 17–24.

8. Democratic Party, "Party Organization," www.democrats.org/about/our-party -organization.

9. Gary C. Jacobson, *The Politics of Congressional Elections*, 6th ed. (New York: Pearson Longman, 2004), 88; Davidson et al., *Congress and Its Members*, 77–78; New York City Campaign Finance Board, *2013 Post-Election Report* (New York: New York City Campaign Finance Board), 2014, 75.

10. OpenSecrets, "Presidential Pre-Nomination Campaign Disbursements."

11. New York City Campaign Finance Board, *2013 Post-Election Report*, 11–12.

12. *Politics & Policy*, "Campaigns and Voter Information: Elections in a Digital Age," 2016, http://politicsandpolicy.org/article/campaigns-and-voter-information-elections -digital-era; Max Willens, "Election 2016 Ads: Xaxis Will Target Voters Using Their Digital and Real-Life Data," *ibtimes*, November 9, 2015, www.ibtimes.com /election-2016-political-ads-xaxis-will-target-voters-using-their-digital-real-life -2176196; DSPolitical, "Voter Targeted Digital Ads at Fingertips of Thousands of Democratic Campaigns," 2016, http://dspolitical.com/press-releases/voter-targeted -digital-ads-now-fingertips-thousands-democratic-campaigns

13. Hari Sreenivasan, "The Digital Campaign," *Frontline*, PBS, 2012, www.pbs.org/wgbh /frontline/film/digital-campaign/transcript.

14. Harry Davies and Danny Yadron, "How Facebook Tracks and Profits from Voters in a $10bn Election," *Guardian*, January 28, 2016, www.theguardian.com/us-news/2016 /jan28/facebook-voters-us-election-fed-cruz-targeted-ads-trump.

15. Donald P. Green and Michael Schwam-Baird, "Mobilization, Participation, and American Democracy: A Retrospective and Postscript," *Party Politics* 22, no. 2 (March 2016): 158–64.

16. Willens, "Election 2016 Ads."

17. DSPolitical, "Voter Targeted Digital Ads."

18. Davies and Yadron, "How Facebook Tracks."

19. Corey Robin, "The Big-Donor Math," *Jacobin*, June 2016, www.jacobinmag.com/2016 /06/money-politics-donors-trump-clinton-business-campaign-finance.

20. Lipow, *Political Parties and Democracy*, 81.

21. US Census Bureau, *Statistical Abstract of the United States, 2012*, 264.

22. Federal Election Commission, "Presidential Pre-Nomination Campaign Disbursements," June 30, 2000, June 30, 2008, June 30, 2012, June 30, 2016.

23. Erie, *Rainbow's End*, 183–90; Judd and Swanstrom, *City Politics*, 69.

24. Jewell and Morehouse, *Political Parties and Elections*, 47.

25. Smith and Greenblatt, *Governing States and Localities*, 168–69.

26. Jewell and Morehouse, *Political Parties and Elections*, 49.

27. National Institute on Money in State Politics, "Candidate Elections Overview," 2015, 2014, 2000, www.followthemoney.org/research/institute-reports/2014-candidate -elections-overview.

28. Federal Election Commission, "Party Table 2," "Party Table 3," 2016; US Census Bureau, *Statistical Abstract of the United States, 2001*, 254.

29. Quoted in Jason Schulman, "Bernie Sanders and the Dilemma of the Democratic Party," 8.

30. New York City Campaign Finance Board, *2013 Post-Election Report*, 26–40.

31. Judd and Swanstrom, *City Politics*, 68–69.

32. Federal Election Commission, "National Party Committees," 2008–2014, Tables 2 and 3, 2016; US Census Bureau, *Statistical Abstract of the United States, 1990*, 266.

33. OpenSecrets, "Democratic National Committee," 2016.

34. Will Tucker, "Personal Wealth: A Nation of Extremes, and a Congress Too: A Yearly Report from the Center for Responsive Politics, *OpenSecrets*, 2015.

35. Ballotpedia, "Ballot Access for Major and Minor Party Candidates," https://ballotpedia .org/Ballot_access_for_major_and_minor_party_candidates; Federal Reserve System, "Changes in U.S. Family Finances from 2010 to 2013: Evidence from the Survey of Consumer Finances," *Federal Reserve Bulletin*, 100, no. 4 (September 2014), 8.

36. Davidson et al., *Congress and Its Members*, 57.

37. Federal Election Commission, "National Party Committees"; US Census Bureau, *Statistical Abstract of the United States, 1990*, 266.

38. OpenSecrets, "Who's Up and Who's Down?"

39. OpenSecrets, "Democratic Congressional Campaign Committee, Receipts by Sector," 2014, 2016; "Democratic Senatorial Campaign Committee, Receipts by Sector," 2014, 2016.

40. SourceWatch, "Building."

41. Jacobson, *Politics of Congressional Elections*, 23.

42. Davidson et al., *Congress and Its Members*, 94.

43. Davidson et al., *Congress and Its Members*, 70–71.

44. Jacobson, *Politics of Congressional Elections*, 41.

45. Davidson et al., *Congress and Its Members*, 75–77.

46. Ballotpedia, "New Democratic Coalition," Candidate Profiles, 2016; Tim Canova for Congress, "Debbie Wasserman Schultz Fails to Receive AFL-CIO Endorsement," 2016, https://timcanova.com/news/debbie-wasserman-schultz-fails-receive-afl-cio -endorsement.

47. Dan Roberts, Ben Jacobs, and Alan Yuhas, "Debbie Wasserman Schultz to Resign as DNC Chair as Email Scandal Rocks Democrats," *Guardian*, July 25, 2016; Peter Nicholas, "Hillary Clinton Backs Debbie Wasserman Schultz during Florida Campaign Stop," *Wall Street Journal*, August 9, 2016, http://blogs.wsj.com/washwire /2016/08/09/hillary-clinton-backs-wasserman-schultz-during-florida-campaign-stop; Michael Sainato, "Wasserman Schultz's Primary Challenger Petitions Joe Biden to Rescind Endorsement," *Observer*, August 4, 2016, http://observer.com/2016/08/wasserman -schultzs-primary-challenger-petitions-joe-biden-to-rescind-endorsement.

48. Election Projection, "2014 Open Seat Elections," 2014, www.electionprojection.com /2014-elections/2014-open-seat-elections.php.

49. Jacobson, *Politics of Congressional Elections*, 99.

50. Davidson et al., *Congress and Its Members*, 76; Jacobson, *Politics of Congressional Elections*, 98–100.

51. OpenSecrets, "Massachusetts Senate Race," 2012.

52. National Institute on Money in State Politics, "2014 Candidate Elections Overview."

53. Timothy B. Krebs and John P. Pelissero, "City Councils," in *Cities, Politics, and Policy: A Comparative Analysis*, ed. John P. Pelissero (Washington, DC: CQ Press, 2003), 177–78.

54. National Institute on Money in State Politics, "2013 and 2014: Money and Incumbency in Legislative Races," 2016.

55. National Institute on Money in State Politics, "2014 Candidate Elections Overview."

56. OpenSecrets "Democratic National Campaign Committee, Receipts by Sector," 2016.

57. James Vlisela Jr., "Michael Madigan is the King of Illinois," *Chicago Magazine*, November 20, 2015, www.chicagomag.com/Chicago-Magazine/December-2013/michael -madigan.

58. Jewell and Morehouse, *Political Parties and Elections*, 98

59. Schulman, "Bernie Sanders and the Dilemma of the Democratic Party," 9

60. Schulman, "Bernie Sanders and the Dilemma of the Democratic Party," 9.

61. Jacobson, *Politics of Congressional Elections*, 229.

62. Davidson et al., *Congress and Its Members*, 258.

63. Harrison, "Breaking Through by Breaking Free," 213.

64. Sarah A. Binder, Thomas E. Mann, Norman J. Ornstein, and Molly Reynolds, *Mending the Broken Branch: Assessing the 110th Congress, Anticipating the 111th* (Washington, DC: Brookings Institution, 2009), 8.

65. Smith and Greenblatt, *Governing States and Localities*, 209.

66. Perlstein, Rick, "It Goes Way, Way Back," *New Republic*, June 14, 2016, https:// newrepublic.com/article/133776/split; Projects Five Thirty-Eight, "The Endorsement Primary," 2016. http://projects.fivethirtyeight.com/2016-endorsement-primary.

67. *Daily Kos*, "Many Progressive Caucus Members Have Endorsed Hillary and Here's the Corrected List," October 1, 2015, www.dailykos.com/story/2015/10/11/1430646/-Many -Progressive-Caucus-members-have-endorsed-Hillary-and-here-s-the-corrected-list.

68. Projects Five Thirty-Eight, "The Endorsement Primary"; Congressional Progressive Caucus, "Caucus Members."

69. NCSL, "State Partisan Composition"; Wikipedia, "Endorsements for the Democratic Party Presidential Primaries, 2016," https://en.wikipedia.org/wiki/Endorsements _for_the_Democratic_Party_presidential_primaries,_2016.

70. Gloria Pazmino, "After Public Anguish, Bronx Councilman Endorses Sanders on Eve of Primary," *Politico*, April 18, 2016, www.politico.com/states/new-york/city -hall/sotry/2016/04/after-publ;ic-anguish-bronx-councilman-endorses-sanders -on-eve-of-primary-033574#izz4MU94Mdbk; Will Bredderman, "Jumaane Williams Endorses Bernie Sanders' Political Revolution," *New York Observer*, April 17, 2016,

http://observer.com/2016/04/jumaane-williams-endorses-bernie-sanders-political
-revolutionary-moonshot/; Ross Barkan, "Meet the Only Member of the New York
City Council Endorsing Bernie Sanders," *New York Observer,* January 6, 2016, http://
observer.com/2016/01/meet-the-only-member-of-the-new-york-city-council
-endorsing-bernie-sanders/; *Daily Kos,* "New York City Council Member Jumaane
Williams Endorses Bernie Sanders at Prospect Park Rally," April 18, 2016, www
.dailykos.com/story/2016/4/17/1516643/-BREAKING-NY-City-Council-Member
-Jumaane-Williams-Endorses-Bernie-Sanders-at-Prospect-Park-Rally.

71. Chicago City Council Progressive Caucus, "Who We Are," Progressive Caucus
Members, 2016, www.chicagoprogressivecaucus.com/who-we-are; Lynn Sweet,
"Sweet Exclusive: Who's on Sanders' Illinois Delegate Slate?" *Chicago Sun-Times,* January 5, 2016, http://chicago.suntimes.com/politics/sweet-exclusive-whos-on-sanders
-illinois-delegate-slate.

72. Amie Parnes and Kevin Cirilli, "The $5 Billion Presidential Campaign," *The Hill,*
January 21, 2015.

73. OpenSecrets, "Lobbying Database."

74. Paul Blumenthal, "Crowdpac Helps Small Donors Find a Perfect Match in Politics,"
Huffington Post, October 7, 2014, www.huffintotonpost.com/2014/10/07/crowdpac
_donots_n_5943022.html.

75. ActBlue, "About Us."

76. Shane Goldmacher, "Bernie's Legacy: One of the Most Valuable Donor Lists Ever,"
Politico, June 6, 2016.

77. Roberts et al., "Debbie Wasserman Schultz"; *New York Times,* "Debbie Wasserman
Schultz Wins."

78. OpenSecrets, "Lobbying Database"; Ballotpedia, "New Democratic Coalition."

79. OpenSecrets, "PAC Contributions to Federal Candidates," 2016.

80. Social Enterprise Conference, "Erin Hill: ActBlue, Executive Director," 2014, https://
thesocialenterpriseconferen2014.sched.org/speaker/erin_hill.1s3ffr3m.

81. OccupyForum, "Don't Give Money to Democratic Party Front Group ActBlue,"
forum post, 2011, http://occupywallst.org/forum/dont-give-money-to-democratic
-party-front-group-ac.

82. Gerstle, "Resilient Power of the States," 320; SourceWatch, "Bundling," November 3,
2010, www.sourcewatch.org/index.php/Bundling.

83. BEA, "Corporate Profits before Taxes by Industry," Table 6.17D, August 3, 2016.

84. Saez and Zucman, "Wealth Inequality in the United States," Table 1, 42; Shah,
"America's Net Worth."

85. Schulman, "Bernie Sanders and the Dilemma of the Democratic Party," 12.

86. Bhaskar Sunkara, "Bernie for President?," *Jacobin,* May 1, 2015, www.jacobinmag.com
/2015/05/bernie-sanders-president-vermont-socialist.

87. Heideman, "It's Their Party."

88. Our Revolution, "Candidates," 2016.

89. Adam Gabbatt, "Is Bernie Sanders' Our Revolution Over before It Even Began?," *Guardian,* August 26, 2016, www.theguardian.com/us-news/2016/aug/26/bernie-sanders
-our-revolution-grassroots-jeff-weaver; Edward-Issac Dovere and Gabriel Debene-

detti, "Bernie Sanders' New Group Is Already in Turmoil," *Politico*, August 23, 2016, www.politico.com; Steven Rosenfeld, "Why the New Sanders Group Our Revolution Is Leaving Many Bernie Backers Scratching Their Heads," *Alternet*, August 31, 2016.

90. Sean Sullivan, "What Is a 501(c)(4), Anyway?" *Washington Post*, May 13, 2013.

91. Our Revolution, "Candidates"; Catherine Schuknecht, "City Council Candidates Get Boost from Bernie Sanders," *Richmond Confidential*, September 8, 2016.

92. Rosenfeld, "Why the New Sanders."

93. Ballotpedia, "New Democratic Coalition."

94. Our Revolution, "Election 2016 Our Revolution Live Tracker," 2016, https://ourrevolution.com/election-2016; Jessica Taylor, "Taking Aim at Money in Politics, Feingold Announces Comeback Bid," NPR, May 14, 2015, www.npr.org/sections/itsallpolitics/2015/05/14/406700612/taking-aim-at-money-in-politics-feingold-announces-comeback-bid.

Chapter Ten: Electoral Politics from a Socialist Perspective

1. See, for example, Luke Stobart, "Can Podemos Reclaim Its Earlier Momentum?" in *Europe in Revolt*, ed. Catarina Príncipe and Bhaskar Sunkara (Chicago: Haymarket Books, 2016), 175–90.

2. Watkins, "Oppositions," 6, 27.

3. Watkins, "Oppositions," 7.

4. Watkins, "Oppositions," 28.

5. Stobart, "Can Podemos Reclaim," 179.

6. Stobart, "Can Podemos Reclaim," 181–83.

7. Clément Petitjean, "What Happened to the French Left?," in *Europe in Revolt*, Príncipe and Sunkara, 87–106.

8. Mark Dudzik and Katherine Isaac, "Labor Party Time? Not Yet," in *Empowering Progressive Third Parties in the United States: Defeating Duopoly, Advancing Democracy*, ed. Jonathan H. Martin (New York: Routledge, 2016), 170.

9. Early, *Refinery Town: Big Oil, Big Money, and the Remaking of an American City* (Boston: Beacon Press, 2017), 2.

10. Feinstein, "A Green Becomes Mayor," 27

11. Early, *Refinery Town*, 3.

12. Early, *Refinery Town*, 128–29.

13. Early, *Refinery Town*, 1.

14. Early, *Refinery Town*, 125–26.

15. Early, "In Bay Area Refinery Town," October 21, 2016

16. Dan Cantor, "A New Progressive Party," in *Empowering Progressive Third Parties in the United States*, ed. Jonathan H. Martin (New York: Routledge, 2016), 204.

17. Molly Ball, "The Pugnatious, Relentless Progressive Party that Wants to Remake America," *Atlantic*, January 7, 2017, https://www.theatlantic.com/politics/archive/2016/01/working-families-party/422949.

18. Ramy Khalil, "How a Socialist Won: Lessons from the Historic Victory of Seattle City Councilmember Kshama Sawant," in *Empowering Progressive Third Parties*, 17–19;

Harrison, "Breaking Through by Breaking Free," 209.

19. Jonathan H. Martin, ed., *Empowering Progressive Third Parties in the United States* (New York: Routledge, 2016), 262.

20. Martin, *Empowering Progressive Third Parties*, 243; Ballotpedia, "Population Represented by State Legislators," 2016, https://ballotpedia.org/Population_represented _by_state_legislators.

21. John Halle, "Don't Wait for Labor: The Necessity of Building a Left Third Party at the Grassroots," in Martin, *Empowering Progressive Third Parties*, 184–203.

22. Russell Saltamontes, "A Union County," *Jacobin*, October 6, 2014, www.jacobinmag .org/2014/a-union-county.

23. Samantha Winslow, "Safety Is Life or Death, Say Refinery Strikers," *Labor Notes*, February 26, 2015; Ballotpedia, "Susan Sadlowski Garza," 2015, https://ballotpedia.org /Susan_sadlowski_garza.

24. Martin, *Empowering Progressive Third Parties*, 86.

25. Ballotpedia, "Ballot Access for Major."

26. Mike McAndrew, "Could You Run for New York State Legislature?," Syracuse.com, 2016, www.syracuse.com/politics/index.ssf/2016/06.will_ny_lawmakers_run_unopposed __for_re-election.html

27. Martin, *Empowering Progressive Third Parties*, 87.

28. Ballotpedia, "Population Represented by State Legislatures."

29. Martin, *Empowering Progressive Third Parties*, 86.

30. Sean McElwee, "Why the Voting Gap Matters," *Demos*, October 23, 2014, www.demos .org/publication/why-voting-gap-matters; McElwee, "Why Non-Voters Matter"; Pew Research Center, "The Party of the Nonvoters," October 11, 2014, www.people-press .org/2014/10/31/the-party-of-nonvoters-2; Green and Schwam-Baird, "Mobilization, Participation, and American Democracy," 158–64.

31. Board of Elections, City of New York, *Annual Report 2012*; Sam Roberts, "New York: Voter Turnout Appears to Be Record Low," *New York Times*, November 6, 2013, www .nytimes.com/news/election-2013/2013/11/06/new-york-turnout-appears-headed -for-record-low.

32. *New York Times*, "City Council," November 5, 2013, www.nytimes.com/projects /elections/2013/general/city-council/results.html.

33. Chicago Board of Election Commissioners, *Tabulated Statement*, 2.

34. Ballotpedia, "Los Angeles, California Mayoral Election, 2013," https://ballotpedia.org /Los_Angeles,_California_mayoral_election,_2013.

35. Javier C. Hernández, "Once Again, City Voters Approve Term Limits," *New York Times*, November 3, 2010, www.nytimes.com/2010/11/03limits.html; New York City Campaign Finance Board, 2014, 26.

36. Judd and Swanstrom, *City Politics*, 213–22, 358–61.

37. Judd and Swanstrom, *City Politics*, 222, 311; US Census Bureau, 2015b)

38. New York City Campaign Finance Board, *2013 Post-Election Report*, 26-40, 74.

39. New York City Campaign Finance Board, *2013 Post-Election Report*, 26-40.

40. Illinois PIRG, *The Money Primary: Money in the 2015 Chicago Aldermanic Elections* (Illinois PIRG Education Fund, 2015), www.illinoispirgedfund.org/sites/pirg/files

/reports/The%20Money%20Primary%20Final%204.1.15_0.pdf, 1–6.

41. NYC Department of Finance, *Annual Report on Tax Expenditures,* Fiscal Years 2009–2016 (New York: Tax Policy Division, 2009–2016), 5.

42. Moody, *Welfare State to Real Estate,* 74–80, 231.

43. Adrienne Kivelson, *What Makes New York City Run?* (New York: City of New York Education Fund, 2001), 49–53.

44. Progressive Caucus, "Making the City Stronger," *Huffington Post,* June 1, 2012, www.huffingtonpost.com.new-york-city-council-progessive-caucus/new-york-city-economic-development-corporation_b_156057.html; Progressive Caucus, "13 Bold Progressive Ideas for NYC in 2013," 2013, http://13boldideas.org/wp-content/uploads/2013/03/13boldideas_depth.pdf.

45. Joshua B. Freeman, "De Blasio's New York," *Dissent,* Winter 2015, www.dissentmagazine.org/article/de-blasio-year-one-new-york-city.

46. Chicago City Council Progressive Caucus, "Who We Are."

47. Sarina Trangle, "Now a Dominant Force, the Progressive Caucus Finds Its Vision Complicated," *City & State,* September 25, 2015, http://cityandstateny.com/articles/politics/new-york-city/now-a-dominant-force-the-progressive-caucus-finds-its-vision-comlicated.html#.V_ZwxugrKM8.

48. Bredderman, "Jumaane Williams Endorses"; Pazmino, "After Public Anguish"; Barkan, "Meet the Only Member."

49. Ross Barkan, "BDS Vote Shows City Council Progressives Are Out of Touch on Israel," *NY Slant,* September 27, 2016, http://nyslant.com/article/opinion/bds-vote-shows-city-council-progressives-are-out-of-touch-on-israel.html.

50. Halle, "Don't Wait for Labor," 190.

51. *Politics & Policy,* "Campaigns and Voter Information."

52. McElwee, "Why the Voting Gap Matters"; McElwee, "Why Non-Voters Matter"; Green and Schwam-Baird, "Mobilization, Participation, and American Democracy," 158–64.

53. Marx, *Capital,* vol. 1, 450.

54. Draper, *Socialism from Below: Essays,* edited by E. Haberkern (Atlantic Heights, NJ: Humanities Press, 1992), 13.

55. Draper, *Socialism from Below,* 30–33.

56. Gallup, "In U.S., Socialist Presidential Candidates Least Appealing," 2010. www.gallup.com/poll/183713.

57. Gallup, "June Wave 1," Princeton Job # 15-06-006, 2015, http://cns7prod.s3.amazonaws.com/attachments/gallup-historical_trend-june_2015.pdf.

58. Hinton, *First Shop Stewart's Movement*; Broué, *The German Revolution,* 67–68; Hoffrogge, *Working-Class Politics*; Spriano, *Occupation of the Factories.*

59. Montgomery, *Fall of the House of Labor,* 425–38.

60. Gramsci, *Antonio Gramsci: Selections from Political Writings, 1910–1920* (New York: International Publishers, 1977), 100.

61. Gramsci, *Antonio Gramsci,* 100.

Conclusion: Pulling the Analysis Together

1. Hobsbawm, *Labouring Men*, 126–39.

Postscript: Who Put Trump in the White House?

1. Nate Silver, "The Mythology of Trump's 'Working Class' Support," *FiveThirtyEight*, May 3, 2016, http://fivethirtyeight.com/features/the-mythology-of-trumps-working-class-support/; CNN Politics, "National President," 2016, http://edition.conn.com/results/exit-polls.

2. US Census, Table 1, "Educational Attainment of the Population 18 Years and Over, by Age, Sex, Race, and Hispanic Origin: 2014," CPS, 2014, www.census.gov/hhes/socdemo/education/data/cps/2014/tables.html.

3. National Small Business Association, *2016 Politics of Small Business Survey*, 4–6; Small Business Administration, *Demographic Characteristics of Business Owners and Employees: 2013*, 1; BLS, "Occupational Employment Statistics: May 2015," *Indeed*, "Small Business Owner Salary," 2016, www.indeed.com/small-business-owner.htm.

4. CNN Politics, "National President."

5. BLS, "Occupational Employment, Job Openings and Worker Characteristics," Table 1.7, 2014, www.bls.gov/emp/ep_table_107.htm.

6. BLS, *Union Members—2015*.

7. Harry Enten, "How Much Do Democrats Depend on the Union Vote?," *FiveThirty-Eight*, July 1, 2014, http://fivethirtyeight.com/datalab/supreme-court-ruling-wounds-both-democrats-and-unions-neither-fatally; CNN Politics, "National President."

8. Moody, *US Labor in Trouble and Transition*, 145.

9. Roper Center, "How Groups Voted," Cornell University, 1976–2012, http://ropercenter.cornell.edu/polls/us-elections/how-groups-voted/how-groups-voted; CNN Politics, "National President."

10. Roper Center, "How Groups Voted," 1996, 2000.

11. McElwee, "Why Non-Voters Matter."

12. *Economist*, "Where Donald Trump's Support Really Comes From," April 20, 2016, www.economist.com/blogs/graphicdetail/2016/04/daily-chart-14?zid=297&ah=3ae0fe266c7447d8a0c7ade5547d62ca.

13. Davis, "Not a Revolution—Yet," *Jacobin*, November 16, 2016, www.jacobinmag.com/2016/11/trump-election-clinton-sanders-whites-turnout.

14. Cook, "2016 National Popular Vote Tracker," December 15, 2016, http://cookpolitical.com/story/10174; US Electoral College, 2012; CNN Politics, 2012; CNN Politics, "Ohio President."

15. Cook, "2016 National Popular Vote Tracker"; US Electoral College, "Presidential Election."

16. CNN Politics, "Election Center, President, Ohio"; CNN Politics, "Ohio President."

17. Davis, "Not a Revolution—Yet."

18. *New York Times*, "President, 100% Reporting," 2012, http://elections.nytimes.com/2-12/results/states/ohio; *New York Times*, "Ohio Results," November 15, 2016, www.nytimes

.com/elections/results/ohio.

19. US Census, "Quick Facts, Lorain County, Ohio," 2016, www.census.gov/quickfacts /table/PST045215/39093; Saltamontes, "A Union County."

20. Lorain County Board of Elections, "2016 Primary Election," "2016 General Election," 2016, http://media.wix.com/ugd/2568d0_45e5b97f36b54098befa5ee19cb7f8e3.pdf.

21. Lorain County Board of Elections, "2012 General Election," http://media.wix.com /ugd/2568d0_45e5b97f36b54098befa5ee19cb7f8e3.pdf; Lorain County Board of Elections, "2016 Primary Election," "2016 General Election."

22. Lorain County Board of Elections, "2016 Primary Election," "2016 General Election"; US Census, "Quick Facts, Lorain City, Ohio," 2016, www.census.gov /quickfacts/table/PST045215/3944856; US Census, "Quick Facts Elyria City, Ohio," 2016, www.census.gov/quickfacts/table/PST045215/3925256.

23. Cook, "2016 National Popular Vote Tracker"; US Electoral College, "2012 Presidential Election," 2012, www.archives.gov/federal-register/electoral-college/2012 /results/state/OH/president/; CNN Politics, "Election Center, President, Ohio"; CNN Politics, "Ohio President."

24. *New York Times*, "Election 2012, Pennsylvania," http://elections.nytimes.com/2012 /results/states/pennsylvania; *New York Times*, "Ohio Results."

25. Gabriel, "How Erie Went Red."

26. US House of Representatives, "Party Divisions of the House of Representatives." 2016. http://history.house.gov/Institution/Party-Divisions/Party-Divisions; Thom File, *Who Votes? Who Votes? Congressional Elections and the American Electorate: 1978–2014* (Washington, DC: US Department of Commerce, 2015), 3.

27. National Conference of State Legislatures, "2009 State and Legislative Partisan Composition," National Conference of State Legislatures, www.ncsl.org/documents /statevote/legiscontrol_2009.pdf; "2015 State and Legislative Partisan Composition," National Conference of State Legislatures, www.ncsl.org/documents/statevote /legiscontrol_2015.pdf.

28. Federal Election Commission, "PAC Financial Activity," 2014; Marcin, "Latest Popular Vote Election Results: Clinton Leads Trump by 2.5 Million as Recount Effort Continues," *International Business Times*, December 1, 2016, www.ibtimes.com/latest -2016-popular-vote-election-results-clinton-leads-trump-25-million-recount.

29. John Nichols, "Hillary Clinton's Popular-Vote Victory Is Unprecedented—and Still Growing" *Nation*, November 17, 2016, www.thenation.com/article/hillary-clintons -popular-vote-victory-is-unprecedented-and-still-growing.

30. Cook, "2016 National Popular Vote Tracker," January 2, 2017, http://cookpolitical.com /story/10174.

31. *New York Times*, "Election 2016, New York Results," www.nytimes.com/elections/results /new-york.

32. US Electoral College, "2012 Presidential Election"; Cook, "2016 National Popular Vote Tracker."

33. United States Elections Project, "2016 November General Election Turnout Rates," www.electproject.org/2016g.

34. File, *Who Votes?*, 3.

35. McElwee, "Why the Voting Gap Matters"; McElwee, "Why Non-Voters Matter"; Pew Research Center, "Party of the Nonvoters."

36. Davis, "Not a Revolution—Yet."

37. Green and Schwam-Baird, "Mobilization, Participation, and American Democracy," 158–64; NCSL, "Voter Identification Requirements/Voter ID Laws," National Conference of State Legislatures, 2016, www.ncsl.org/research/elections-and-campaigns /voter-id.aspex.

38. File, *Who Votes?*, 1–4.

39. For a liberal Republican account of much of this history, see Geoffrey Kabaservice, *Rule and Ruin: The Downfall of Moderation and the Destruction of the Republican Party from Eisenhower to the Tea Party* (New York: Oxford University Press, 2012).

40. Charlie Post, "The Future of the Republican Party," *Jacobin*, December 23, 2014, www.jacobinmag.com/2014/12/republican-party-tea-party.

Appendixes

1. BLS, *Productivity and Costs by Industry: Manufacturing Industries, 2007.*

2. BLS, "Labor Productivity and Costs," August 9, 2016, https://data.bls.gov/cgi-bin /print.pl/lpc/prodybar.htm.

3. BLS, *Productivity and Costs by Industry: Manufacturing Industries, 2005–2007.*

4. Jack Metzgar, *Striking Steel: Solidarity Remembered* (Philadelphia: Temple University Press, 2000), 121; ArcelorMittal, *Driving Solutions*, 21.

INDEX

Bold page numbers refer to tables

273

ALSO AVAILABLE
FROM HAYMARKET BOOKS

Bananeras: Women Transforming the Banana Unions of Latin America
Dana Frank

The Civil Wars in U.S. Labor: Birth of a New Workers' Movement or Death Throes of the Old?
Steve Early

Disposable Domestics: Immigrant Women Workers in the Global Economy
Grace Chang, Foreword by Alicia Garza, Afterword by Ai-jen Poo

Doing History from the Bottom Up: On E.P. Thompson, Howard Zinn, and Rebuilding the Labor Movement from Below
Staughton Lynd

In Solidarity: Essays on Working-Class Organization and Strategy in the United States
Kim Moody

Poor Workers' Unions: Rebuilding Labor from Below (Completely Revised and Updated Edition)
Vanessa Tait, Foreword by Bill Fletcher Jr., Afterword by Cristina Tzintzún

Rank and File: Personal Histories by Working-Class Organizers
Alice and Staughton Lynd

Subterranean Fire: A History of Working-Class Radicalism in the United States
Sharon Smith

US Politics in an Age of Uncertainty: Essays on a New Reality
Edited by Lance Selfa

Why Bad Governments Happen to Good People
Danny Katch

ABOUT HAYMARKET BOOKS

Haymarket Books is a radical, independent, nonprofit book publisher based in Chicago.

Our mission is to publish books that contribute to struggles for social and economic justice. We strive to make our books a vibrant and organic part of social movements and the education and development of a critical, engaged, international left.

We take inspiration and courage from our namesakes, the Haymarket martyrs, who gave their lives fighting for a better world. Their 1886 struggle for the eight-hour day—which gave us May Day, the international workers' holiday—reminds workers around the world that ordinary people can organize and struggle for their own liberation. These struggles continue today across the globe—struggles against oppression, exploitation, poverty, and war.

Since our founding in 2001, Haymarket Books has published more than five hundred titles. Radically independent, we seek to drive a wedge into the risk-averse world of corporate book publishing. Our authors include Noam Chomsky, Arundhati Roy, Rebecca Solnit, Angela Y. Davis, Howard Zinn, Amy Goodman, Wallace Shawn, Mike Davis, Winona LaDuke, Ilan Pappé, Richard Wolff, Dave Zirin, Keeanga-Yamahtta Taylor, Nick Turse, Dahr Jamail, David Barsamian, Elizabeth Laird, Amira Hass, Mark Steel, Avi Lewis, Naomi Klein, and Neil Davidson. We are also the trade publishers of the acclaimed Historical Materialism Book Series and of Dispatch Books.